P9-DWX-844

LITERARY ESSAYS

LITERARY ESSAYS

BY

DAVID DAICHES

OLIVER AND BOYD
EDINBURGH: TWEEDDALE COURT
LONDON: 39A WELBECK STREET, W.I.
1956

FIRST PUBLISHED . . . 1956

English
80829
DEC 13 '56
PR
99
D13

PRINTED IN GREAT BRITAIN BY ROBERT CUNNINGHAM AND SONS LTD., ALVA
FOR OLIVER AND BOYD LTD., EDINBURGH

56 - 4933
11-30-56

PREFACE

THESE TWELVE essays were written for various periodicals and occasions, on both sides of the Atlantic, during the past six years. They reflect three of my principal interests—English literature, Scottish literature and modern American literature and criticism. The essay on translating the Bible derives from a concern with this question which first led me to write my doctoral dissertation at Oxford on English Bible translation some twenty years ago. The one essay in this collection which cannot properly come under the general title of 'Literary Essays' is the light-hearted Cambridge piece I wrote to provide an ironic note for the Cambridge number of the *Twentieth Century*. When it first appeared, everybody assumed that Mr Brightly spoke for myself, and I take this opportunity of pointing out that I was mocking all the speakers in the dialogue equally and that none speaks for me though each does occasionally say something with which I agree. What my own views are on some of the questions discussed in the Cambridge dialogue may perhaps be gathered from the final essay.

Acknowledgements are due to the periodicals and institutions which first published or commissioned these essays; their names appear in the text, though I should add here that the essay on Scott, while it first appeared in print in *Nineteenth Century Fiction*, was originally delivered as a lecture at the English Institute, New York.

DAVID DAICHES

St. John's College,
Cambridge.

CONTENTS

GUILT AND JUSTICE IN SHAKESPEARE[1]

IN PROPOSING TO DISCUSS guilt and justice in Shakespeare, I am aware that I am asking for trouble from two quarters. There are those who believe that the only way to understand fully the general ideas which underlie Shakespeare's plays is first to familiarize oneself with the Elizabethan view of the world and the moral order, and then to apply this view to an interpretation of the plays. There is, of course, much common sense in this position, and I for one am not disposed to deny that if we understand what Dr Tillyard has called 'the Elizabethan world picture' we shall see clearly certain patterns of meaning in Shakespeare that would otherwise remain obscure. But we must beware of laying the dead hand of historical uniformity on a great poetic dramatist. There is always some disparity between the view of the age and the individual poetic vision; Shakespeare's universe is not Kyd's or Marlowe's or Fletcher's, and his plays present a picture of the world that we will not find in the work of any other Elizabethan. We distort the meaning of Shakespeare's plays sadly if we lay them on the Procrustean bed of a synthetic 'Elizabethan point of view'. I should plead that we should listen to what the plays say, as carefully and sensitively as we can, and rely on what we learn that way for our primary understanding of Shakespeare, using our knowledge of the period as a help and a corrective where helps and correctives are needed, but not imposing that knowledge in such a way as to blur Shakespeare's individual meaning.

The second source of objection to my title might well be that kind of modern critic who insists on the uniqueness of the individual play and who deprecates any generalizations about the author's attitude based on his work as a whole. Each play creates

---

[1] A talk delivered in the Conference Hall of the Shakespeare Memorial Theatre, Stratford-upon-Avon, on 25th August 1954.

its own moral universe, such critics would maintain, not only by
the pattern of action but by the pattern of imagery and symbol
which runs through it, and evidence of meaning cannot be carried
over from one play into another. Again, I concede the element
of sense in this position; obviously plays are plays, individual
works of dramatic art, not merely documents illustrating the
history of a mind; but it is a curious kind of nominalism which
denies that the total impression of a group of plays by a single
great writer is of interest or value or asserts that one somehow
does violence to the aesthetic uniqueness of the individual work
by going on to discuss some of the dominant attitudes revealed by the author in several of them. I believe that we can
work from the individual plays to a larger view of how Shakespeare's mind and imagination were moving during certain periods
of his career, and thence back to the individual plays with
heightened interest and enlarged understanding.

So much by way of preliminary defence of my approach. Let
me now begin my inquiry by asking: What is guilt? If we assume
that there are forces of good and of evil both at work in the world,
then we might say that the guilty man is one who co-operates
with the forces of evil to increase evil's effectiveness in human
affairs. Innocence is on the side of the good, guilt on the side of
evil. Or so it would be pleasant to believe. A closer look at life
convinces us that innocence often achieves evil. If Brutus had
been a less simply virtuous man, he would not have helped to
kill one of his best friends and brought tyranny to Rome (the
opposite of what he intended). If Othello had been less innocent,
he would not have trusted Iago and so he would not have been
brought to murder his wife. If Hamlet had been less of a sensitive
idealist, he would not have destroyed his own house as well as the
house of Polonius. A more worldly Brutus, a less morally sensitive Hamlet, a tougher and more cunning Othello, would have
done less harm in the world. The first tragic problem faced by
Shakespeare in his maturity concerns the ambiguity of innocence.

This problem goes far deeper than the relation between private
and public virtue, which is in some degree the theme of *Julius*

Caesar. It includes, among other problems, that of the relation between innocence and virtue, or at least between innocence of character and effectiveness of moral action. It is an old dilemma. Milton was to treat it, in his own way, in *Paradise Lost*, where 'our credulous mother, Eve' allowed herself to be fooled by Satan into tasting of the forbidden tree. If Satan, in the form of the serpent, had been telling the truth, then Eve would have done right to believe him and to eat of the fatal fruit. Eve's real fault was lack of sophistication; she was unsuspicious of what the serpent told her; she was, to use the American slang term, a 'sucker' and swallowed his story. But is it morally wrong to be a sucker—as Eve was with respect to the serpent, as Othello was with respect to Iago, as Brutus was with respect to such political sophisticates as Antony, as Hamlet was, we might almost say, with respect to life?

Innocence plays into the hands of evil; only the tarnished and sophisticated mind can achieve that approximate good which alone lies within human reach. Is this one of the themes of Shakespearean tragedy? Perhaps; but before we conclude that it is we must inquire a little more closely. The case of Brutus is that of the liberal intellectual in a world of *Realpolitik*—a familiar enough case in the modern world. Cassius is the co-hero of the play, and, skilled politician though he is, with little scruple in playing on Brutus' finer feelings, he admires Brutus and cannot help allowing Brutus to achieve moral ascendancy over him, once the murder of Caesar is accomplished. The coarser nature is dominated by the finer, to the destruction of both of them and of the ideal to which they had sacrificed everything. In the quarrel scene it is Cassius who first gives way, and it is under the influence of this moral domination by Brutus that, against his better judgment, Cassius allows Brutus to have his way in the ill-advised plan of seeking immediate battle at Philippi. Nowhere is the Epicurean Cassius more like the Stoic Brutus than when he commits suicide because he is ashamed of having lived 'so long, to see my best friend ta'en before my face'. And that suicide, rather than military defeat, seals the doom of the republican cause.

But Cassius is not as unlike Brutus as he thinks he is. Though he is the shrewder and the more practical, he is basically an idealist too, an intellectual, whom Caesar had come to suspect because 'he thinks too much'. If he appears as a cunning man of action beside Brutus, he is almost equally a babe in the wood when seen beside Antony, the man without innocence, the man who knows how to unite his personal affections with his political ambitions. (Though Shakespeare shows us in *Antony and Cleopatra* what happens when that unstable equilibrium collapses.) In *Julius Caesar* Antony's is the success story; he is the tarnished man who knows how to come to terms with life. He is not evil—he is generous, noble and kind-hearted—but he lacks innocence: he is postlapsarian man, who has adapted himself to life after the Fall.

Wherein lies Antony's success? Is it not in his ability to manipulate people, to act the puppeteer and utilize the worthy emotions of innocent people for his own purposes? Cassius does this in a very mild way with Brutus, but Antony is the great puppeteer of the play, and his famous oration is the work of a supreme puppet master. He manipulates other people's innocence. So does Richard III, and Edmund in *King Lear*, and Iago. But we are not to conclude from this that Antony is intended to be a villain like these characters: that would be manifestly absurd. Richard III and Edmund and Iago are evil; Antony is sophisticated and cunning, but far from evil. All four manipulate the innocence of others for their own ends. Antony stands midway between innocence and evil, the tarnished sensual man, the man whose way of life is—to use a term the politicians are now so fond of—above all *viable*. 'Human nature being what it is', Antony's way is not to be rejected out of hand. But I have a friend who says that whenever he has had a guest at dinner who has begun a political conversation with the remark, 'human nature being what it is', he always counts the spoons. The argument is an excuse for being content with imperfection: one could not imagine Brutus or Hamlet using it.

Antony manipulates his self-interest and his ideals into a compromise that is above all practicable. He is too good to be a tragic villain, too bad to be a tragic hero. Are we to say, then, that he is Shakespeare's ideal practical man? Shakespeare answers that question for us in his *Antony and Cleopatra*, which shows us, as Granville-Barker has said, the nemesis of the sensual man. The unstable equilibrium cannot last; Antony in the end surrenders wholly to his passions and loses the political world to young Octavius Caesar, the man whose fortunes he had earlier saved. *There*, perhaps, is Shakespeare's ideal practical man, Octavius Caesar, shrewd, cool-headed, altogether a cold fish. Obviously it is not the ideal practical man who is the glory of the human species, and we do not need Octavius to tell us that practical success was not, for Shakespeare, the greatest thing in life. But to return to Antony. *Antony and Cleopatra* is—among many other things—the story of a tawdry sensual love raised to tragic heights by sheer poetry. Antony, who had formerly manipulated the passions of the Roman crowd with such success, now manipulates his own emotions, even though he is not really in control over them. And while most at their mercy, he seems to be exploiting them most. The poetry is no longer rhetoric, designed to influence other people, but that enlarging and exploratory poetry whose function is to raise human passion above its lonely and trivial reality. Here is love without innocence, in sharp contrast to the love of Romeo and Juliet. This affair between an ageing roué and a royal prostitute is, from one point of view, sordid and ludicrous. Cleopatra is shrewish, hysterical, sadistic, dishonest and cowardly, as well as beautiful, queenly and heroic. Antony is selfish and fatuous as well as generous and noble. Are they great lovers or merely great sensualists? They are both experienced in the ways of sexual pleasure and often talk as though that is all that love involves. Yet this is far from being a disillusioned or a cynical play. We are continually fascinated by the richness and variety of character and the way in which history is bound up with psychology. There is little pity or fear in the play, but rather a lively humane curiosity throughout. And the poetry keeps enlarging the moment, showing experience as ever livelier and richer. We watch fascinated as Antony, most Roman when

B

most enslaved by Egypt, goes to his self-inflicted death, and then follow Cleopatra's twistings and turnings with ever-increasing interest and wonder. We make no new moral judgments on either, because that is decided at the beginning and is never in question: they are neither innocent nor admirable. But perhaps they are admirable in the literal Latin sense of the word, something to wonder at. For there is a wonder in it all, and Cleopatra in her death finds, as it were, the objective correlative of that wonder. The sensual life ends in a blaze of ritual pageantry: it has its own amoral nobility.

So Antony in some sense controls his destiny after all, which is one thing the innocent man cannot do. Antony's kind of failure is at least redeemable; it ends with a bang, not a whimper, striking a blow for human glory. Can we say this of the ends of Shakespeare's innocents, of Brutus and Hamlet and Othello, who are destroyed by their own naïve idealism? Let me pause for a moment at *Hamlet*, and say a word about the play from this point of view. The central problem of the play is that knowledge of guilt has destroyed the hero's innocent picture of the world, and it can never be restored. What can one do about evil? One can ignore it, or come to terms with it, or *use* it in the creation of a workable compromise world. One thing one cannot do is *undo* it. Evil, once performed, is irrevocable. And that is one thing that the wholly innocent man cannot accept. Of the many meanings that can be extracted from the action of *Hamlet*, perhaps the most tragic, and the one which fits in best with what appears to have been Shakespeare's view of the essential tragedy of human life at this time, is that here is a presentation of the paradox of guilt and justice. Justice demands appropriate action where a crime has been committed, but in fact *no action is ever appropriate*. The tragedy of *Hamlet*, as in some degree of *Othello*, is that moral outrage as seen by the innocent demands action, when no action can be of any use. In a sense, we can say that the Ghost was at fault in appearing to Hamlet in the first place, and setting him, for what might be called purely selfish reasons, a task which, even if accomplished, could do no possible good. When Hamlet's whole nature was outraged by his mother's behaviour and then by the news of his father's murder, he naturally felt that something must be done. But what? What could be done that would make any difference—any difference at all to the things that really mattered? Would a dagger through Claudius' ribs restore Hamlet's shattered universe? Would it restore the earlier idealized image of his mother or remove the 'blister' that had been set on innocent love? This is a tragedy of moral frustration. What are you going to do about past crimes which have shattered your preconceptions about the nature of life? There is nothing you can ever do about the past: 'forget it, brother', is the only possible advice. And yet of course Hamlet could not forget. Revenge is no real help: what sort of action, then, *is* of help? None that is directed towards undoing the past: only purposive action directed towards the future can ever get anywhere. Antony would have seen that; so would Octavius Caesar. The real problem is not to restore your private image of the world, but to make an imperfect world a degree or two better than it is. But the moral innocent can never accept this view. And that is at least one explanation of Hamlet's long delay in carrying out the Ghost's command: he wanted action that would undo the past, and no action could do that, revenge least of all, for that would only re-enact the past.

The punishment can never fit the crime, for it can never undo it. We may think we may be able to find appropriate action, as Lear thought:

> I will have such revenges on you both
> That all the world shall—I will do such things—
> What they are, yet I know not; but they shall be
> The terrors of the earth;

but in fact we never do, and it is impossible that we ever should. Lear's frustration at feeling a deep moral indignation which can have no 'objective correlative' in action is, in part, the cause of his madness, as it is of Hamlet's moods and Othello's self torture (for in *Othello* there is no action that can take care of the supposed fact of Desdemona's infidelity). Only when he gives up the whole idea of action does Lear recover and achieve redemption.

The morally outraged man, the finer and more sensitive he is, will feel all the more need for action, the need to do something about his shocking revelation; and his frustration at finding no adequate action produces one kind of tragedy. As I have suggested, the Ghost is in a sense the real villain in *Hamlet*, for he destroys his son by setting him an impossible task. And the Ghost learns, perhaps sooner than Hamlet himself, the futility of trying to undo the past by physical action. He declines from the armed warrior whom we first see to become on his last appearance a pathetic domestic figure ('enter the ghost in his night gown'), only interested in trying to make contact with his morally lost wife and in saving her from Hamlet's morbid rage, the rage of outraged innocence. True, he states that his object is to whet Hamlet's almost blunted purpose, but his manner and behaviour belie this: he is there to try and save his family. This remarkable scene—the only one in which we see the Hamlet family together, father, mother and son—has a strange kind of pathos, with the Queen unable because of her guilt to see her husband's spirit, so that the Ghost, after a vain effort to re-establish the family unit, as it were, departs in silence for ever. On the other side is the Polonius family, all destroyed too through involvement in this tragedy of outraged innocence, guiltless involvement on Ophelia's part, almost guiltless on Laertes', and only relatively guilty on the part of Polonius. We last see *them* together fairly early in the play, when Laertes is being seen off by his devoted father and sister—also a touching domestic tableau, with its own meaning in the play. The tragedy of Hamlet concerns more than the wreck of a noble spirit, and the longer he dwells on the past and searches for a way of undoing it, the more do guiltless, as well as guilty, people become involved in it.

In *Othello* the hero's romantic innocence is clearer and more bound up with ignorance of the world than in any of the other tragedies. Iago is Othello's anti-type, the 'realist', the man who thinks he knows how to get on in the world, who knows that innocence is folly. He is more than a mere device to set the plot in motion, as some modern critics have seen him, or than the embodiment of 'motiveless malignity' that Coleridge saw: he is both the disgruntled professional soldier and the hard-boiled cynic who feels personally outraged when a simple-minded hero like Othello gets ahead in the world and he, who knows the world so much better, fails to get on. By all the rules, which Iago knows so well, innocence *ought not* to prosper, and Iago cannot be happy until he manipulates Othello to his destruction. The dignity and self-confidence that Othello displays in the first act must be destroyed. And because Othello is a Moor, and noble, and so deeply in love with Desdemona that he can scarcely believe his good fortune, and inexperienced and therefore self-distrustful in domestic matters (especially where Venetians are concerned), Iago succeeds in destroying him. That he destroys Desdemona too is incidental; he has no malice against her; he is out to destroy successful innocence, which to him ought to be a contradiction in terms, and he can only get at that through Desdemona. He wants nothing out of it all except the destruction of Othello: he makes this heroic figure dance to his piping, makes a puppet out of him—and what is to happen after that, he scarcely thinks about. If he had thought, he would have known that sooner or later the truth would come to light, but he never looked beyond his immediate aim.

What makes it all possible is Othello's incredulity in the face of his own supreme happiness—a kind of modesty, which makes him vulnerable to Iago's suggestion that he does not in fact enjoy the happiness he has thought was his.

> If it were now to die
> 'Twere now to be most happy; for, I fear,
> My soul hath her content so absolute
> That not another comfort like to this
> Succeeds in unknown fate.

Desdemona does not share his sense of insecurity, and replies:

> The heavens forbid
> But that our loves and comforts should increase
> Even as our days do grow.

She has defied her father and chosen Othello, and takes her

happiness as a right. She is no innocent idealist, but an enterprising and practical young woman who went after the man she wanted. When Othello, inflamed by Iago's cunning and plausible lies, turns on her, she is hurt and bewildered, but her world does not come crashing about her ears. She goes to her death puzzled and horrified, but confident that Othello's behaviour is all due to some terrible mistake. She loses faith neither in life nor in him.

Othello is not a study in jealousy. For that, as Coleridge pointed out, we must go to Leontes in *The Winter's Tale*. Iago has to work desperately hard to catch Othello in his trap, and even then he is helped by coincidence before he can succeed. It is not jealousy, but anguish that this beautiful and virtuous-seeming creature, whom he loved, could be so horribly guilty, that so torments him. It is an offence against his picture of the universe. All reason and order and beauty are shattered: 'chaos is come again.' A soldier, a man who was used to meeting a situation with the appropriate action, he here confronts a situation so monstrous, so destructive of reason, that nothing can be done about it. Something had to be done, but nothing could be done. Othello was not a philosopher like Hamlet, who could at least mark time by introspection and speculation while pondering the problem of the irrevocability of performed evil. The man of action must do something—but what? 'Othello's occupation's gone', his world is shattered, here was the outrage of irreversible evil. Something had to be done, and the only action that seemed at all relevant and proper in the circumstances was to kill Desdemona. He did not kill her in jealous rage. He made no move himself to kill his supposed rival Cassio. He killed Desdemona for the sake of his moral universe, as the only action somehow appropriate to the situation. 'It is the cause, it is the cause, my soul.' And when the truth is finally known, though it cannot make life tolerable for Othello, it at least restores his moral universe and he can resume his former dignity of bearing before performing the now inevitable act of self-slaughter. Iago becomes for him simply the Devil, expelled from the world he had destroyed, so that that world can exist again.

I asked a little while back: 'What can one do about evil?' and I replied that one can ignore it, or come to terms with it, or make use of it, but one can never undo it. I might have added that one can punish it. After all, does not justice reside in the punishment of the wicked? Punishment is, from one point of view, a form of revenge—an impersonal form of revenge, shall we say—and to the outraged innocent who demands the rehabilitation of his lost world it is as barren. Other Elizabethan dramatists than Shakespeare had been concerned to show that revenge was stultifying. Shakespeare, in several of his plays, goes further and suggests that punishment might be stultifying too. If one of his tragic themes was outraged innocence becoming the tool of evil, another was the futility of the quest for punishment. If human affairs can be successfully managed only by the tarnished man, the man who compromises in some degree with evil, who has the right to administer justice?

Measure for Measure is, of course, the play which handles this theme most directly. Its basic plot is an old one, which goes back into the mists of folklore: the story of the judge or ruler who offers to save a girl's lover or husband or brother if she will yield herself to him, and who, after the girl has yielded, deliberately breaks his promise. In pre-Shakespearean versions the girl does yield to the ruler, but Shakespeare, by means of a device he had already used in *All's Well*—the secret substitution of one girl for another in the bed of the seducer—keeps his heroine chaste throughout; further he follows George Whetstone rather than Geraldi Cinthio in saving the girl's brother and having the ruler only imagine that he has been put to death.

Several themes are woven together in this apparently simple story. In the first place there is the ironical theme of the judge himself guilty of what he has others punished for. *Quis custodiet ipsos custodes?* Who shall guard the State's guardians, and what happens when the judge is more guilty than the man he condemns? This is bound up with a theme not unrelated to the deep-seated Oedipus motif: the ruler, in an honest attempt to uncover guilt, reveals that he is himself the guilty one. This is the detective story where the detective, conscientiously following the clues, proves himself to be the criminal. Such a notion has both its comic and its tragic side. The uncovering of the hypocritical judge as the true villain can easily be made the subject of pure comedy, as was done by Heinrich von Kleist in his comedy *Der zerbrochene Krug* (The Broken Jug), in which a judge is forced by circumstances to conduct a careful cross-examination which proves himself to have been the criminal in the case under investigation. Finally, there is the Christian element in the story, which Shakespeare emphasizes in the title. (Cf. Luke, Chapter 6: 'Judge not, and ye shall not be judged; condemn not, and ye shall not be condemned: forgive, and ye shall be forgiven. . . . For with the same measure that ye mete withal it shall be measured to you again.') In *Measure for Measure* everybody is in some degree guilty, and it is only after the much-injured heroine has pleaded for mercy for the man who has injured her that it is revealed that the injury was in intention only. All are guilty, and mercy rather than justice saves the day.

Shakespeare further complicates the story by having a disguised duke, the real ruler, watch over the proceedings unknown to the actors. The Duke, before leaving the country on a temporary absence, gives over his rule to Angelo, hoping that Angelo, a sternly puritanical character, will have the firmness to revive laws which the Duke himself has been too kind-hearted to enforce, with a resulting increase in sexual immorality among all classes. Angelo begins by sentencing to death young Claudio for intercourse with his fiancée and refusing to listen to any pleas for mercy. Claudio's sister Isabella, passionately chaste and about to enter a nunnery, pleads with Angelo for her brother's life, and Angelo, suddenly smitten with lust for Isabella, agrees to save him if she yields herself to him for one night. She of course refuses, but the Duke, disguised as a friar, persuades her to agree to a plot whereby Mariana, formerly betrothed to Angelo but later deserted by him when her dowry was not forthcoming (Angelo's original sin), is substituted for Isabella without Angelo's being aware of the substitution. After spending some hours secretly at night with the supposed Isabella, Angelo goes back on his word and orders Claudio to be immediately executed, but the disguised Duke arranges for the head of a man who has died in prison to be brought to Angelo as Claudio's, and Claudio is spared. Finally, in a carefully contrived dénouement, Angelo is exposed, and, after a plea for forgiveness made by Isabella while she still thinks Claudio has been executed, forgiven. Behind this main action runs a stream of sordid low life, with bawds, brothels and much talk of venereal disease.

The play has puzzled some, largely because of the different and sometimes apparently conflicting themes bound up in the story as Shakespeare develops it. The 'gulling' of the hypocrite (in the manner of Ben Jonson's comedies) is one way of treating Angelo, but he is at the same time presented as a genuinely puritanical character who suddenly discovers, to his dismay and even horror, that he is as much subject to sensual temptation as ordinary men. He might even be said to be a man who has sublimated his tendencies towards sadistic sensuality in the practice of stern justice, but who, on being faced with a beautiful woman pleading for mercy for a brother condemned to death, regresses into the sensualist and sadist. Similarly, Isabella is both a stern, other-worldly character who fiercely abuses her brother for a momentary lapse in his desire to face death rather than have his sister lose her chastity and at the same time cheerfully plays the procuress with Mariana, and a symbol of radiant purity who, at the end of the play, embodies its Christian moral of mercy before strict justice. The gulling of the hypocrite, the testing of the puritan, the revelation of the judge as the criminal, the discovery that all are guilty and none has the right to judge, and that mercy rather than justice is the proper 'measure for measure' as between man and man—here is indeed an intermingling of comic and tragic themes. No wonder that *Measure for Measure* has elements of Jonsonian comedy, Sophoclean irony and Christian morality.

But the play is a unity nevertheless, and underlying the whole complex action is the question: How can we forgive each other? Only by realizing that we all in some degree partake of the nature of the guilty. The theme is that of Dostoievsky's *Brothers Kara-mazoff*, the morality Sossima's. Yet not quite. There is no passion of saintliness in Shakespeare's play. The dark theme of sex misused—the forces of life used to produce disease—runs through it like a stain. And the mockery of human designs and pretensions by the event emphasizes the impossibility of judging the human heart. There is, I suppose, no point in complaining that no character in the play seems wholly sympathetic, that even virtue is made to appear uncongenial, if one realizes that a basic theme in it is precisely that none are guiltless and that in judging one another we have no right to condemn but only to forgive. This is in a sense a deeply pessimistic position, and it implies at one level the denial of the possibility of order and justice.

We see the implications of this in *King Lear*, when Lear's moral insight is achieved at the expense of his pretensions to kingship. *Lear* is a complex and tremendous play, which I cannot attempt to deal with here. I want to draw attention only to the point that as Lear's madness grows he acquires a new moral vision which ends in the recognition that there is no division into the just and the unjust. 'None does offend, none.' This is the other side of the medal presented by *Measure for Measure*, the obverse of the view that we all share in everybody else's guilt, we *all* offend. The artifice of rank can produce an apparent division into judge and criminal, but with the 'natural' vision of madness this is seen to be a false picture. This is more than the movement from vengeance to compassion, which it is often taken to be; the statement that 'none does offend' follows a fierce picture of universal lechery and deceit which shows the same kind of bitter disgust with sex that some of Hamlet's speeches show. It is because all are equally guilty that none does offend. The road to true humility runs through these bitter insights.

But are such bitter insights any more helpful in living than the naïve idealism of the innocent? If all are guilty and none does offend, if judge and criminal can change places at will, what becomes of human society? Lear's vision may be the way to his personal redemption, but it is not the road back to efficient

kingship. Ignorant innocence and bitter knowledge are two extremes, one deriving from too little experience and the other
from too much, and neither is a viable human attitude. The old
argument about whether Lear should have been restored to his
throne could have been answered simply on these grounds: the
restoration of a man who had reached his point of view about the
nature of justice was *morally* impossible. Hamlet was no fit prince
because his moral innocence made him believe that evil was
always *other people's* evil, destroying his own moral world; he
never saw himself in Claudius; but the view that other people's
evil is always your own evil is equally untenable in a ruler. I am
not suggesting that Shakespeare's plays are concerned with the
ideal ruler—Shakespeare found great failures more interesting
than prim success stories—but an extension of the argument in
this way does help, I think, to show some of the moral patterns in
some of the plays.

In his final plays, the so-called romances or tragi-comedies,
Shakespeare tackled these problems from a quite different point
of view. Is moral innocence always self-destructive? In Marina
and Imogen and Perdita and Miranda Shakespeare said 'no'. Is
the administration of justice by humans to humans possible? In
the character of Prospero he gave a rather dubious 'yes'. Can
past evil be undone? It can, symbolically, if we find the proper
ritual. In *Pericles*, *Cymbeline*, *The Winter's Tale* and *The Tempest*
Shakespeare deals, in one way or another, with evil and innocence,
guilt and atonement, uncorrupted youth undoing original sin and
starting afresh. Mythology, folklore and magic find their way
into these plays to a greater degree than in any other of Shakespeare's mature work, so that it can hardly be claimed (as many
have asserted) that they represent a new faith in the essential
goodness of man: the remoteness of the setting and the introduction of the magical element indicate a different level of probability from that found in *Hamlet* or *Othello*, a symbolic world
where (unlike the real world) innocence can triumph and the gods
enable the past to be undone. In *Pericles*, Marina and her mother,
both assumed to be dead, are found in the end alive and innocent;

in *Cymbeline* Imogen similarly comes alive again; in *The Winter's Tale* the statue of Hermione proves in the end to be the living Hermione, long thought dead; and in *The Tempest* Alonso and his company are miraculously redeemed from drowning to find repentance and new virtue. The dramaturgy in these plays is relaxed, almost casual, with masque elements and other spectacular devices introduced to emphasize the note of symbol and ritual. Shakespeare has done with probing directly the tragic paradoxes of human nature, and he now reaches out to a larger poetic symbolism through which the moral patterns and possibilities of human life can be presented with the calm beauty of one who is no longer tortured by his own involvement.

Pericles, with its corrupt text and composite authorship, is the least satisfactory of these plays, and the story, deriving ultimately from a widely dispersed tale of Greek origin, is too crowded with incident to be easily rendered dramatically. Since it is not a commonly read play, let me give a brief summary of its plot. Antiochus, king of Antioch, has incestuous relations with his own daughter; Pericles, prince of Tyre, discovers this, thereby arousing Antiochus' anger. To avoid the effects of Antiochus' wrath, Pericles flees from his own kingdom of Tyre and after succouring starving Tarsus sets sail again, is shipwrecked, lands at Pentapolis, where he marries the King's daughter, Thaisa, then sets off by sea again for Tyre. But he is again shipwrecked; during the storm Thaisa gives birth to a daughter, Marina, before apparently dying, and her body is committed to the sea in a chest. The chest is washed up at Ephesus, where Cerimon restores the apparently dead Thaisa to life and she becomes a priestess of Diana. Meanwhile, Pericles and Marina arrive at Tarsus, where Pericles stays a year before returning to Tyre, leaving Marina in the care of Cleon, governor of Tarsus, and Cleon's wife Dionyza. But Dionyza grows jealous of Marina, who outshines her own daughter, and plans her murder. Before she can be murdered, however, she is carried off by pirates to Mytilene, where she is sold to a brothel, but her angelic innocence converts the customers to virtue and she retains her chastity. Pericles is told by Cleon and Dionyza that his daughter is dead, and he devotes himself to grief. But fate brings his ship to Mytilene, where he finds Marina in a moving scene of mutual discovery. Finally, under Diana's guidance, he proceeds to Ephesus, where he finds his wife, long supposed dead.

To get the whole of this complicated story across requires the use of choruses and dumb-shows, employed clumsily enough. But the main theme centres on Marina, lost and found again, subjected to the corrupting influence of the brothel yet preserving always her shining innocence. And the sea, on which Marina was born and into which Thaisa disappears to be cast up later alive, dominates the play, a symbol of purification, of 'death by water' which precedes resurrection. T. S. Eliot's poem 'Marina' distills the essential meaning:

> What seas what shores what grey rocks and what islands
> What water lapping the bow
> And scent of pine and the woodthrush singing through the fog
> What images return
> O my daughter.

Pericles is a symbolic play, a religious play, dealing with death and resurrection, with ritual purification and the redemptive power of innocence. Uneven and botched up in places as it is, it has its Shakespearean moments of grave beauty, and though by itself, so uncertain is the text and the authorship, it could tell us little about the direction in which the later Shakespeare's imagination was moving, with the following three plays it helps to build up a picture of a Shakespeare who has turned away from what (with all the necessary qualifications) might be called the psychological realism of the great tragedies to a new, more symbolic kind of play in which he could come to terms with the problem of evil in a different way.

Cymbeline is another curiously complicated story, with elements from Holinshed and from folklore. A strain of fairy tale runs right through the play. The princess who marries against her parents' wishes, the wicked stepmother, the potion which brings apparent death but which really only sends the drinker into a prolonged swoon, the 'Snow White' theme of the apparently dead girl being covered with flowers by her simple companions —these are familiar enough elements in any folk literature. The evil Cloten, son of the wicked stepmother, is also a folk-character, though Shakespeare gives him a fully individualized personality. Imogen herself is pure Shakespeare, idealized yet real, one of those spirited heroines whom he created so happily in his 'middle comedies' and who here is subjected to much more grievous trials than anything which befell Rosalind or Viola. For the theme of this play, as of *Pericles*, is innocence triumphant, emerging victorious from the darkest possible circumstances.

Evil mounts to an ugly climax before the counter-movement sets in, and Shakespeare leaves us in no doubt of its reality. Iachimo, the subtle Italian, is as nasty a case of small-minded pride and perverted ingenuity as one can find in literature, and Cloten is a sadistic boor. Only the Queen, the wicked stepmother, with her stagey asides and her poison potions, remains a purely fairy tale character, and her final suicide is as unreal as the rest of her actions. This is tragi-comedy, where all the terror of tragedy is given full vent before the tide is allowed to turn. Those who maintain that Shakespeare now felt in a kindly mood towards life have surely paid too little attention to Cloten or to the tortured speech that Posthumus makes when he thinks his wife has betrayed him, a speech full of the sex nausea we find in *Hamlet*.

Of course, tragi-comedy had become the fashion; the Blackfriars audiences wanted all the thrills of tragedy with the happy ending of comedy, and they wanted, too, the masque-like devices, the music and pageantry, which Shakespeare, yielding to public taste, now freely gave them. It may be that this is the only explanation one needs for these final romances or tragi-comedies: Shakespeare the professional playwright was changing his style in response to public demand. Yet one cannot be satisfied with this explanation. The themes of these final plays are too similar, and the ritual of forgiveness runs too persistently through them all, for this not to be a reflection in some way of Shakespeare's mind at this time. The point is, however, that it was not an easy forgiveness resulting from a new optimistic belief that vice is always defeated by virtue. Evil in all its horror is confronted directly in these plays. Salvation comes by magic or coincidence, and the ritual of pardon is performed in the serenity of a brave new world in which we cannot literally believe. Even so, the grosser villains are exempt from pardon. In *Pericles* the incestuous Antiochus and his daughter are destroyed by a blast from heaven; Cloten in *Cymbeline* has his head cut off by Guilderius with gruesome cheerfulness, and the Queen conveniently ends her own life. Those who are pardoned are those whose acts, in spite of themselves, turn out to have brought forth nothing but good. As in *Measure for Measure*, time has brought good results out of evil intentions, and no one standing on the stage in the remarkable last act of *Cymbeline* has managed to achieve any lasting evil. That is their good luck, or rather the playwright's magical manipulation of events. And so, as Cymbeline says, 'Pardon's the word to all'.

This bringing of good out of evil is, of course, a theological theme, the theme of the fortunate fall. '*O felix culpa!*' When, in *Paradise Lost*, Adam hears from Michael God's plan for the redemption of mankind, he replies:

> O goodness infinite, goodness immense!
> That all this good of evil shall produce,
> And evil turn to good.

In *Pericles*, *Cymbeline* and *The Winter's Tale* it is the playwright who demonstrates this goodness, who brings good out of all this evil; in *The Tempest*, it is one of his characters, Prospero, who plays God within the play and arranges his own scheme of redemption for the little society which comes under his control. This is the precise reverse of the tragic theme Shakespeare had handled so profoundly in earlier plays—the theme of innocence unwittingly co-operating with evil, of moral idealism playing into the hands of the Iagos of the world. With luck, with magic, with constant divine control, innocence is saved from betraying itself and others, and evil can be made to bring forth good. But not in the real world, only in the wish-fulfilment world, the symbolic world where the sea gives back its dead and the murdered god comes to life again. Shakespeare in these plays has made contact with that archetypal myth with which man has always consoled himself for the harsh paradoxes of the human situation as we know it.

The Winter's Tale is the greatest of Shakespeare's tragicomedies, and the play where the implications of his attitude at this time can be most clearly seen. The first three acts constitute a complete tragic play in themselves. Leontes, obsessed with his self-begotten notion that his wife has played him false with his friend Polixenes, brings her savagely to trial, thus causing the death of their young son Mamillius; orders the destruction of her new-born baby on the grounds that it must be Polixenes' bastard; and only realizes the monstrous fatuity of his obsession when he has been shocked out of it by the report of his wife's death. Shakespeare spares us nothing. The presentation of Leontes' sudden access of jealousy, and its wildfire growth, is brilliant and accurate; Mamillius, before he goes to his death, gives us the best and most attractive child scene in Shakespeare; Paulina, faithful and outspoken, the only one who says what *we* want to say throughout, meets nothing but rebuffs; and Hermione's splendid dignity does not save her. At the end, Mamillius dead, Hermione dead, and her infant daughter on the way to destruction, the consequences of Leontes' wicked jealousy appear to have worked themselves out. He knows better now, but it is too late to do anything about it.

This is a tragedy, yet a simple tragedy, resulting from the destruction done by evil, Leontes' jealousy. Virtue does not destroy itself; Leontes' jealousy is not, like Othello's rage, dependent for its existence on his very virtue. It is a pity that the innocent are destroyed by the guilty, but it is less disturbing than that the innocent should produce evil by their very innocence. The first movement of *The Winter's Tale* would, indeed, be like the first part of a melodrama—with evil triumphant and the machinery of saving coincidence not yet set in motion—were it not that it ends with evil subdued, only too late. Leontes is no longer the villain, but a sadder and a wiser man.

Part of the essential tragedy of *Hamlet* and *Othello*, I have suggested, is that one cannot undo the past; evil once done is done, and there is no way of restoring the lost world of innocence. But in these last plays Shakespeare finds a way of at least partially undoing evil. It is done by trickery, one might say—Hermione is not really dead, but hidden by Paulina; the infant daughter is saved and brought up as a shepherdess—but it is a symbolic trickery, whose function is to suggest, once again, a ritual of redemption. Act IV of *The Winter's Tale* takes us to Bohemia sixteen years later, and it is a new world, where even roguery is innocent. The lost princess is now Perdita, a shepherd's supposed daughter, and, true to the logic of fairy tale, she bears in her face and manners the hereditary stamp of her royal birth, so that she attracts Prince Florizel, Polixenes' son, and the two fall in love. Bohemia is fairyland, real enough in its pastoral atmosphere, its sheep-shearing feast and its flowering countryside, but fairyland none the less, where Time keeps Innocence until the opportunity has come for sending it back to do its redeeming work in the real world. When Polixenes breaks up the idyllic pastoral to discover Florizel's identity and abuses both Florizel and Perdita for daring to fall in love so out of their degree, his vile temper and cruel threats do not seriously disturb us: fairy tale fathers are always angry in such circumstances, and Polixenes' anger, though mean-spirited and selfish, has not the tragic overtones of Leontes' jealousy.

In the end we come back to the real world. The young lovers flee to Sicily, pursued by Polixenes, and eventually the discovery of Perdita's identity makes all well. But this, significantly, is not the end of the play, and the climax of reconciliation between the young lovers and their parents is not presented on the stage, only related in conversation between other characters. The climax is reserved for the discovery by Leontes that Hermione is still alive. Paulina introduces her as a newly-finished statue of the dead queen, but the statue turns out to be the living queen, kept in

c

seclusion all these sixteen years. But is the past really undone? Are we back before Leontes' fatal outburst of jealousy? For sixteen years Hermione has deliberately allowed her husband to think her dead, and she returns to life now to greet her long-lost daughter. The text gives her no greeting to her husband; her first words are to ask a blessing on Perdita. And there is no return to life for Mamillius. The curse is not fully lifted from the older generation: what Leontes has done he has done, and it cannot after all be undone. The younger generation can do better; they bring new innocence and new hope, and Hermione returns from the grave to give her blessing to them. She says to Perdita:

> thou shalt hear that I,
> Knowing by Paulina that the oracle
> Gave hope thou wast in being, have preserv'd
> Myself to see the issue.

She says nothing about being happy to live with Leontes again, or of the waste of those sixteen years: all her thought is for her daughter. The play ends with Leontes trying in his pattering speech to act the part of the leader of this group who have eyes for one another rather than for him. Murdered innocence comes to life again, with promise of a happy future, but the murderer can never again be the man he was before the crime.

So one cannot altogether undo the past, after all. Or perhaps, if we stay in Bohemia and instead of sending our innocents back to Sicily bring the guilty over to the Bohemian fairyland, the past can be undone for all. But at a cost. A solution that is valid for fairyland may not be valid for the real world. We cannot help wondering what is going to happen to the characters in *The Tempest* when they return from the magic isle to Italy.

In *The Tempest* Shakespeare pushes the theme of forgiveness farthest of all: there is no Antiochus, no Cloten, no dead Mamillius. Prospero's island is not subject to the normal laws of human destiny, for Prospero controls all with his magic and he can set the stage for the desired solution. In a sense the play is less Christian than any of Shakespeare's earlier treatments of guilt and justice. *Measure for Measure* leaves us with a sense of identity with the guilty, and we forgive each other for that reason. But Prospero has no real kinship with the other characters; he stands outside the action and stage-manages it, with Ariel's help. The ritual of forgiveness is conducted by a priest who is not himself in need of pardon. That is perhaps why many readers and spectators of *The Tempest* have found Prospero a pompous bore, with his prosy expositions of earlier events to both Miranda and Ariel and his easy loss of temper with inattention or weakness. Though he may not be, as was once widely thought, Shakespeare himself taking his farewell of the stage, he is certainly in a sense the creator of the other characters in the play, controlling them from above, a god-like figure who renounces his godhead only at the end of the play when, the action satisfactorily concluded, he breaks his magic staff to take his place among common humanity. He is in some respects like the Duke in *Measure for Measure*, for both manipulate the other characters in a god-like way (perfect contrast to the malevolent puppeteering of Iago), but the Duke is involved in his world more than Prospero is, and symbolizes that involvement by marrying Isabella in the end.

Miranda is youth and innocence, and her union with Ferdinand has the same symbolic meaning as that of Florizel and Perdita. Trinculo and Stephano represent gross animality, mankind at its lowest, and the spirits that serve them are not like Ariel, but alcoholic spirits which destroy the judgment—and it is the alcohol that attracts Caliban:

> That's a brave god and bears celestial liquor.
> I will kneel to him.

Ariel is the wise man's spirit, representing the scientist's control over nature, almost a Baconian symbol. The other characters represent different degrees of good and evil at the human level—except for Caliban, who remains a somewhat puzzling character. He is the conquered savage who has rejected the education of his master and is punished by slavery for that rejection. Yet the island was his, 'by Sycorax my mother', and Prospero took it from him by force. Prospero, as the superior order of being, would have, on the Elizabethan view, the right to dominate the inferior, so Shakespeare seems to be posing no ethical problem here. Caliban, savage son of a witch, the denier of civilization who refuses to fit into Prospero's scheme of things and is punished for his refusal, is in a strange way both evil and innocent. He is, in his own way, a child of nature; he loves music, he is credulous, and easily fooled by human art. There is perhaps more to be said for him than for the human villains whose treachery to each other constitutes a deeper evil than Caliban's crude villainy: *corruptio optimi pessima*.

The action takes place throughout on the island, washed by the purifying sea. It is shipwreck that saves Alonso and Antonio from their wickedness; as in *Pericles*, death by water proves to be redemption. It is shipwreck, too, that brings Ferdinand to Miranda, and having done that, brings to her gaze other representatives of the outside world, causing her to exclaim:

> O wonder!
> How many goodly creatures are there here!
> How beauteous mankind is! O brave new world,
> That has such people in't!

She is deceived: it is not a brave new world but a shabby old one. Her innocence is ignorance; she takes the motley assortment of schemers and traitors to be angels; and one is left wondering how she will cope with the realities of the everyday world when she has left the island for Italy. We remember that it was Othello's ignorance of the 'civilized' way of life that led him to trust Iago.

So in the end Shakespeare avoids tragedy by shifting his action to a magic island in which all can be controlled by a benevolent will: *The Tempest* is a magical play, full of grave beauty and rich poetry, a play out of this world, a wish-fulfilment play in which virtue has all the power and innocence meets its appropriate destiny. This is the Garden of Eden, with God, as Prospero, personally in charge to prevent Satan from prevailing; Miranda is a prelapsarian character who, as the play ends, is about to leave the shelter of Paradise to test her virtue in the wicked world. When Eve, 'our credulous mother', left Paradise she had already been tempted and had fallen, and she and Adam went out into the world disillusioned and knowledgeable. But credulous Miranda goes out unfallen into the world, whither Shakespeare refuses to follow her. His last gesture is to avert his eyes from the workaday world at the same time as he sends his characters back into it. There they may become figures in other plays, tragedies no less than comedies, since they will now be unprotected by Prospero's magic.

Shakespeare's last word can hardly be Prospero's:

> We are such stuff
> As dreams are made on, and our little life
> Is rounded with a sleep,

for if that is all that life is, it is an odd thing to spend one's career interpreting it dramatically. No; life is worth something after all. The characters in *The Tempest* leave the magical island of redemption to go back into civilization with all its imperfections and temptations, and this is a good thing, for man belongs with his kind, and there is a glory even in the tragic paradoxes of the human situation. In the Epilogue Prospero asks to be released, by the applause of the audience, from 'this bare island', and the adjective is significant. 'Let me not', he says,

> Let me not,
> Since I have my dukedom got
> And pardon'd the deceiver, dwell
> In this bare island by your spell; . . .

The magic world is but a 'bare island' after all, compared with the ordinary world of men. Just as, in *Paradise Lost*, 'all th' Eastern side of Paradise, so late their happy seat', appeared to Adam and Eve as flaming and terrible when they looked back for a moment before going down into the world that was all before them, so Prospero's Eden becomes uninhabitable in the end. Perhaps Shakespeare's last word, like Milton's, was that man cannot live in Paradise.

SAMUEL RICHARDSON[1]

EW WRITERS have suffered as much as Richardson for their
historical importance. He is, we all know, 'the father of the
English novel'. Generations of students have noted the fact
at university lectures. *Pamela*, they will confide in examinations,
is the first true English novel; it is written in epistolary form and
tells the story of a virtuous maid who resisted her wealthy master's
advances to the point where she won his hand in marriage.
Clarissa is longer, and tells the story of an equally virtuous lady
who was dishonoured by a rake while under the influence of
drugs and who consequently died, life after dishonour being
impossible. *Sir Charles Grandison*, also long, gives the picture of
an ideal gentleman and his ultimate happy marriage with one of
the many females who adore him. So much is common knowledge. Most of the students will go on to add that Richardson's
morality is bourgeois in the extreme; that Pamela, whose whole
endeavour is to sell her chastity in the dearest market, is more of
a designing minx than a paragon of virtue, and that Clarissa's
languishing into her grave after a purely technical loss of chastity
is a typical example of the unacceptable Puritan attitude to sex.
Nevertheless, the report will conclude, the fact that all three
novels are told in the form of letters passing between the characters
enables Richardson to give a fine psychological immediacy to the
action; he did understand the female heart, if not the male, and
records with commendable subtlety its fluctuations and vagaries;
and after all he *is* the father of the English novel. A few more
enterprising students might perhaps go on to vindicate Richardson's progenitive claims against those of Defoe or to contrast
Richardson's hot-house atmosphere with the fresh air of Fielding.
None of them will have read Richardson.

[1] An address given to the National Book League, London, on 23rd September
1954.

26

This has been the authorized version of Richardson for some time now, and of course there is some truth in it. Richardson *is* historically important, his morality *is* typical of the middle class of his day, his understanding of the female heart *is* impressive. But the true nature and value of his achievement can be obscured by these parrotted generalizations: it is time we removed the literary historian's ticket from the novels and read them with attention. And it would be as well if in reading them we forgot about 'the novel', about the subsequent history of the literary form which Richardson pioneered in England, and concentrated on what was before us. If we did that, we should find, I think, many unexpected patterns of meaning, particularly in *Pamela* and *Clarissa*. We should find that these works were in some ways more closely related to mediaeval saints' lives than to the novel as we now know it, or that they are a kind of *Paradise Lost* and *Paradise Regained*, set not in Eden or the wilderness but in the mundane world of social convention and obligation. Milton and Bunyan were concerned, in their different ways, with the exercise of free-will in resisting temptation and thus achieving salvation, Richardson is concerned with the exercise of prudence in order to achieve success through virtue and thus attain salvation in both worlds. Where the wiles of the devil make this double achievement impossible, as in *Clarissa*, prudence yields to saintliness and the next world provides the only refuge.

The ideas that Richardson employs and manipulates in his novels are: prudence and virtue, gentility and morality, reputation and character. The relation between them is often complex. Gentility is sometimes opposed to morality, sometimes a sign of morality. Reputation is generally the reward of good character but not always a guarantee of it. Prudence and virtue often go together, but sometimes (as in the latter part of *Clarissa*) lead in opposite directions. Richardson is very much aware of the social context; he is, one might say, obsessed with it. Rank mattered to him; the difference between classes was something he could never forget, and his moral patterns are built up against a background of social relationships which provide the most real and ineluctable facts about human life. For Richardson, all the tests of life are public, carried out in full view of society and conditioned by the structure of society. Eden for him is no garden but an estate, and Adam is a landlord with tenants, Eve a lady with social duties and dangers, and the serpent a neighbouring squire who violates the rules of the game by combining the genuine attractiveness of rank with an immoral character. There is no private wrestling with one's soul or with the devil here; Richardson's moral dramas are acted out on a public stage, and any moments of private anguish are promptly communicated by the sufferer to a friend in a letter. The epistolary technique is no incidental device: it is bound up with the social context of Richardson's moral patterns. And if there is no purely private anguish, there is similarly no purely private victory. Virtue must be recognized to be real, and Clarissa's death is made into a moral victory and indeed a beatification in virtue of the universal recognition of her saintliness which it produces. Richardson was the first important English writer to deal with basic moral problems imaginatively in a detailed social context.

This, then, is what is meant by the claim that Richardson's novels enshrine an eighteenth-century bourgeois morality. Virtue is consistently related to prudence on the one hand and to reputation on the other, and the arena of moral struggle is the stratified society of contemporary England. Further, in the eyes of Richardson and his fellows the aristocracy is still a class to be envied and aspired to. Pamela, the serving maid, has her virtue rewarded by marrying into the squirearchy; Clarissa's upper middle class family want to consolidate their position as property owners and achieve a title, and Clarissa's pursuer, the aristocratic Lovelace, has never any doubt that marriage to him is a desirable thing for her. Prosperous tradesmen and master craftsmen may have believed that their class was the sole repository of true virtue and respectability in the nation, but the aristocracy was still admired and looked up to as the class which the successful bourgeois hoped ultimately to enter. The implications of this double view of the aristocracy—as representing both rakishness and the heights of that worldly felicity which was the proper reward of a life of combined prudence and virtue—can be seen again and again in the working out of Richardson's plots.

Richardson more than once stated that his primary aim in writing these novels was moral instruction rather than mere entertainment. It is perhaps worth quoting his own summary of his intentions, which he gives us retrospectively in the preface to *Sir Charles Grandison*. *Pamela*, he tells us, 'exhibited the beauty and superiority of virtue in an innocent and unpolished mind, with the reward which often, even in this life, a protecting Providence bestows on goodness. A young woman of low degree, relating to her honest parents the severe trials she met with from a master who ought to have been the protector, not the assailer of her honour, shows the character of a libertine in its truly contemptible light. This libertine, however, from the foundation of good principles laid in his early years by an excellent mother; by his passion for a virtuous young woman; and by her amiable example and unwearied patience, when she became his wife, is, after a length of time, perfectly reclaimed.' *Clarissa*, he goes on, 'displayed a more melancholy scene. A young lady of higher fortune, and born to happier hopes, is seen involved in such variety of distresses as lead her to an untimely death; affording a warning to parents against forcing the inclinations of their children in the most important article of their lives, and to children against hoping too far from the fairest assurances of a man void of principle. The heroine, however, as a truly *Christian heroine*, proves superior to her trials; and her heart, always excellent, refined and exalted by every one of them, rejoices in the approach of a happy eternity. Her cruel destroyer appears wretched and disappointed, even by the boasted success of his vile machinations: but still (buoyed up with self-conceit and vain presumption) he goes on, after every short fit of imperfect, yet terrifying conviction, hardening himself more and more; till, unreclaimed by the most affecting warnings and repeated admonitions, he perishes miserably in the bloom of life, and sinks into the grave oppressed with guilt, remorse and horror. His letters, it is hoped, afford many useful lessons to the gay part of mankind against that misuse of wit and youth, of rank and fortune, and of every outward accomplishment, which turns them into a curse to the miserable possessor, as well as to all around him.' And now, he tells us, he presents in *Sir Charles Grandison* 'the example of a man acting uniformly well through a variety of trying scenes, because all his actions are regulated by one steady principle; a man of religion and virtue; of liveliness and spirit; accomplished and agreeable; happy in himself, and a blessing to others.'

Thus there can be no doubt that Richardson saw his novels as essentially moral works, comparable, as I have suggested, to mediaeval saints' lives. But of course a writer's statement of his intentions never tells us all the important things about a work, particularly when it is made, as here, after the books have been completed. There was, no doubt, a certain amount of complacent rationalization about Richardson's descriptions of the nature and purpose of his novels. The novels themselves are more complex than he ever seems to have realized, works of art by accident, one might almost say, like Bunyan's *Pilgrim's Progress*. The subtle moral and emotional pattern in *Clarissa*, which the modern reader finds so brilliant, derives from areas of Richardson's mind of which he cannot have been fully conscious. I shall return to this point when I come to discuss in more detail the individual novels.

Richardson was a printer by trade, and a good and prosperous one. He was born in 1689, and produced *Pamela*, his first novel, in 1740, when he was fifty-one years old. His belated discovery of his talent as a novelist emerged when he was in the process of compiling a volume of letters designed to serve as models for humble people not sufficiently educated to be able to write easily and confidently on those occasions when letters might be called for. He was working on this collection in 1739—probably writing letter no. 138, entitled 'A Father to a Daughter in Service, on hearing of her Master's attempting her Virtue'—when it occurred to him that he might work up a complete novel out of a series of letters written by a virtuous servant girl to her parents in the

intervals of dodging her master's attempts at rape. He remembered a true story of a virtuous servant girl who eventually
married her master after successfully repulsing his more irregular
approaches, and this exemplary combination of prudence and
virtue appealed to him. He dropped his collection of letters, and
embarked at white heat on *Pamela*, Part I of which he finished in
a couple of months.

The original volume of letters was then completed, and published in 1741, entitled *Letters Written to and for particular friends,
Directing the Requisite Style and Forms To be Observed in writing
Familiar Letters*. It is more than a collection of model letters.
Some of his friends, Richardson tells us in his preface, 'are of
opinion, that they will answer several good ends, as they may
not only direct the *forms* requisite to be observed on the most
important occasions; but, what is more to the purpose, by the
rules and instructions contained in them, contribute to *mend the
heart, and improve the understanding....* The writer ... has endeavoured ... to inculcate the principles of virtue and benevolence; to describe properly, and recommend strongly, the
social and relative duties; and to place them in such practical
lights, that the letters may serve for rules to think and act by, as
well as forms to write after.' The titles of the letters indicate the
sort of thing. 'To a Father, against putting a Youth of but
moderate Parts to a Profession that requires more extensive
Abilities.' 'From an Uncle to a Nephew, on his keeping bad
Company, bad Hours, etc., in his Apprenticeship.' 'General
Rules for agreeable Conversation in a young Man. From a
Father to a Son.' 'A young Man in Business, to a Father, desiring
Leave to address his Daughter.' 'From a young Lady to her
Father, acquainting him with a Proposal of Marriage made to her.'
'The Father's Answer, on a Supposition, that he approves *not* of
the young Man's Addresses.' 'A Father to a Son, to dissuade him
from the Vice of drinking to Excess.' 'A young Woman in Town
to her Sister in the Country, recounting her narrow Escape from
a Snare laid for her, on her first arrival, by a wicked Procuress.'
'To rebuke an irregular Address, when it is not thought proper

wholly to discourage it.' 'An Excuse to a Person who wants to borrow Money.' 'A Lady to her Friend, a young Widow Lady, who, having buried a polite and excellent Husband, inclines to marry a less deserving Gentleman, and of unequal Fortune.' There is only one letter that has no moral relevance at all; that is 'A humorous Epistle of neighbourly Occurrences and News, to a Bottle-Companion abroad', and here we see Richardson trying his hand at something rather in the Lovelace manner. Some of the letters almost sketch out an incipient plot, but the plan of the book does not allow Richardson to pause long enough over any situation to develop it into a story. But clearly he was itching to do so.

Perhaps it is relevant to add that Richardson had always been an assiduous letter-writer, and not only on his own behalf. For, according to his own account, when still 'a bashful and not forward boy' of not more than thirteen, three young women entrusted him with their love secrets in order to have him write answers to their lovers' letters. 'I have been directed to chide and even repulse when an offence was either taken or given, at the very time that the heart of the chider or repulser was open before me, overflowing with esteem and affection; and the fair repulser, dreading to be taken at her word, directing *this* word or *that* expression to be softened or changed.' This was good training for the future novelist of the female heart, and helps to explain why Richardson understood women—at any rate, certain kinds of women—so much better than he understood men. Men for Richardson the novelist were interesting only in so far as they aroused emotion in women; like Harriet Byron in *Sir Charles Grandison*, he first reacted to a new male character by imagining him in the rôle of a lover or a husband and estimated his character in the light of his probable behaviour in that rôle. That, incidentally, is the trouble with *Sir Charles Grandison*: in a novel whose object is to depict the ideal gentleman, Richardson could only achieve his purpose by introducing a sufficient number of female characters whose unanimity in worshipping the hero would sufficiently testify to his qualities. But a handsome, virtuous and wealthy baronet who is surrounded by females who are all in love with him and eventually coolly chooses as his bride the one who wins on points, as it were, is neither a very interesting nor a very edifying spectacle.

Richardson's volume of model letters reveals, or at least suggests, the moral world in which his novels take place. It is a world in which *relationships* are of the first importance: the relation between master and servant, between parents and children, between debtor and creditor, between suitor and sought—these and other relationships condition what is proper in human behaviour, and they are all, in some sense, symbolic of the relationship between man and God. They reveal a nexus of rights and duties, the rights being parental and proprietary, the duties being filial and, in a sense, feudal. Interspersed with the letters revealing, and indeed commanding, these rights and duties, are calls to repentance and amendment addressed to those who have gone astray. We thus have both the Law and the Prophets. The rewards for duty well done are clearly defined; they are both earthly and heavenly. Family and social relationships in this world being a microcosm of the larger relationship between man and God, there is an obvious analogy between prosperity in this world (the result of the proper management of human relationships) and eternal felicity in the next. The analogy between the two worlds is, throughout Richardson's work, complex but consistent. One moves into the next world only if the present world fails one. Pamela was able to combine prudence with virtue and, literally, make the best of both worlds. The title of the novel is *Pamela: or, Virtue Rewarded*. Clarissa, cheated out of prudence, fails to secure earthly prosperity but is instead rewarded in Heaven. I have already suggested that Richardson manipulated such ideas as prudence and virtue, gentility and morality, with considerable subtlety. Prudence guarantees earthly happiness, while virtue guarantees heavenly happiness, and the truly fortunate are those to whom circumstances allow both. Respectability is the outward and visible sign of prudence, and often, but not always, of true virtue. (Clarissa loses her external respectability while fully preserving her true virtue.) Similarly, gentility is the social behaviour and the conventions within which virtue is likely to flourish but does not necessarily flourish. *Clarissa* shows that otherworldliness is not a virtue until this world has failed one. Good management, economy, methodical disposition of one's time, prudence and efficiency in managing property and business are important qualities in all Richardson's heroes and heroines; Clarissa has them all at first, and, though Lovelace cheats her into the imprudent act of going off with him, she retains them to the end, changing only the objects to which she applies them: she gets ready for death with exemplary efficiency, even ordering and paying for her coffin in advance. It might well be asked whether Richardson is playing fair in endowing his heroines also with inimitable beauty. What has beauty to do with moral patterns he is tracing? The answer, I think, is simply that beauty is dangerous; it is more difficult to be virtuous with beauty than without it, because beauty attracts impure desire and provokes outrage. If, therefore, like Pamela, one can combine prudence, virtue and beauty, one is truly secure in both worlds. If, like Clarissa, one has virtue and beauty but is cheated by the devil out of the exercise of prudence on one critical occasion, one can compensate by raising virtue to the level of saintliness and, confident of the next world, cheerfully repudiate this one. Pamela is held up for our imitation (though Richardson makes it very clear that only a most exceptionally gifted servant can hope to marry her master), Clarissa for our adoration. The latter's is the true saint's life.

Richardson's epistolary method was not only a natural one for him, and an inevitable one in view of the road by which he approached the novel; it was also the appropriate one for a novelist concerned with the moment-to-moment recording of the fluctuations of emotion in the midst of moral struggle. It serves a similar purpose to that of the soliloquy in drama and the so-called stream of consciousness technique in modern fiction. We are brought immediately and directly into the consciousness of the character. It is, of course, a convention, in itself no better and no worse than other conventions in fiction. There is no point in speculating on how the characters could possibly have found time to write their hundreds of thousands of words, or how they could have had the presence of mind, in the midst of so much anguish, to sit down to write out everything, recalling every word spoken by themselves and by those with whom they have conversed; nor should we be distressed to find that they managed even to make copies of their letters and send them to other correspondents, and to transcribe other people's letters to them, and send them around. That Lovelace, rake and daredevil and man of action, impatient of delay and control, should in his turn find both the time and the inclination to write to his friend in the most intimate detail all his nefarious designs against Clarissa, and give a play-by-play account of everything he and she do and say, is of course improbable, but this kind of improbability does not touch the level of probability on which the novel moves. Quite apart from the fact that in the eighteenth century people wrote letters oftener and in more detail than could be imagined in our own age, there is the basic fact that all art requires conventions, and the criterion to be applied is the degree to which the author's use of the convention enables him to build up the proper life in the work. The letters do indeed take the reader into the heart of the developing situation and enable him to follow with extraordinary immediacy the psychological implications of the working out of the moral pattern.

One great difference there is between the epistolary technique and the stream of consciousness method: the latter emphasizes the privateness, the uniqueness, of individual experience, and is therefore appropriate for novels in which the essential loneliness of the individual is stressed and the possibility of adequate communication between individuals is a major problem (as it is, for example, in the novels of Virginia Woolf). The great theme of the eighteenth and often of the nineteenth century novelist is the relation between gentility and virtue; that of the modern novelist is the relationship between loneliness and love. The former theme requires a more public kind of elaboration than is appropriate for the latter, and letters are a most effective way of publicizing private experience. Publicity is important for Richardson. For him, virtue is not a matter between oneself and God; it must be publicly known and admired. Clarissa's death scene, for example, is most carefully staged; it is a device for demonstrating saintliness in action. For the saint to arrange such a demonstration implies a certain degree of self-approval, but that was no problem for Richardson, for whom self-approval must always co-exist with virtue, even with modesty. Clarissa is humble, yet she is full of conscious superiority, which she expresses quite unaffectedly, and the same can be said of Sir Charles Grandison. The moral life is a public life; it is an *exemplum*, something to be seen, approved and imitated or at least admired. Martyrdom would be useless if no one knew of it, and the exemplary life could not be exemplary if no one observed it. Clarissa represents the former, Pamela the latter.

Pamela, which came out in 1740 (though dated 1741), is an altogether simpler novel than *Clarissa*. Its theme is a folk theme, but the treatment is very different from anything one will find in folk literature. The class background is far from being the simple one of low-born maiden and high-born lord. Richardson's class was committed to the view that worth depended on individual effort rather than on status, yet they were fascinated by status and could not help admiring and envying it. This gives an ironic ambivalence to the whole moral pattern of the novel. Squire B. is bent first on seduction and then on rape; he is dishonest, malevolent, cruel and persecuting. He does everything he can to get Pamela into his physical power, and at one stage is on the point of committing rape when Pamela providentially falls into fits and scares him off. (All the while the horrible Mrs Jewkes, the housekeeper to whom Mr B. had entrusted Pamela in the hope of softening her up for seduction, looks on with glee and exhorts her master not to 'stand dilly dallying' but to get the act of violation over with at once. Likewise, in *Clarissa*, the rape of the heroine is watched and encouraged by Mrs Sinclair and her band of trollops. Even rape must be public in Richardson.) Yet, after Mr B. has relented and sent Pamela home, she returns voluntarily when he sends for her, loving and admiring him all the time, though disapproving of his attempts to dishonour her. Whenever he relaxes his attempts for a moment, she is all respect and admiration for him; and when he finally convinces her that her continued successful resistance has led him to offer marriage, she is all humble love and passionate gratitude. Successful resistance turns lust to love; once Squire B. has got over his weakness for seduction and rape he is seen by Richardson as a wholly admirable person, not only worthy of the love of a virtuous girl like Pamela but deserving of her humblest obedience and veneration. She considers herself unworthy of him. 'My good master,' she writes, 'my kind friend, my generous benefactor, my worthy protector, and oh! all the good words in one, my affectionate husband, that is soon to be (be curbed in, my proud heart, know thyself, and be conscious of thy unworthiness!) has just left me, with the kindest, tenderest expressions, and gentlest behaviour that ever blest a happy maiden.' If a man is a wealthy landowner, and handsome and graceful in manners to boot, he must be considered wholly good so long as he is not being actively bad. Printers do not become angels by merely ceasing to threaten girls with sexual violence, but evidently squires do. Richardson, of course, would have been horrified by such a comment. He claimed that he was showing a genuine reformation of character, wrought by Pamela's virtue in a young man who had the advantage of an excellent moral grounding in childhood. But we know better, and I suspect Pamela did.

This counter pattern which crosses the moral pattern which Richardson consciously planned for the work does not, of course, spoil the novel; on the contrary, it makes it richer and truer. Human nature is like that; motivation is complex, and the relation between our moral professions and the full psychological explanation of our actions is far from simple. Sometimes it almost seems that Richardson knew this and was deliberately writing a sly, ironic novel. After Mr B.'s first attempts on her, before she has been deceitfully carried off to the country house where Mrs Jewkes presides, Pamela very properly decides to go

D

home to her parents and leave the scene of temptation; but she finds excuse after excuse for not going, and postpones her departure until Mr B. has managed to mature his plan for tricking her into going instead to the house he has waiting for her. And though she professes to prefer honest poverty to vicious luxury, she makes it quite clear in her letters home that she has grown used to a much better way of life than they can afford in their humble cottage. She notes all the fine clothes given her by her late mistress and her master, and, having completed an inventory of what she has, noting what she can in conscience retain, makes such remarks as: 'Here is a calico night-gown, that I used to wear o' mornings. 'Twill be rather too good for me when I get home; but I must have something. . . . And here are four other shifts, one the fellow to that I have on; another pretty good one, and the other two old fine ones, that will serve me to turn and wind with at home, for they are not worth leaving behind me; and here are two pairs of shoes; I have taken the lace off, which I will burn, and may-be will fetch me some little matter at a pinch, with an old silver buckle or two.' Most suggestive of all, she gives up the fine clothes her lady had given her, determined not to sail under false colours, and provides herself with a new, simpler outfit.

And so when I had dined, up stairs I went, and locked myself up in my little room. There I dressed myself in my new garb, and put on my round-eared ordinary cap, but with a green knot, my home-spun gown and petticoat, and plain leather shoes, but yet they are what they call Spanish leather; and my ordinary hose, ordinary I mean to what I have been lately used to, though I should think good yarn may do very well for every day, when I come home. A plain muslin tucker I put on, and my black silk necklace, instead of the French necklace my lady gave me; and put the ear-rings out of my ears. When I was quite equipped, I took my straw hat in my hand, with its two blue strings, and looked in the glass, as proud as any thing. To say truth, I never liked myself so well in my life.

O the pleasure of descending with ease, innocence, and resignation! Indeed, there is nothing like it! An humble mind, I plainly see, cannot meet with any very shocking disappointment, let Fortune's wheel turn round as it will.

And down she trips, looking, as she very well knows, more

ravishing than ever, and runs straight into her master, who pretends not to recognize the 'pretty neat damsel'.

He came up to me, and took me by the hand, and said, 'Whose pretty maiden are you? I dare say you are Pamela's sister, you are so like her. So neat, so clean, so pretty! Why, child, you far surpass your sister, Pamela!'

I was all confusion, and would have spoken, but he took me about the neck: 'Why,' said he, 'you are very pretty, child: I would not be so free with your *sister*, you may believe; but I must kiss *you*.'—'O Sir,' said I, 'I am Pamela, indeed I am: indeed I am Pamela, *her own-self*!'

This, and scenes like this, are admirably done, whatever Richardson thought he was really doing. It is as though Richardson knows Pamela so well that he has simply to let himself *be* Pamela in order to write the letters. He does not have to understand her or to analyse her motives, any more than she understands and analyses herself. She sets herself out to attract her master from the beginning, though she herself does not realize it and perhaps her creator does not; but prudence as well as morality demands that she keep herself unravished while keeping his interest in her at fever pitch. She thinks she is trying to escape his clutches, but allows herself to be deflected from her attempts at escape by the slightest obstacles (even to the point of supposing an inoffensive cow to be a fierce bull), and when he finally lets her go she flies back to him at his summons.

When he releases her, she leaves with a reluctance that surprises herself. 'I think I was loth to leave the house. Can you believe it? —What could be the matter with me, I wonder? I felt something so strange at my heart! I wonder what ailed me.' She writes home in this troubled state of mind from a village where the coach has paused. 'Here I am, at a little poor village, almost such a one as yours!' The smallness and poverty of the village (and by implication of her parents' home) are mentioned more than once. And when Mr B.'s letter arrives, asking her to return (though only in the most oblique way promising marriage) she writes in her journal, 'O my exulting heart!' She knows now what she has wanted all along.

The rest of Part I and all of Part II are much less interesting.

The marriage duly takes place, and there is a lively scene a little while afterwards when, the Squire being temporarily away from home, his sister Lady Davers calls and, assuming that Pamela is her brother's mistress and not his wife, abuses her with fine snobbish scorn. But after this the book swells into a chorus of admiration from the neighbouring gentry. Pamela's story is known, and she is trotted around aristocratic drawing-rooms to be admired for her successful defence of her chastity and her nobility of character. She has perfect manners, and conducts herself everywhere with model decorum. Lady Davers is reconciled and joins the chorus of admiration. One of Pamela's last acts in Part I is to exercise her benevolence on an illegitimate daughter of her adoring husband, product of an early and fully confessed amour.

Part II, added in 1742, to replace and discredit continuations (both serious and satirical) by other hands, is a dull marriage manual showing the ideal couple in action, with a mild and temporary break in perfect felicity when Squire B. becomes involved with a widowed countess at a masked ball. (Thus showing the immorality of masked balls, which Richardson was never tired of preaching.) Pamela becomes the oracle, dispensing wisdom in her letters on everything from the state of the drama to Locke's views on education. The most interesting part of *Pamela* is over by the time her marriage is accomplished.

Pamela is thus a psychologically realistic fairy tale grounded in middle class morality which achieves a level of ironic counter-statement by the sheer honesty and accuracy of its heroine's self-revelation. Mr B. is less successful than the heroine; Richardson had little first-hand knowledge of the manners and conversation of the higher squirearchy and nobility, and Mr B. is interesting only for the reactions he produces in Pamela. It has long been the fashion to complain about the morality of the book, with its attempt to reconcile virtue with material self-interest. But what is wrong with reconciling virtue with self-interest if you can? There are three factors involved: what you are really like (psychology); what will get you success in this life (prudence);

what will get you success in the next life and may with luck also do so in this (virtue). Pamela is true to her psychology (as one might say) and manipulates her virtue into prudence with unconscious art. (One assumes that it is unconscious.) All one can say is: nice work if you can get it.

There is surely nothing immoral in refusing to have sexual relations with the man you are in love with until marriage secures you a permanent relationship with him. It is not *that* which seems to me the moral flaw in the novel. What I object to is something that appears equally clearly in *Clarissa*, namely Richardson's narrow and mechanical view of sex, and indeed of love. Pamela's love for Squire B. cannot be easily dissociated from her admiration of his position and wealth; once he has been prevailed on to behave decently his position and wealth can be allowed to make him desirable. It is not that Squire B. marries Pamela because he cannot satisfy his lust outside marriage; it is rather that her continued defence of her chastity, and his reading of her letters and journal, have aroused in him a moral admiration of her character which changes his sexual desire into moral approval. Sex, wherever it is treated in Richardson, is presented as something violent and violating. The notion of mutual sexual satisfaction never seems to have occurred to him. None of Richardson's rakes seeks such satisfaction; they want to rape; they are not sensualists but competitive collectors of virginities by violence. In *Clarissa*, Lovelace achieves his nefarious purpose on a drugged and passive victim. It is a purely quantitative business, a matter of arithmetic: the more people you can violate, the greater your glory as a rake. This is a Kinsey report view of sex, a mechanical as well as an unrealistic view. And the rake's view of sex as violence done by the man to the woman is lower even than Kinsey. The woman is sacrificed to male violence, and even marriage but provides the proper arena for such a sacrifice. In *Clarissa* images of the victim stretched out before the knife recur again and again, directly and obliquely. In *Sir Charles Grandison* the wedding night of the hero and heroine is described in terms suggestive of the bride as a sacrifice. Richardson understood the housemaid's quiver of joy at the thought of marrying her handsome master, and reproduces this kind of sensibility with great brilliance. But that has as little to do either with sex or with love as has the attitude of his rakes, for whom a seduction or a rape (it is all one to them) is, like climbing Mount Everest, a matter of planning and stamina. There is no pleasure in it: the pleasure lies in the satisfaction of having done it. One can, if one likes, relate this characteristic of Richardson's to the Puritan suspicion of sex, but I for one am dissatisfied with such easy generalizations. Many Puritans, because of their very suspicion of sex perhaps, had an uncanny insight into its nature and working. I suspect it has something to do with Richardson's own temperament and history.

Clarissa appeared in eight volumes in 1748. It is a subtler and profounder work than *Pamela*, and by general agreement Richardson's masterpiece. It is impossible to give an adequate account of this long and complex novel here, and I must be content with noting aspects which I think interesting and significant. In the first place, the deployment of the plot is a remarkable achievement. Clarissa, the virtuous, beautiful, talented younger daughter of the wealthy Harlowes, with a fortune of her own left her by her grandfather (but which she has filially surrendered to her father), is manipulated from a position which combines the height of virtue with the height of material good fortune to one in which she is despised and rejected, becoming an almost Christ-like figure of the Suffering Servant. This is achieved by no sudden *peripeteia*, no dramatic reversal, but by a brilliantly deployed series of little incidents which combine to deny Clarissa the fruits of prudence without actually making her an imprudent character and eventually close in on her to prevent any return to the world of material happiness. Clarissa is manoeuvred into sainthood by a cunningly woven mesh of circumstance which seems always until almost the very end to allow the possibility of escape back into the world of lost prosperity. She is given the appearance of guilt without real guilt; she is made to appear to fall without having really fallen; almost everybody comes at one time or another to doubt the purity of her motives or the perfection of her character. Then, in the end, when public opinion seems to have disposed of her for ever, she rises in death from her degradation to shine on high in glorious resurrection.

Let me briefly recall the main movements of the story. The first major phase of the action concerns the Harlowe family's sustained attempt to force Clarissa to marry the stupid, ugly and mean-spirited Mr Solmes. The leading spirit here is her contemptible brother, who sees financial advantage to himself in the match, while her jealous sister Arabella, suspicious that Clarissa is in love with Lovelace (whom she loves but pretends to hate), is equally determined to have her married off to Solmes. Her father, a gouty autocrat, finds his authority and what he calls his honour involved, and insists on the match. Her mother, weakly giving in to pressure from the rest of the family, adds her persuasions. Meanwhile, Clarissa's brother has insulted Lovelace, who has overcome and wounded him in a duel, while Clarissa reluctantly consents to a clandestine correspondence with Lovelace in order to prevent him from taking a bloody revenge on the Harlowe family. Clarissa is in continuous correspondence with her friend Anna Howe, to whom she recounts each day's events.

The situation here developed enables Richardson to develop a much richer moral pattern than anything to be found in *Pamela*. Clarissa, the perfection of whose character is made clear from the beginning, finds herself obliged to disobey her parents and at the same time involved in clandestine correspondence with a rake. Richardson is here exploring, as fully as he can, the borderland of his moral universe. Children must obey their parents; but on the other hand parents must never force a child into marriage against the child's inclinations. These principles Richardson had already made clear elsewhere, but they are clear enough in the story. Clarissa offers to give up all thoughts of marriage and to live single either on the estate her grandfather had left her or anywhere else acceptable to her parents. She is suspected of being really in love with Lovelace, but she protests that she will have nothing more to do with him or any other man if she is allowed to remain free of Solmes. But her brother has organized the family to press for her marriage with Solmes, and she is confined to her room and subjected to every kind of pressure in the hope that she will consent to the marriage, in connection with which the most elaborate and (to the Harlowe family) favourable settlements have been drawn up. The picture of family pressure operating on Clarissa is drawn with magnificent vividness. The spiteful brother and sister, the tender but insistent mother, the hectoring uncles, and in the background the father egotistically insistent on his parental rights—all this comes through with vividness and immediacy from Clarissa's letters to Anna Howe. At the same time Anna herself is revealed in her replies as a sprightly and witty girl whose chief pleasure in life (to Clarissa's distress) is teasing the worthy gentleman whom her mother wants her to marry and whom, it is clear, she will eventually marry. (Another piece of evidence, incidentally, that Richardson did not understand the nature of love between the sexes.)

We also get occasional glimpses of Lovelace, who is revealed as the master mind behind the preposterous behaviour of the Harlowe family. By bribing servants to report his determination to perform various rash acts in pursuit of his vengeance against the Harlowes and his love for Clarissa, he whips them into a fury of determination that Clarissa shall marry the odious Mr Solmes at the earliest possible moment. Pressure on Clarissa grows stronger and stronger; Lovelace presents himself continually as a source of refuge, offering to provide unconditional sanctuary for the persecuted girl among the ladies of his family (who, of course, all adore her, though by reputation only). Finally, when it looks as though Clarissa is to be forced by physical compulsion into marriage with Solmes, she momentarily yields to Lovelace's suggestion of rescue, only to revoke her acceptance of his offer shortly afterwards. But Lovelace refuses to take cognizance of her letter of revocation and awaits her at the garden gate with all necessary equipment for escape. On her going out to inform him that she cannot take advantage of his offer, he contrives a scene which enables him to whisk her off, and henceforth she is in Lovelace's power.

The second movement of the story deals with the struggle between Clarissa and Lovelace. He is a rake, and therefore is reluctant to marry, though he adores Clarissa. He contrives matters so that she is made more and more dependent on him, and eventually brings her to London, to an apparently respectable lodging house which is in fact a brothel run by an old friend of his and staffed by girls whom he has ruined. After much coming and going, and a complex series of movements in Clarissa's heart towards and away from Lovelace—the documentation of this shows us Richardson at the height of his powers—he attempts her virtue by arranging a mock fire and bringing her out of her room in her night dress to escape the supposed conflagration. She sees his purpose, discovers his trick, and successfully repulses him, shaken to the core by his villainy. He is repentant and offers immediate marriage, which she proudly rejects. She despises him, and will not marry a man whom she despises. He exerts himself to restore himself to favour in her eyes, arranging for friends of his to play the part of an emissary from her relatives offering reconciliation if only she is married to the man she eloped with, and even to personate his own noble relations. He succeeds to the point of manoeuvring her back to the house of ill fame, and there, with the co-operation of the inmates, he first drugs and then violates her. Now that he has climbed his Everest and proved that it cannot be done without carrying oxygen, as it were, he is prepared to concede her true virtue and to marry her. (Of course he had pretended to be dying to marry her all the time, but had adroitly phrased his offers so as to compel her refusal on each occasion.) After illness and hysteria, she escapes from him, and ignores his frenzied appeals for forgiveness and immediate marriage. Meanwhile her friends and relations consider her a ruined woman who has wilfully contributed to her own dishonour. Her family regard her as a wicked runaway who deliberately chose ruin at the hands of a rake.

The third and final movement of the book deals with Clarissa's vindication and sanctification. By means of letters appropriately copied and circulated the truth begins to emerge. But her family are prevented from knowing the truth until after her death, while her dear friend Anna Howe is kept from her by a number of contrived circumstances, and even her sympathetic cousin Morden, who finally arrives home from Italy, is not allowed to come to see her until her death is inevitable. All this time the unfortunate Lovelace is frantically pleading for forgiveness and marriage, backed by his powerful family. But Clarissa remains alone, in lodgings, befriended by strangers, cut off from friends and relations. And there, having made all suitable preparations, she dies, before an audience of new-found admirers. Her death is a studied presentation of *ars moriendi*, a high example of the art of dying like a Christian. Her family, on finally learning the whole truth about her conduct, are consumed by remorse, and her funeral is the occasion of its exhibition. Every single wicked character in the book then meets an appropriate sticky end.

Such a sketchy account of the plot can give no impression of the book's richness and subtlety, nor can it illustrate the effective way in which Richardson moves his heroine from the context of this world to her glorious martyr's inheritance of the next. And almost until the end he keeps the possibility of marriage with Lovelace open. Her friend Anna Howe urges her that this is the way to bring everything to a reasonably happy ending, and the Lovelace family, who love and admire her, plead with her to reform by marriage the attractive but wayward author of all the mischief. At one time she had been prepared to marry him in order to reform him, and she admitted, if not love for him, at least a predisposition in his favour. But there is no forgiveness for violation; she cannot marry a man so wicked, nor can she consider herself, a violated woman, as someone who ought to marry. The grave, and Heaven beyond it, are now her only resource. The book, which had begun as an exercise in Holy Living, ends as a case history of Holy Dying.

Before her violation Clarissa had been prepared to consider marriage to the fascinating Lovelace for the purpose of reforming him, and Lovelace himself cunningly played on his need for reformation by such means. But that temptation is over once the rape has taken place; marriage is henceforth unthinkable to Clarissa (but not to her friends), whose thoughts are more and more centred on the next world. Attempted violation (such as Pamela met with) is one thing; successful violation is another. Richardson is not as clear as he might be on the relation between guilt and misfortune. Sometimes he suggests that Clarissa (though through no fault of her own) is 'ruined', made permanently unfit for matrimony by having been forcibly rendered a fallen woman. Like so many of his generation and later, Richardson had a purely technical view of chastity. Clarissa, though a saint, had lost her chastity, so she must give up any hope of accommodation with this world. She could not, of course, consider marriage with her violator (and Richardson is a cut above many nineteenth-century moralists in this), but neither could she respect any other man willing to marry a woman who had lost her 'honour' however innocently.

Perhaps Clarissa could have escaped Lovelace's clutches in time if she had really tried. She could easily, it has been suggested, have put herself under the protection of the nearest magistrate. But to look at her confinement in Mrs Sinclair's house in this way is to misunderstand what Richardson is doing. That house has by this time become a microcosm of the world, and Clarissa's confinement in it is a symbol of her confinement in this wicked mundane sphere; the only escape now can be into the next world. After her violation, *all* men are vile. Nothing in this remarkable book is more psychologically convincing than Clarissa's horror of anything in trousers after her experience at the hands of Lovelace. She uses the word 'man' as a term of abuse and contempt, and at first refuses to have a doctor in her room during her final illness because he is of the male sex. This world, in whose social duties man may, with luck, imitate heavenly felicity and anticipate his ultimate reward, has become for Clarissa a den of iniquity. Her family, obedience to whom is a condition of earthly prosperity, have made her obedience impossible. She cannot go back to them. She is going home to her father, as she tells Lovelace in a deliberately ambiguous note, but it is her Heavenly Father; her family relationship is subsumed in the higher relationship to God, the Father of all.

It might be argued that by making Clarissa perfect in beauty, virtue and wealth Richardson was deliberately restricting the implications of the story. What universal application can be drawn from the fate of a character who is endowed with all possible good qualities of character and fortune? It can, however, be argued with equal plausibility that Richardson, by putting the extreme case, by showing how even this perfect creature can be caught in the mesh of the wicked world, is extending rather than limiting his context. But this whole argument is academic. *Clarissa* is a novel both realistic in its psychology and symbolic in its scope and meaning: it elaborates the conditions under which virtue can be driven to sainthood. Further it must be remembered that for all her saintliness Clarissa is human. She can be proud and obstinate, and she has her moments of weakness. And the origin of her troubles lay in her breaking of the social rules, however innocently.

Lovelace is a more interesting character than Mr B., though no more convincing. He is a mild and timid man's picture of the ideal rake, of Satan as gentleman, witty, boisterous, adventurous, courageous, ruthless. His letters to his friend Belford are pre-posterous enough, showing him as they do congratulating him-self on being a rake and introspecting on his rakishness with incredible self-consciousness. To us he is less a fascinating villain than a cad and a fool, who does not even know how to handle his women. But he serves his purpose, which is after all little more than that of a catalyst.

There is much more to be said about *Clarissa*—indeed, I feel that I have only touched the fringe of its meaning and its interest —but I must say a brief word about Richardson's last novel, *Sir Charles Grandison*, published in seven volumes in 1754. The relative lack of moral conflict in this work makes it less interesting than the other two. Further, Richardson is here concerned ex-

clusively with high life, which was unfamiliar to him, and the
result is a stiffness that compares most unfavourably with Pamela's
vulgar self-revelations. Who can be convinced by a hero who
has absolutely everything life has to offer—fortune, supreme good
looks, perfect virtue and perfect prudence? He goes through life
settling other people's affairs with calm assurance, making friends
of enemies, disarming those who seek duels with him by a flick
of his wrist (for he disapproves of duelling), arranging marriages,
making up quarrels, mingling seemly mirth with grave reproof.
Nowhere else in Richardson is the public nature of the emotional
life made so apparent. Everyone reveals his (or, more often, her)
inmost emotions to everyone else. Letters are shown, copied,
exchanged. Sir Charles, who first meets the beautiful and virtuous
Harriet Byron through rescuing her from being carried off by
the villainous Sir Hargrave Pollexfen, soon reveals to her the
complicated story of his emotional entanglements in Italy, and
she is referred to letters in the hands of the Rev. Dr Bartlett, Sir
Charles' chaplain, for further details. The Italian subplot is melodramatic and artificial, and the lovely Clementina, who would
have married Sir Charles but for a difference in religion, is an odd
creature to find in Richardson's pages. But in high life anything
can happen, and Sir Charles speaks Italian perfectly. The book is
not, however, as dull as this description might lead one to suppose.
Lady G.'s accounts of her tiffs with her husband are often lively
and amusing, and there are other 'humours' in the book to relieve
the complacent virtue of the hero.

But if Richardson had written only *Sir Charles Grandison* he
would not be remembered today as a novelist. The detail here,
which is profuse, does not weave the fine psychological and moral
mesh of *Clarissa*, nor has it the naïve conviction of *Pamela*. I
could make a case for *Sir Charles Grandison*, but it would be
disproportionate to attempt to do so here at the end of an already
too crowded discussion of the other novels. I would rather end
by returning to *Clarissa*, and urge you to forget what the textbooks
of literary history say and read this brilliant and original novel
with a fresh mind.

THE POETRY OF DYLAN THOMAS[1]

THE SUDDEN and premature death of Dylan Thomas produced elegies and appreciations in extraordinary numbers on both sides of the Atlantic. Thomas was the most poetical poet of our time. He talked and dressed and behaved and lived like a poet; he was reckless, flamboyant, irreverent, innocent, bawdy and bibulous. His verse, too, had a romantic wildness about it that even the reader who could make nothing of it recognized as 'poetic'. In the February 1954 issue of the *London Magazine* a twenty-six-year-old poet wrote a letter saying that Thomas represented the 'archetypal picture of the Poet' for his generation, and that the death of this wild and generous character produced 'something like a panic' in the world of letters. He was answered in the next issue of the magazine by a thirty-one-year-old poet who said that this was puerile nonsense and deplored what he called the 'fulsome ballyhoo' which Thomas's death evoked in both England and America. There was perhaps an element of ballyhoo in the spate of articles about Thomas, but sober critical judgment is difficult when one is writing of a brilliant young man who has died at the very height of his career (or at the very height of his promise; we shall never tell now). And surely the exaggeration of the sense of loss at the death of a poet is a sign of health in any culture? Now that the shock has worn off, however, we can turn more soberly to ask the question: What sort of poetry did Dylan Thomas write, and how good is it?

In a note to the collected edition of his poems, Thomas wrote: 'These poems, with all their crudities, doubts, and confusions, are written for the love of Man and in praise of God. . . . ' And in his prologue to the same volume he proclaimed his intention of celebrating the world and all that is in it:

[1] First published in *The English Journal* (Chicago), October 1954.

> . . . as I hack
> This rumpus of shapes
> For you to know
> How I, a spinning man,
> Glory also this star, bird
> Roared, sea born, man torn, blood blest.
> Hark: I trumpet the place,
>
> From fish to jumping hill! Look:
> I build my bellowing ark
> To the best of my love
> As the flood begins,
> Out of the fountainhead
> Of fear, rage red, manalive, . . .

This prologue is a great hail to the natural world, and man as a part of it, and might be taken by the careless reader as an impressionist outpouring of celebratory exclamations:

> Huloo, my prowed dove with a flute!
> Ahoy, old, sea-legged fox,
> Tom tit and Dai mouse!
> My ark sings in the sun
> At God speeded summer's end
> And the flood flowers now.

Yet in fact this spontaneous-seeming poem is a cunningly contrived work in two movements of fifty-one lines each, with the second section rhyming backwards with the first—the first line rhyming with the last, the second with the second last, and so on, the only pair of adjacent lines which rhyme being the fifty-first and the fifty-second. Whether the ear catches this complicated cross rhyming or not, it is part of a cunning pattern of ebb and flow, of movement and counter-movement, which runs through the poem. This single piece of evidence is perhaps enough to prove that, for all the appearance of spontaneity and sometimes of free association that his poems present to some readers, Thomas was a remarkably conscientious craftsman for whom meaning was bound up with pattern and order. No modern poet in English has had a keener sense of form or has handled stanzas and verse paragraphs—whether traditional or original—with more deliberate cunning.

It is worth stressing this at the outset because there are still some people who talk of Thomas as though he were a writer of an inspired mad rhetoric, of glorious, tumbling, swirling language which fell from his pen in magnificent disorder. He has been held up by some as the antithesis of Eliot and his school, renouncing the cerebral orderliness of the 1920s and the 1930s in favour of a new romanticism, an engaging irresponsibility. On the other hand there are those who discuss his poems as though they are merely texts for exposition, ignoring the rhyme scheme and the complicated verbal and visual patterning to concentrate solely on the intellectual implications of the images. The truth is that Thomas is neither a whirling romantic nor a metaphysical imagist, but a poet who uses pattern and metaphor in a complex craftsmanship in order to create a ritual of celebration. He sees life as a continuous process, sees the workings of biology as a magical transformation producing unity out of identity, identity out of unity, the generations linked with one another and man linked with nature. Again and again in his early poems he seeks to find a poetic ritual for the celebration of this identity:

> Before I knocked and flesh let enter,
> With liquid hands tapped on the womb,
> I who was shapeless as the water
> That shaped the Jordan near my home
> Was brother to Mnetha's daughter
> And sister to the fathering worm.

Or again:

> The force that through the green fuse drives the flower
> Drives my green age; that blasts the roots of trees
> Is my destroyer.

And most clearly of all:

> This bread I break was once the oat,
> This wine upon a foreign tree
>
> Plunged in its fruit;
> Man in the day or wind at night
> Laid the crops low, broke the grape's joy . . .

This flesh you break, this blood you let
Make desolation in the vein,
Were oat and grape
Born of the sensual root and sap;
My wine you drink, my bread you snap.

Man is locked in a round of identities; the beginning of growth
is also the first movement towards death, the beginning of love
is the first move towards procreation, which in turn moves
towards new growth, and the only way out of time's squirrel-cage
is to embrace the unity of man with nature, of the generations
with each other, of the divine with the human, of life with death,
to see the glory and the wonder of it. If we ignore the cosmic
round to seize the moment when we think we have it, we are
both deluded and doomed:

I see the boys of summer in their ruin
Lay the gold tithings barren,
Setting no store by harvest, freeze the soils;
There in their heat the winter floods
Of frozen loves they fetch their girls,
And drown the cargoed apples in their tides.

Those boys of light are curdlers in their folly,
Sour the boiling honey; . . .

This is from an early poem; and several of these early poems strike
this note—the note of doom in the midst of present pleasure, for
concealed in each moment lie change and death. Thomas did not
rush towards the celebration of unity in all life and all time which
later became an important theme of comfort for him; he moved
to it through disillusion and experiment. The force that drives
the flower and the tree to full burgeoning and then to death
would destroy him also. Only later came the realization that such
destruction is no destruction, but a guarantee of immortality, of
perpetual life in a cosmic eternity:

And death shall have no dominion.
Dead men naked they shall be one
With the man in the wind and the west moon;
When their bones are picked clean and the clean bones gone,
They shall have stars at elbow and foot;

E

> Though they go mad they shall be sane,
> Though they sink through the sea they shall rise again;
> Though lovers be lost love shall not,
> And death shall have no dominion.

It is this thought that sounds the note of triumph in 'Ceremony after a Fire Raid' and which provides the comfort in 'A Refusal to Mourn the Death, by Fire, of a Child in London'.

'A Refusal to Mourn' is a poem worth pausing at, for it illustrates not only a characteristic theme of what might be called the middle Thomas, but also a characteristic way of handling the theme. The poem is ritualistic in tone; its dominant images are sacramental; and the cunningly contrived rise and fall of the cadence of each stanza adds to the note of formal ceremony. There are four stanzas, the first two and one line of the third containing a single sentence which swells out to a magnificent surge of meaning. Then, after a pause, the final stanza makes a concluding ritual statement, an antiphonal chant answering the first three stanzas. The paraphrasable meaning of the poem is simple enough: the poet is saying that never, until the end of the world and the final return of all things to their primal elements, will he distort the meaning of the child's death by mourning. One dies but once, and through that death becomes reunited with the timeless unity of things. But the paraphrasable meaning is not, of course, the meaning of the poem, which is expanded at each point through a deliberately sacramental imagery while at the same time the emotion is controlled and organized by the cadences of the stanza. The first stanza and a half describe the end of the world as a return from differentiated identity to elemental unity:

> Never until the mankind making
> Bird beast and flower
> Fathering and all humbling darkness
> Tells with silence the last light breaking
> And the still hour
> Is come of the sea tumbling in harness
>
> And I must enter again the round
> Zion of the water bead

> And the synagogue of the ear of corn
> Shall I let pray the shadow of a sound
> Or sow my salt seed
> In the least valley of sackcloth to mourn
>
> The majesty and burning of the child's death . . .

There is no obscurity here, to anybody who knows Thomas's idiom. We have only to recall 'This bread I break was once the oat' to realize the significance of the first three lines of the second stanza. The water bead and the ear of corn are symbolic primal elements, to which all return at the end. But why '*Zion* of the water bead' and '*synagogue* of the ear of corn'? The answer is simply that these are sacramental images intended to give a sacramental meaning to the statement. It is a kind of imagery of which Thomas is very fond (one can find numerous other examples, among them such a phrase as 'the parables of sun light' in 'Poem in October' or his use of Adam and Christ in his earlier poems). One might still ask why he says 'synagogue' and not 'church'. The answer, I think, is that he wants to shock the reader into attention to the sacramental meaning. A more everyday religious word might pass by as a conventional poetic image, but 'synagogue' attracts our attention at once; it has no meaning other than its literal one, and therefore can be used freshly in a non-literal way. The third stanza continues:

> I shall not murder
> The mankind of her going with a grave truth
> Nor blaspheme down the stations of her breath
> With any further
> Elegy of innocence and youth.

Here words like 'mankind', 'blaspheme', 'stations of her breath' (recalling 'station of the Cross') play an easily discernible part in the expansion of the meaning, while the pun in 'grave truth' represents a device common enough in modern poetry. The concluding stanza gives the reason, the counter-statement:

> Deep with the first dead lies London's daughter,
> Robed in the long friends,
> The grains beyond age, the dark veins of her mother,

> Secret by the unmourning water
> Of the riding Thames.
> After the first death, there is no other.

This echoes, in its own way, the opening stanza; but its tone is new; it is that of liturgical proclamation. We need not wince at the suggestion that 'long friends' means (among other things) worms; worms for Thomas were not disgusting, but profoundly symbolic: like maggots they are elements of corruption and thus of reunification, of eternity.

How much a poem of this kind owes to the imagery and to the cadence, as well as to the careful patterning, can be seen at once if one takes the perhaps extreme method of turning its paraphrasable content into conventional rhymed verse:

> Not until doomsday's final call
> And all the earth returns once more
> To that primaeval home of all,
> When on that insubstantial shore
> The tumbling primal waters foam
> And silence rules her lonely home,
>
> And I return to whence I came,
> The sacramental child of earth,
> Joining with nature to proclaim
> A death that is a second birth—
> No, not until that final sleep
> Will I for this dead infant weep.
>
> She lies with her ancestral dead,
> The child of London, home at last
> To earth from whence all life is bred
> And present mingles with the past.
> The unmourning waters lap her feet:
> She has no second death to meet.

This is doggerel, of course, but it contains, in however crude a form, the essential paraphrasable meaning of the Thomas poem —yet misses everything of any significance about it. The note of ritual, of sacrament, of celebration, achieved through his special use of imagery and by other devices, is central in Thomas's poetry.

I have not given a critical analysis of the poem, but merely suggested a way of looking at it. 'A Refusal to Mourn' is a characteristic poem of one phase of Thomas's career, during which he was drawing together his impressions of the unity of all creation and all time to serve the purpose of a specific occasion. His earlier poems often fail by being too packed with metaphor suggestive of identity. Words like 'Adam', 'Christ', 'ghost', 'worm', 'womb', phrases like 'the mouth of time', 'death's feather', 'beach of flesh', 'hatching hair', 'half-tracked thigh', abound, and though each has its orderly place in the poem the reader often feels dulled by the continuous impact of repeated words of this kind. The sonnet-sequence, 'Altarwise by owl-light', contains some brilliant identifying imagery (suggesting the identity of man with Christ, of creation with death, of history with the present), but it is altogether too closely packed, too dense, to come across effectively. The opening is almost a self-parody:

> Altarwise by owl-light in the halfway house
> The gentleman lay graveward with his furies;
> Abaddon in the hangnail cracked from Adam,
> And, from his fork, a dog among the fairies,
> The atlas-eater with a jaw for news,
> Bit out the mandrake with tomorrow's scream. . . .

The careful explicator will be able to produce informative glosses on each of these phrases, but the fact remains that the poem is congested with its metaphors, and the reader is left with a feeling of oppression. A fair number of Thomas's earlier poems are obscure for this reason. It is not the obscurity of free association or of references to private reading, but an obscurity which results from an attempt to pack too much into a short space, to make every comma tell, as it were. With his continuous emphasis on birth, pre-natal life, the relation of parent to child, growth, the relation of body and spirit, of life to death, of human and animal to vegetable, and similar themes, and his constant search for devices to celebrate these and identify them with each other, he does not want one word to slip which may help in building up the total pattern of meaning. One of his poems shows how the

making of continuous connections and identities can bewilder
the reader:

> Today, this insect, and the world I breathe,
> Now that my symbols have outelbowed space,
> Time at the city spectacles, and half
> The dear, daft time I take to nudge the sentence,
> In trust and tale have I divided sense,
> Slapped down the guillotine, the blood-red double
> Of head and tail made witnesses to this
> Murder of Eden and green genesis.

He is saying here, in his compact metaphorical way, that expression in language (which means expression in time) breaks up and so distorts the original vision. In his desire to avoid that breaking up he sometimes piles up the images and metaphors until the reader simply cannot construe the lines (as in the sixth stanza of 'When, like a Running Grace'). But it must be emphasized that this is not the fault of a bad romantic poetry, too loose and exclamatory, but comes from what can perhaps be called the classical vice of attempting to press too much into a little space.

Thomas progressed from those poems in which his techniques of identification are sometimes pressed too far, through a period of 'occasional' verse in which he focussed his general notions on particular incidents and situations to give a grave and formal ceremonial poetry ('A Refusal to Mourn', 'Do not go gentle into that good night', 'On the Marriage of a Virgin', etc.) to a period of more limpid, open-worked poetry in which, instead of endeavouring to leap outside time into a pantheistic cosmos beyond the dimensions, he accepts time and change and uses memory as an elegiac device ('Poem in October', 'Fern Hill', 'Over Sir John's Hill', 'Poem on His Birthday'). But these divisions are not strictly chronological, nor do they take account of all the kinds of verse he was writing. There is, for example, 'A Winter's Tale', a 'middle' poem, which handles a universal folk theme with a quiet beauty that results from perfect control of the imagery. It is far too long a poem to quote, and it needs to be read as a whole to be appreciated; it is one of Thomas's half dozen truly magnificent poems.

Another remarkable poem, which does not quite fit into my threefold classification is 'Vision and Prayer', a finely wrought pattern-poem in two parts of six stanzas each. In no other poem has Thomas so successfully handled the theme of the identity of himself, everyman, and Christ. He imagines himself addressing the unborn Christ, who, in his mother's womb, seems separated from himself by a 'wall thin as a wren's bone'. The infant in the next room replies, explaining that it is his destiny to storm out across the partition that separates man from God, and the poet identifies himself with the glory and suffering of Christ's redemptive career. The first part of the poem blazes to a conclusion with a vision of the triumph and pain of Christ's death. The second movement begins in a slow, hushed, almost muttering cadence: the poet prays that Christ remain in the womb, for men are indifferent and wanton and not worth redemption. Let the splendour of Christ's martyrdom remain unrevealed; 'May the crimson/ Sun spin a grave grey/ And the colour of clay/ Stream upon his martyrdom'. But as he ends this sad prayer the sun of God blazes forth and takes up the poet in its lightning. 'The sun roars at the prayer's end.' No summary or partial quotation can do justice to the force and brilliance of this most cunningly modulated poem. The stanzas of the first part are diamond-shaped, and those of the second part shaped like an hour-glass, and this visual device is not arbitrary but reflects and answers the movement of the thought and emotion at each point.

Of the more limpid, open-worked poems of the third period, 'Poem in October', though written earlier than the others in this group, can stand as an excellent example. The poet, on his thirtieth birthday, is remembering his past and seeing himself in the familiar Welsh landscape as a boy with his mother:

> It was my thirtieth year to heaven
> Woke to my hearing from harbour and neighbour wood
> And the mussel pooled and the heron
> Priested shore
> The morning beckon
> With water praying and call of seagull and rook

> And the knock of sailing boats on the net webbed wall
> Myself to set foot
> That second
> In the still sleeping town and set forth.

Again we have the sacramentalizing of nature ('heron priested shore') and we have also a sense of glory in the natural world which Thomas learned to render more and more effectively as his art matured. Again, one cannot see the quality of the poem from an extract; elegy is combined with remembrance and commemoration, and the emotion rises and falls in a fine movement.

Thomas's radio play, *Under Milk Wood*, was broadcast by the B.B.C. and won instant approval among professional critics and laymen alike. In writing for the radio Thomas naturally avoided any too close packing of the imagery, and chose a style closer to that of 'Poem in October' than to that of his earlier poems. In spite of an occasional touch of sentimentality *Under Milk Wood* is a remarkable performance, one of the few examples in our time of spoken poetry[1] which is both good and popular. In estimating the loss to literature caused by Thomas's early death, I should be inclined to put the cutting short of his career as a poet for the radio as the most serious of all. Thomas was by instinct a popular poet—as he wrote:

> Not for the proud man apart
> From the raging moon I write
> On these spendthrift pages
> Nor for the towering dead
> With their nightingales and psalms
> But for the lovers, their arms
> Round the griefs of the ages,
> Who pay no praise or wages
> Nor heed my craft or art.

He had no desire to be difficult or esoteric. He drew on the Bible and on universal folk themes rather than on obscure late classical

---

[1] I call the language of *Under Milk Wood* poetry, though it is prose to the *eye*. When I wrote this I had *heard* the play twice but I had not read it, and there is no doubt that to the ear it is poetry. The opposite is true of T. S. Eliot's later plays, where the language is verse to the eye but prose to the ear.

writers or Jessie Weston's *From Ritual to Romance*. In *Under Milk Wood* he puts into simple yet powerful and cunning words a day in the life of a Welsh village, with each character rendered in terms of some particular human weakness or folly. Unlike Eliot, Thomas accepted man as he was: he had a relish for humanity. By the end of his life he had learned to be both poetically honest and poetically simple—a difficult combination, especially in our time. And in choosing the spoken verse of the radio as a medium he was pointing the way towards a bridging of the appalling gap in our culture between professional critic and ordinary reader.

Was he a great poet? Against him it can be argued that his range was severely limited, that (in his earlier poems) he overdid a handful of images and phrases to the point almost of parodying himself, that many of his poems are clotted with an excess of parallel-seeking metaphors. I doubt if he wrote a dozen really first-rate poems; these would include, among those not hitherto mentioned here, 'In the White Giant's Thigh' and 'In Country Sleep'. In his favour it can be claimed that at his best he is magnificent, as well as original in tone and technique, and that he was growing in poetic stature to the last. Perhaps the question is, in the most literal sense, academic. It is enough that he wrote some poems that the world will not willingly let die.

WALT WHITMAN'S PHILOSOPHY[1]

POETS ARE RARELY systematic philosophers. Their vision of life is embodied in their poetry, with all the rich overtones of symbolic meaning which poetic statement can provide; to paraphrase their ideas in prose generalizations is to risk losing all that is most valuable in the original. How can we ever discuss the philosophy of a poet apart from his poetry? In 'Song of Myself' Whitman warned us: 'I have no chair, no church, no philosophy.' And although, with his characteristic disregard for mere consistency, he made many other statements with an exactly contrary meaning, the fact remains that to treat Whitman as a systematic philosopher is an unrealistic and unprofitable procedure. He did, however, have a vision of man, and throughout his life he kept exploring ways of communicating it. We can, I think, helpfully discuss that vision, examine the ways in which he sought to project it and the fundamental attitudes which it implies. When Whitman said, 'I have no chair, no church, no philosophy,' he continued:

> I lead no man to a dinner-table, library, exchange,
> But each man and each woman of you I lead upon a knoll,
> My left hand hooking you round the waist,
> My right hand pointing to landscapes of continents and the public road.
>
> Not I, not any one else can travel that road for you,
> You must travel it for yourself.

This is not a philosophical formulation, but a symbolic gesture, in which the poet's self is linked both to other selves and to the world of external nature; it is a gesture which brings into one relationship the three factors of individual identity, love, and 'landscapes of continents'. Whitman's most memorable utter-

[1] A lecture delivered at the Library of Congress, Washington, D.C., in January 1955, as part of the celebrations commemorating the 100th anniversary of the publication of *Leaves of Grass*.

ances are all symbolic gestures—of embracing, pointing, hailing; devices for joining the unique and mystical identity of the self with the world of his fellow men, of the other unique and mystical identities. In the well-known words of his opening 'Inscription':

> One's-self I sing, a simple separate person,
> Yet utter the word Democratic, the word En-Masse.

I am not here concerned with questions of poetic style, and I shall not comment on the perhaps embarrassing term 'En-Masse' except to note in passing that the strange foreign and supposedly foreign words which Whitman scattered throughout his poetry, often so unhappily, represent a device which he hoped would enable him to move from the literal to the symbolic, to shock the reader into recognition of what is really there, to give a new tilt to the vision. The simple point about this familiar declaration to which I wish to draw attention is that it presents a polarity which is a basic preoccupation of Whitman's. The uniqueness and all-importance of the identity of the individual, and the human necessity of contact—both are basic. This is not, perhaps, a philosophical tenet; but it is a central part of Whitman's vision.

> Underneath all, individuals,
> I swear nothing is good to me now that ignores individuals,
> The American compact is altogether with individuals,
> The only government is that which makes minute of individuals,
> The whole theory of the universe is directed unerringly to one single
>   individual—namely to You.

But a few lines further on in the same poem he declares:

> Underneath all is the Expression of love for men and women.

The dialectic consists sometimes of two terms (the 'Me' and the 'Not-Me'), sometimes of three (the self, other selves, Nature). The poet, says Wordsworth, carries 'everywhere with him relationship and love'. With this Whitman (who, incidentally, refers to Wordsworth very rarely) would have thoroughly agreed. He would have agreed, too, with Wordsworth's statement that the poet 'considers man and nature as essentially adapted to each other, and the mind of man as naturally the mirror of the fairest

and most interesting properties of nature'. But he was more insistent than Wordsworth ever was on the compelling mystery of
identity, and thus knew from the beginning that relationship and
love involve a paradox. In one of the many advertising blurbs
for *Leaves of Grass* which Whitman himself wrote anonymously,
he said:

That he *writes about himself* [Whitman's italics]—a criticism often sneeringly
brought against him—is, in fact, the very object of his appearance in literature,
which is, briefly, to formulate in a poem, with unprecedented candor, a complete human being, body, mind, emotions, soul.

But he goes on to add:

The book weaves and twines in everywhere the different products, climates,
and all and each of the several United States, by their nomenclature, the South
as much as the North—not a single State or city, and hardly a river or mountain
left out; all knitted and twisted together, so that their entire geography and
hydrography are fused in its pages.

That was in 1873. In 1882, in *Specimen Days*, he wrote:

The most profound theme that can occupy the mind of man . . . is doubtless
involved in the query: What is the fusing explanation and tie—what is the
relation between the (radical, democratic) Me, the human identity of understanding, emotions, spirit, &c., on the one side, of and with the (conservative)
Not-Me, the whole of the material universe and laws, with what is behind
them in time and space, on the other side?

It is the old Cartesian dilemma, of the relation between the
perceiving mind and external reality, complicated by the fact
that for Whitman external reality included both 'the whole of the
material universe and laws' and the world of other perceiving
selves. He solved his dilemma, not philosophically, but poetically.
The sympathetic imagination, which was the poetic mind at
work, was by a process of *Einfühlung*, of empathy, able to project
the poet's self into other selves. 'I am the man, I suffer'd, I was
there,' Whitman exclaims in 'Song of Myself' after listing varieties of individuals and their experiences. Indeed, that is the very
theme of 'Song of Myself', paradoxical though it may sound. It
is a song of identification. 'I am the hounded slave, I wince at the
bite of the dogs,' or again, 'Not a mutineer walks handcuff'd to

jail but I am handcuff'd to him and walk by his side'—we all know the familiar passages in which Whitman projects himself into other identities. The poetic imagination both realizes the full, unique identity of the self, and identifies that self with other selves. The same point is made, again and again, in that strangely moving poem, 'The Sleepers':

> I go from bedside to bedside, I sleep close with the other sleepers each in turn,
> I dream in my dream all the dreams of the other dreamers,
> And I become the other dreamers. . . .
>
> I am the actor, the actress, the voter, the politician,
> The emigrant and the exile, the criminal that stood in the box,
> He who has been famous and he who shall be famous after today,
> The stammerer, the well-form'd person, the wasted or feeble person.

Just as the sympathetic imagination helps Whitman to solve one aspect of his dilemma, so sensation and memory together help to solve the other, to join man and Nature. Here again he would have agreed with Wordsworth, that the poet 'will follow wheresoever he can find an atmosphere of sensation in which to move his wings.' Sensation for Whitman was not merely a bridge between the self and the external world; it was a method of learning to know the external world from the inside, so that it ceases to be external and becomes part of one's self:

> There was a child went forth every day,
> And the first object he look'd upon, that object he became,
> And that object became part of him for the day or a certain part of the day,
> Or for many years or stretching cycles of years.

This sense of an identity between man and Nature is familiar enough in Romantic poetry, and Emerson has his own version of it. But, however much Emerson may have influenced Whitman—and Whitman contradicted himself more than once on this question —Whitman's view of the relation between man and Nature is essentially his own. Perception of Nature, and remembered perception of Nature, help at the same time to disperse identity, as it were, among different natural scenes and objects, and to enrich personality by making those scenes and objects part of the self.

So by love the individual both disperses and fulfils himself, both scatters his ego and concentrates it.

The true personality is thus a microcosm, containing within itself potential identification with all other true personalities and (in a somewhat obscure sense, it is true) all of Nature. His well-known description of himself as

> Walt Whitman, a kosmos, of Manhattan the son,
> Turbulent, fleshy, sensual, eating, drinking and breeding,
> No sentimentalist, no stander above men and women or apart from
> them, . . .

emphasizes the paradox: in being most himself, his complete bodily self, without repression or emotional over-compensation, he becomes the proper equal of others and can, by the exercise of the sympathetic imagination, identify himself with them. The complete self is both bodily and spiritual, and Whitman is emphatic in declaring that both aspects are equal:

> I have said that the soul is not more than the body,
> And I have said that the body is not more than the soul. . . .

To be capable of the proper kind of imaginative expansion, the self must not deny any of its aspects. All human functions, all human capabilities, are sacred, and the fulfilled personality—who is at once most himself and most capable of entering into the lives of others—denies none. Sex is thus accepted frankly and freely, in its physical as well as its other aspects; and, by the same token, as he insists so often, the woman is without any possible reservation the complete equal of the man.

Though parts of this doctrine were far enough removed from the view of the New England Transcendentalists, there were some interesting similarities. In 1836 Orestes Brownson had described the Transcendentalists' mission as the reconciliation of spirit and matter. 'We cannot . . . go back either to exclusive Spiritualism, or to exclusive Materialism. . . . Both have their foundation in our nature, and both will exist and exert their influence. . . . Is the bosom of Humanity to be eternally torn by these two contending factions? No. It cannot be. The war must end. Peace must be made. This discloses our Mission. We must reconcile spirit and matter; that is, we must realize the atonement.' This was precisely Whitman's view. The individual whose true self combined equally body and soul was for him the root fact of existence. The 'rapport'—to use one of Whitman's favourite words—between such individuals and between each individual and Nature provides the basis of true civilization; it is a prerequisite of the good society. 'Produce great Persons, the rest follows,' he declared in 'By Blue Ontario's Shores', and great persons for him were *real* persons, not marionettes, not—to use another of his favourite terms—'dandified' persons, mechanical slaves of fashion or dupes of their own narrow and unrealized selves. Everyone is capable of self-realization if not narrowed and corrupted by bad influences and bad habits, and that, I think, is what Whitman means when he talks about the importance of the 'average'. He has been accused of putting the average man on a pedestal, of being the precursor of those opinion-seekers and pollsters who search after a statistical norm and then idolize it as the typical American. But clearly Whitman had no such idea in his head. No one would have been more horrified than he by that modern advertising which suggests that because more people are buying x or y then *you* will naturally want to buy it, or with the notion of keeping up with the Joneses. What Whitman meant was that the formal attributes of greatness believed in by what he liked to call the feudal ages had no necessary connection with real human greatness, which was independent of birth, social position, formal education, or conventional 'talents'. Political democracy provides the framework, the possibility—and only that—for the full development of personality without regard to traditional advantages of rank and so on. Any man engaged in his chosen work amid America's teeming society could be a 'great person' in Whitman's sense. The stereotype, the parroter of clichés, the man who organizes his thinking (in Matthew Arnold's phrase) in terms of catchwords rather than of of ideas, the party man, have nothing to do with Whitman's 'average'.

Whitman's conception of the 'average' is, of course, closely related to his view of democracy and of the potentialities of America as the home of democracy. Perhaps the most superficial aspect of Whitman's political thought was his more or less routine acceptance of the notion that free, progressive America could look back with scorn on the tyrannies of the European past and equally deride the inequalities of the present-day European class system. This was a standard enough American doctrine by Whitman's day, and he showed no great originality in taking it over. Nor was he especially original in demanding a great new truly American literature instead of a pallid imitation of English writers. Emerson, as we all know, had announced at the end of his address on 'The American Scholar' that 'we have listened too long to the courtly muses of Europe', and Whitman followed with his 'Come Muse migrate from Greece and Ionia', his call to the American Muse to take up her habitation in the 'better, fresher, busier sphere', the 'wide, untried domain', that awaited her. I do not mean that Whitman was not in earnest when he said things like this; of course he was; but he had more original and profounder things to say about the possibilities of American democracy. Nothing could be farther from the truth than Sidney Lanier's remark that 'Whitman's argument seems to be, that, because a prairie is wide, therefore debauchery is admirable, and because the Mississippi is long, therefore every American is God'. In the letter to Emerson which he included in the 1856 edition of his poems he talked of 'that new moral American continent without which, I see, the physical continent remained incomplete, may be a carcass, a bloat'. The physical grandeur of America was a challenge to its inhabitants to achieve a comparable grandeur of personality, while the growth of the country's population gave unprecedented scope to the individual's capacity for imaginative understanding and sympathy. Again, in the 1855 preface he stated emphatically: 'The largeness of nature or the nation were monstrous without a corresponding largeness and generosity of the spirit of the citizen.'

It is in the light of such remarks that we must read Whitman's rapt descriptions of the ideal American. He proclaims triumphantly of the ordinary men and women of America: 'Their shadows are projected in employments, in books, in the cities, in trade; their feet are on the flights of the steps of the Capitol; they dilate, a larger, brawnier, more candid, more democratic, lawless, positive native to The States, sweet-bodied, completer, dauntless, flowing, masterful, beard-faced, new race of men.' But of course this is not a description of the America he sees; it is a prophetic vision of the America he believes in, the America which, he feels, will one day come into being. He begins the paragraph which contains this description by declaring, 'I am a man of perfect faith.' And he adds: 'We have not come through centuries, caste, heroisms, fables, to halt in this land today.' His visionary gaze is on the future, and he goes on to call on the American people to justify his faith and embody his vision. Further, for all his loving play with the names and scenes of America, the country is for him a symbol of something larger, of civilization in its ideal development. Just as the individual must fully realize his own personality to fulfil himself *and* to achieve proper 'rapport' with others, so the country must fully realize its own personality before it can stand as a symbol of something larger than itself. In his vision of the Americans of the future, he announces that 'they resume Personality, too long left out of mind'. That is the road to the true American future. It is, moreover, a road to a goal that can perhaps never be fully attained: 'America is not finished, perhaps never will be.'

Political democracy makes it possible for each individual to fulfil his own personality, to realize fully his free self. But political democracy cannot in itself guarantee that such a development will take place. That development needs the assistance of the poet, and to embody a vision of it was, for Whitman, the prime task of the American poet. 'I have allowed the stress of my poems to bear on American individuality and assist it,' he wrote in 'A Backward Glance O'er Travel'd Roads'. The visionary poet often deliberately mixes his tenses, and Whitman does it as visionaries from Isaiah on have done it. In describing his ideal as though it were real, he is behaving as a poet rather than as a

F

sociologist, and to accuse Whitman of naïveté because his ideal-
izing descriptions often do not correspond with fact is itself naïve.
And we must remember that the prose of his prefaces—often
written in the same style as his poetry and sometimes embodied
later in verse—is not, merely because it is prose, to be read as
systematic philosophy or as sociological description: it, too, embodies the vision.

Whitman's idealization of the 'average' is not, then, an endorse-
ment of the Gallup poll or an abandonment to statistics or an
obsession with mediocrity—though some of those who profess
to follow Whitman are guilty of these errors. The average is for
him a symbol of the infinite potential of individual personality.
Political democracy provides the best nursery for personalities,
with the poet as the best nurse. America, which came into being
as a nation dedicated to political democracy, and which, by its
extent, variety and resources, constitutes the best possible arena
for the display and mutual 'rapport' of varied personalities, is the
symbolic home of 'great persons'. America's duty is therefore to
exploit its own potentialities as that symbolic home, rather than
imitate the behaviour of other countries. He was not blind to the
fact that America often seemed to be neglecting that duty. *Democratic Vistas* is full of bitter denunciations of America's failure to
be true to her destiny as he saw it:

> I say we had better look our times and lands searchingly in the face, like a
> physician diagnosing some deep disease. Never was there, perhaps, more
> hollowness at heart than at present, and here in the United States. Genuine
> belief seems to have left us. The underlying principles of the States are not
> honestly believ'd in (for all this hectic glow, and these melodramatic scream-
> ings,) nor is humanity itself believ'd in. What penetrating eye does not every-
> where see through the mask? The spectacle is appalling. . . .

He could even talk (in *Specimen Days*) of 'the supple, polish'd,
money-worshipping, Jesus-and-Judas-equalizing, suffrage-sove-
reignty echoes of current America'—incidentally, this in defence
of Carlyle, the anti-democrat, with whose criticism of democracy
in action he found himself forced to agree, for all his profound
disagreement in principle. He was no happier than many another

observer about the crudities and cruelties of the Gilded Age. America's destiny to produce 'great persons' was being betrayed. 'But sternly discarding, shutting our eyes to the glow and grandeur of the general superficial effect, coming down to what is of the only real importance, Personalities, and examining minutely, we question, we ask, Are there, indeed, *men* here worthy the name?' The Emersonian overtones of this question cannot disguise its heartfelt urgency. 'Is there', he continues, 'a great moral and religious civilization—the only justification of a great material one?' He makes clear, in *Democratic Vistas*, that political democracy was to be only the first stage, the essential foundation. The second stage, also preparatory, was the achievement of material prosperity. The third stage, which he announced in his poetic visions, was the stage when America, having fully realized herself, became the home of great personalities—'these States, self-contain'd, different from others, more expansive, more rich and free, to be evidenced by original authors and poets to come, by American personalities, plenty of them, male and female, traversing the States, none excepted—and by native superber tableaux and growths of language, songs, operas, orations, lectures, architectures—and by a sublime and serious Religious Democracy sternly taking command, dissolving the old, sloughing off surfaces, and from its own interior and vital principles, reconstructing, democratizing society.'

But what of the masses? What of his favourite concept, 'En-Masse'? In a nation of 'rich, luxuriant, varied personalism' to which Whitman looked forward, will we not get something rather more like John Stuart Mill's view of society as expressed in his essay on *Liberty* (which Whitman admired) than the picture of 'the broadest average of humanity' to which Whitman looked forward? I have already given part of the answer to this question, in pointing out that Whitman's notion of the 'average' was perfectly compatible with his desire to see rich and varied personalities. He was, nevertheless, aware of an apparent contradiction in his thought here, for he saw that unlimited and unregulated individualism could lead in its own way to the negation of democracy—something that John Stuart Mill also saw later. 'We shall,' wrote Whitman in *Democratic Vistas*, 'it is true, quickly and continually find the origin-idea of the singleness of man, individualism, asserting itself, and cropping forth, even from the opposite ideas. But the mass, or lump character, for imperative reasons, is to be ever carefully weigh'd, borne in mind, and provided for. Only from it, and from its proper regulation and potency, comes the other, comes the chance of individualism. The two are contradictory, but our task is to reconcile them.' He added an illuminating footnote here:

> The question hinted here is one which time only can answer. Must not the virtue of modern Individualism, continually enlarging, usurping all, seriously affect, perhaps keep down entirely, in America, the like of the ancient virtue of Patriotism, the fervid and absorbing love of general country? I have no doubt myself that the two will merge, and will mutually profit and brace each other, and that from them a greater product, a third, will arise. But I feel that at present they and their oppositions form a serious problem and paradox in the United States.

The relation between the individual and the masses, as Whitman saw it, is thus comparable to the relation between the 'Me' and the 'Not-me' which I have already discussed. The dialectic here is almost Hegelian: out of two apparent opposites a third unity is formed—the sympathetic, all-inclusive personality out of the reconciliation of the 'Me' and the 'Not-me', and the true democratic society out of the reconciliation between individual and mass. If Whitman, in some of his finest poems, hails America in terms which suggest that these reconciliations have already been effected, that is a legitimate device of the poetic visionary.

Whitman's vision of the fulfilled individual, the complete personality, and his place in a democratic American civilization is, as he himself stressed, essentially religious. As he put it in his somewhat odd vocabulary: 'Beyond the vertebration of the manly and womanly personalism of our western world, can only be, and is indeed, to be, (I hope,) its all penetrating Religiousness.' It is not, of course, institutional religion that Whitman is talking about—he joins hands with the Transcendentalists firmly on this point. 'Religion,' he wrote in the same section of *Democratic Vistas* from which I have been quoting, 'although casually arrested, and, after a fashion, preserv'd in the churches and creeds, does not depend at all upon them, but is a part of the identified soul, which, when greatest, knows not bibles in the old way, but in new ways —the identified soul, which can really confront Religion when it extricates itself entirely from the churches, and not before.' Whitman was suspicious of institutions and parties. 'Disengage yourself from parties,' he cried. 'They have been useful, and to some extent remain so; but the floating, uncommitted electors, farmers, clerks, mechanics, the masters of parties—watching aloof, inclining victory this side or that side—such are the ones most needed, present and future.' The institutions of political democracy were necessary to provide an arena in which the individual could work out both his personal and his social destiny, but they were a means, not an end, and a means easily capable of abuse. 'Political democracy,' he wrote, 'as it exists and practically works in America, with all its threatening evils, supplies a training-school for making first-class men. It is life's gymnasium, not of good only, but of all.' Of ecclesiastical institutions, he had not even that to say; he had learned suspicion of them from the Transcendentalists, as well as from the Quaker preference for the 'inner light'.

Whitman's faith in America, his vision of a fulfilled and exemplary American democracy, expressed itself inevitably in a form which involved a certain amount of disparagement of other countries and of the whole past of the Old World, but this is neither his characteristic nor his most eloquently expressed mood. To the polarities in his thought which I have tried to indicate there must be added another—that between America and the world in general. Though he is ready enough to list the weaknesses of older societies ruled by kings or tyrants and highly stratified in their organization, he is remarkably generous in his tributes to what the New World owes to the Old. As he put it in 'Song of the Exposition':

We do not blame thee elder World,
  nor really separate ourselves from thee,
(Would the son separate himself from the father?)
Looking back on thee, seeing thee to thy duties, grandeurs, through
  past ages bending, building,
We build to ours today.

Whitman's vision is essentially cosmic; its identifying gaze moves ever outward from the self, and the observing and imagining self moves progressively across America and across the world. 'Salut au Monde' is rather too much of an exclamatory catalogue to be one of his best poems, but it gives nevertheless an impressive picture of his vision wandering through history and geography, uniting all times and all lands, focussing the cosmos through his own consciousness:

Within me latitude widens, longitude lengthens,
Asia, Africa, Europe, are to the east—America is provided for in the
  west,
Banding the bulge of the earth winds the hot equator,
Curiously north and south turn the axis-ends,
Within me is the longest day, the sun wheels in slanting rings, it does
  not set for months,
Stretch'd in due time within me the midnight sun just rises above the
  horizon and sinks again,
Within me zones, seas, cataracts, forests, volcanoes, groups,
Malaysia, Polynesia, and the great West Indian islands.

There were, of course, contradictions in Whitman's attitude to the non-American world—we all know Whitman's defence of contradictions—as there were bound to be for anyone who saw America both as the blueprint of a new society, freed from the dead hand of old tradition and inequalities, as the symbolic ideal of the community where individuals link their personalities in perfect association, and as one part of history and geography, bound up with the whole world and the whole universe.

'Passage to India' is Whitman's most mature poetic statement on the relation between the New World and the Old. The spanning of the American continent by rail and the linking of Europe to India by the opening of the Suez Canal provided a perfect symbol for the use of his visionary imagination, with its need to explore simultaneously the poet's unique self and the world at large. The poem is partly about contact , 'rapport'.

> Passage to India!
> Lo, soul, seest thou not God's purpose from the first?
> The earth to be spann'd, connected by network,
> The races, neighbors, to marry and be given in marriage,
> The oceans to be cross'd, the distant brought near,
> The lands to be welded together.

But contact is only one of the themes. The poem is also a vision of history, starting with the dawn of civilization in the East and coming up to the modern railway train thundering across the American continent. Old myths of unity now take on new meaning, the past becomes alive in a new way:

> Year at whose wide-flung door I sing!
> Year of the purpose accomplish'd!
> Year of the marriage of continents, climates and oceans!
> (No mere doge of Venice now wedding the Adriatic,)

> I see O year in you the vast terraqueous globe given and giving all,
> Europe to Asia, Africa join'd, and they to the New World,
> The lands, geographies, dancing before you, holding a festival garland,
> As brides and bridegrooms hand in hand.

> Passage to India!
> Cooling airs from Caucasus far, soothing cradle of man,
> The river Euphrates flowing, the past lit up again.

Passage to India is passage to the past, to 'primal thought', and at the same time a challenge for the future. Contemplating the potentialities of modern transport, the poet sees life as adventure, experience as discovery, bringing the whole self into contact with history, geography, society. Characteristically, the great expansive movement of Whitman's vision is linked to an inward movement of self-contemplation—'We too take ship O soul'. In the concluding image of the voyage (a favourite of Whitman's) he sees himself, the past, India, America coming together in one great challenge to further spiritual adventure:

Passage to more than India!
Are thy wings plumed indeed for such far flights?
O soul, voyagest thou indeed on voyages like those?
Disportest thou on waters such as those?
Soundest below the Sanskrit and the Vedas?

Then have they been unleash'd.
Passage to you, you shores, ye aged fierce enigmas!
Passage to you, to mastership of you, ye strangling problems!
You, strew'd with the wrecks of skeletons, that, living, never reach'd
    you.

Passage to more than India!
O secret of the earth and sky!
Of you O waters of the sea! O winding creeks and rivers!
Of you O woods and fields! of you strong mountains of my land!
Of you O prairies! of you gray rocks!
O morning red! O clouds! O rain and snows!
O day and night, passage to you!

O sun and moon and all you stars! Sirius and Jupiter!
Passage to you!

Passage, immediate passage! the blood burns in my veins!
Away O soul! hoist instantly the anchor!
Cut the hawsers—haul out—shake out every snail! . . .

And so to the final cry: 'O farther, farther sail!' A poem about
history and geography, about the past, present and future of the
world, ends as an apostrophe to his own soul: a fine example of
Whitman's counterpointing of the 'Me' and the 'Not-me'.

Whitman's view of the relationship between the individual,
society and the cosmos led him occasionally to see the whole of
life as a sort of cosmic dance in which everyone and everything
moves according to its own laws and both fulfils its own destiny
and plays its proper part in the general movement. This is an old
notion among poets and philosophers, going back to Plotinus
and beyond. When Whitman declares that

All is a procession,
The universe is a procession with measured and perfect motion . . .

he is unconsciously echoing what the Elizabethan poet, Sir John
Davies, had said in his 'Orchestra'. The measured cosmic dance

began, says Davies, when the world first sprang from its primal
seeds:

> Since then they still are carried in a round,
> And changing come one in another's place;
> Yet do they neither mingle nor confound,
> But every one doth keep the bounded space
> Wherein the dance doth bid it turn or trace.
> This wondrous miracle did Love devise,
> For dancing is love's proper exercise.

Yeats, too, influenced by Plotinus, was to see the relation between
the individual and the processes of life symbolized by the dance:

> O chestnut tree, great rooted blossomer,
> Are you the leaf, the blossom or the bole?
> O body swayed to music, O brightening glance,
> How can we know the dancer from the dance?

In his vision of the dance of life, therefore, Whitman is perpetu-
ating an old poetic tradition, and giving it new meaning in the
light of his own preoccupation with identity and relationship.
In 'A Song of the Rolling Earth' we get a similar picture of the
dance of the days and the years and the hours, the stately procession of time in the universe, with its relation to human fate:

> Embracing man, embracing all, proceed the three hundred and sixty-
>   five resistlessly round the sun;
> Embracing all, soothing, supporting, follow close three hundred and
>   sixty-five offsets of the first, sure and necessary as they.

Life is a formal dance; life and death are part of the same continuous process, and immortality is guaranteed because the process *is* continuous:

> Behold this compost! behold it well!
> Perhaps every mite has once formed part of a sick person—yet behold!
> The grass of spring covers the prairies,
> The bean bursts noiselessly through the mould in the garden,
>
> The delicate spear of the onion pierces upward,
> The apple-buds cluster together on the apple-branches,
> The resurrection of the wheat appears with pale visage out of its
>   graves . . .

And again, from the same poem:

> Now I am terrified at the Earth, it is that calm and patient,
> It grows such sweet things out of such corruptions,
> It turns harmless and stainless on its axis, with such endless successions
>   of diseas'd corpses,
> It distills such exquisite winds out of such infused fetor,
> It renews with such unwitting looks, its prodigal, annual, sumptuous
>   crops,
> It gives such divine materials to men, and accepts such leavings from
>   them at last.

Life is process, and the fully realized individual's part in the process is eternal, and thus we get to a view of immortality:

> I believe of all those men and women that fill'd the unnamed lands,
>   every one exists this hour here or elsewhere, invisible to us,
> In exact proportion to what he or she grew from in life, and out of
>   what he or she did, felt, became, loved, sinn'd, in life.

On the purely logical level there are of course some inconsistencies in Whitman's view of immortality; the important thing to note is that in passages such as these Whitman is exploring a symbolic language in which to suggest his vision of life as grand process. We might compare his more conventional use of the image of life as a voyage which never ends.

Another aspect of Whitman's thought which I think is worth some discussion is his view of the function of the poet. By the poet, of course, Whitman generally means Walt Whitman, for, as we have seen, one of his characteristic techniques is to contract everything to the self, and then make the self typical and all-inclusive through its method of observation and of sympathetic identification. The poet for Whitman is, in a sense, the ideal observer both of his fellow men and of the natural world (again, there is a similarity to Wordsworth's view here). The poet's sympathetic identification with what he sees and what he imagines is the source of his poetic vision. 'The known universe has one complete lover and that is the greatest poet', he wrote in the 1855 preface, and this sentiment is echoed again and again in both his verse and his prose. Whitman has been criticized for the indis-

criminate way in which he embraces the universe and everything
that it contains, good and bad, and it has been more than once
pointed out that this pragmatic acceptance of whatever *is* suggests
not only an unrealistic and facile optimism but also a supreme
lack of logic in one who at the same time denounced 'the young
men of These States' as 'a parcel of helpless dandies, who can
neither fight, work, shoot, ride, run, command—some of them
devout, some quite insane, some castrated—all second-hand, or
third or fourth, or fifth hand—waited upon by waiters, putting
not this land first, talking of art, doing the most ridiculous things
for fear of being thought ridiculous, smirking and skipping along,
continually taking off their hats.' How could Whitman take a
normative attitude to the civilization of his day if at the same time
he accepted everything in existence merely because it was in
existence? I think the answer to this question lies in Whitman's
view of the nature of a real person. Inanimate Nature and
animals were all to be accepted; they were what they were, part
of the process of things. But men—who were alone capable of
betraying their identities by leading second-hand lives in which
their real selves were not involved—could be judged in accordance with the degree to which they fulfilled the true laws of
their own personalities. It is significant that after Swinburne
turned against Whitman, to write a stinging attack on the man
and his poetry, Whitman remarked of the furious English poet:
'Ain't he the damndest simulacrum?' Swinburne, in talking this
frenzied nonsense, was acting as a simulacrum, a pale image of
his real self, not in his true capacity as a person. And this is the
way in which Whitman tended to speak of those he disliked and,
indeed, of all evil in the universe. He did not hold simply that
'whatever is, is right', but rather that whatever exists in its true,
undistorted nature is good. The 'parcel of helpless dandies' that
he attacked were denounced as 'all second-hand, or third, fourth,
or fifth hand', and that was the real burden of his complaint.

Now I think that this helps to explain, too, Whitman's increasing insistence on his originality as he grew older. In repudiating an obvious debt to Emerson and—as Esther Shephard

has pointed out—concealing a significant debt to two novels of George Sand, Whitman cannot be acquitted of disingenuousness; but we can see why it was important to him to keep stressing his originality. The real poet was essentially original, true to his own vision, transcribing nothing at second hand. If Whitman had thought more carefully about the problem of originality, he would have seen that it is not necessarily incompatible with borrowing: nobody now denies the originality of Shakespeare's genius because he took his plots from other writers. But he was so obsessed with the importance of renouncing the second-hand, of exploiting only his own true self, that he felt it necessary to repudiate with increasing urgency any suspicion of borrowing. 'Self-reliant, with haughty eyes, assuming to himself all the attributes of his country, steps Walt Whitman into literature, talking like a man unaware that there was ever hitherto such a production as a book, or such a being as a writer.' So Whitman wrote of himself in an anonymous review of *Leaves of Grass* in 1855. The statement is not, of course, literally true, and it is inconsistent with what Whitman later said of his early reading and the admitted influences on him of the Bible, Ossian, Italian opera, and other sources, including the writings of Emerson, which, as he once said, brought him to the boil after he had been long simmering. Whitman insisted on his originality because originality for was him the first prerequisite of the true poet. And, of course, essentially he was right: he was, in all that matters, a truly original poet.

The sharpest, and in many ways the most impressive, attack on Whitman's view of the poet as the universal lover was made by D. H. Lawrence, a man whose vision was in some important respects very similar to Whitman's. Lawrence admired Whitman as a pioneer and a moral leader (for Lawrence, all great poets were moral leaders). 'Whitman, the great poet, has meant so much to me. Whitman, the one man breaking a way ahead. Whitman, the one pioneer.' And again: 'Now Whitman was a great moralist. He was a great leader. He was a great changer of the blood in the veins of men.' But Lawrence could not stomach Whitman's gestures of universal acceptance. ' "I embrace all," says Whitman. "I weave all things into myself." Do you really! There can't be much left of *you* when you've done. When you've cooked the awful pudding of One Identity.' And Lawrence made devastating fun of Whitman's statement, 'I am he that aches with amorous love.' 'Reminds one of a steam-engine,' he said. 'A locomotive. They're the only things that seem to me to ache with amorous love. All that steam inside of them. Forty million foot-pounds pressure.' Lawrence also passionately denounced Whitman's indiscriminate acceptance of all kinds of people.

I think that every one interested in Whitman ought to read and ponder Lawrence's essay in *Studies in Classic American Literature*. This comment by a fellow-genius is full of perception and has a splendid vigour. It also lays its finger on some key aspects of Whitman's thought. Whether we agree with Lawrence or not, we ought to know what to say to his charges, for they spring from a vision as intense as Whitman's own and more like Whitman's than that of any other critic of him. The real difference between them, it seems to me, is that for Lawrence the problem of identity, of the fully realized individual, was related to the equal and opposite problem of the essential and ultimate *otherness* of other individuals. Lawrence and Whitman agreed on the question of identity and self-fulfilment; they differed sharply on what Whitman called 'rapport'. The ideal relation between two individuals was for Lawrence an almost mystical awareness on the part of each of the core of *otherness* in the other. For Whitman, one individual could, as it were, subsume another by sympathy; the poet could symbolically *become* other people without losing his identity—indeed, in the very exercise of it. This was dangerous heresy to Lawrence, to whom the notion of the merging of personalities was disgusting. In talking of these matters, both writers used a symbolic language, and I think myself that Lawrence read Whitman rather too literally. But the difference between the two views remains. And probably no one will deny that on occasion Whitman's gestures of universal acceptance are not adequately related to his gestures of identity, and that this essential polarity in Whitman's vision did not always produce coherent poetic statement.

Another notion that is important in Whitman's view of the poet is that of *simplicity*. 'Nothing is better than simplicity,' he wrote in the 1855 preface. 'Nothing can make up for excess or for the lack of definiteness.' By simplicity he meant the poet's honesty to his vision, his refusal to distort it by following convention or fashion. The poet must distort neither side of the equation—neither himself, the ideally sympathetic observer, nor what he sees. 'Men and women and the earth and all upon it,' he wrote in the same preface, 'are simply to be taken as they are, and the investigation of their past and present and future shall be unintermitted and shall be done with perfect candor.' The poet's personality, though simple in the sense of honest and true to itself, is nevertheless richly endowed. 'The most affluent man is he that confronts all the shows he sees by equivalents out of the stronger wealth of himself.' This most interesting statement (again from the 1855 preface) shows clearly that, in spite of his insistence on simplicity, Whitman did not regard the poet's relation to what he observed as one of naïve confronting, of the bare meeting of eye and object. Nor did he take the view of Francis Bacon, who had defined the poet as one who 'submits the shows of things to the desires of the mind'. For Whitman, the poet's mind, while retaining its simplicity in the sense that it refused to be side-tracked by artistic conventions that bore no relation to its own vision, was richly enough stored to contain within itself what one might call 'objective correlatives' to all that it might see or imagine. It was this that enabled the poet to subsume other characters, and it was precisely on this point that Lawrence so fiercely opposed Whitman.

It is difficult for any poet to bring the life of imagination into contact with daily living. From what little we know of Shakespeare's life, there appears to have been no sign, in his daily behaviour, of the imaginative fire that burned within him. Lawrence, preoccupied throughout his life, as Whitman was, by relationship and love, expressed his affection in real life by throwing crockery and by other kinds of childish violence. But Whitman desired to carry over the symbolic life of the poet's imagination into the daily life of the poet's person. 'First be yourself what you would show in your poem,' he wrote in one of his anonymous reviews of *Leaves of Grass*. This is not as unusual a view as some critics have supposed: it was common enough in Renaissance Europe, as the life of Sir Philip Sidney indicates, and its most eloquent expression is found in Milton's 'Apology for Smectymnuus', where he wrote that 'he who would not be frustrate of his hope to write well hereafter in laudable things, ought himself to be a true poem'. Whitman's attempt to act out his conception of the poet in his daily life resulted in what has been called, with considerable justice, 'Whitman's pose'. Miss Esther Shephard, in her book with this title, makes great play of the fact that Whitman took this pose in large part from a novel by George Sand, whose influence on him he carefully concealed. This side of Whitman is rather childish, it is true, and not particularly admirable. But I cannot bring myself to feel, with Miss Shephard, that it is wholly reprehensible and represents a stain on Whitman's poetic character. If George Sand's novel, *The Countess of Rudolstadt*, fired his imagination, there is nothing wrong in that; if it led him to dress and behave in a certain way, we may smile at the childishness of poets; if Whitman scrupulously concealed the fact that the novel was important for him—well, every writer is entitled to his reticences, and in any case it was not *essentially* important to him. It released something in him; it did not put it there. The same can be said for the influence on him of phrenology. But the point I am concerned with here is that Whitman was a poseur because he felt it necessary to act out in real life his conception of the way a poet's imagination works. It may be naïve in Whitman, as in Milton, to make this simple correlation between man as poet and man in his everyday behaviour; the poetic imagination, we may feel, does not spring in such a simple way from a poet's outward life. But I cannot see why Whitman's childishness as a poseur should affect our view of his poetry or our assessment of his poetic vision.

Another aspect of Whitman's conception of the poet concerns his view of the relation between poetry and religion. He shared fully Matthew Arnold's view that in the modern world poetry was to take over the task hitherto performed by religion. 'View'd today,' he wrote in *Democratic Vistas*, 'from a point of view sufficiently over-arching, the problem of humanity all over the civilized world is social and religious, and is to be finally met and treated by literature. The priest departs, the divine literatus comes.' There were two possible implications of this view. One, suggested by Arnold and developed by Walter Pater, was that religion should be assimilated to poetry, and its true function is to stimulate aesthetic awareness. The other, which represented Whitman's view, was that poetry should be assimilated to religion, the poet becoming the prophet. So that the view that the poet must take over the task of the priest led in Pater to the aestheticizing of religion and in Whitman to the opposite—the making of poetry into prophecy.

I have already noted that for Whitman the poet was the ideal observer, looking at his fellow-men and at the natural world with an all-embracing sympathetic imagination. It is also worth observing that for Whitman the poet's observation had what might be called a supreme normality: the poet saw things as they really were, in their right place. He expressed this thought both in the prose of the 1855 preface and in verse. 'Of all mankind the great poet is the equable man. Not in him but off from him things are grotesque or eccentric or fail of their sanity. Nothing out of its place is good and nothing in its place is bad. He bestows on every object or quality its fit proportions neither more nor less. He is the arbiter of the diverse and he is the key. He is the equalizer of his age and land . . . he supplies what wants supplying and what wants checking.' The poets' vision penetrates to the inner law of things; he sees everything as it truly is. This again is related to Whitman's optimism and his view, which I have already discussed, that whatever exists *in its proper place* is good.

For all the wide-ranging panoramic expansion of Whitman's poetry, we keep being continually impressed as we read by the importance to him of the *centre* (he uses the image of the hub of the wheel). The individual looks out, and the world falls into shape around him. Every real person and concrete thing is the centre of a pattern in the universe, and Whitman comes back again and again to that centre, as in the conclusion to *Democratic Vistas*—'the main thing being the average, the bodily, the concrete, the democratic, the popular, on which all the superstructures of the future are to permanently rest'. Again, this links his view of American democracy with his view of poetry.

For what he called 'dandified' poetry Whitman had a mixture of admiration and contempt. The poetry of Tennyson, for example, he admired as being 'of a very high (perhaps the highest) order of verbal melody, exquisitely clean and pure, and almost always perfumed, like the tuberose, to an extreme of sweetness'. But it was 'a verse of inside elegance and high-life'. As Whitman saw it, poetry to Tennyson was 'a gentleman of the first degree, boating, fishing, and shooting genteelly through nature, admiring the ladies, and talking to them, in company, with that elaborate half-choked deference that is to be made up by the terrible license of men among themselves'. This is perceptive, and true in its way. He goes on to say that Tennyson 'does not ignore courage, but all is to show forth through dandified forms'. 'The models are the same both to the poet and the parlors. Both have the same supercilious elegance, both love the reminiscences which extol caste, both agree on the topics proper for mention and discussion, both hold the same undertone of church and state, both have the same languishing melancholy and irony, both indulge largely in persiflage, both are marked by the contour of high blood and a constitutional aversion to anything cowardly and mean, both accept the love depicted in romances as the great business of a life or a poem, both seem unconscious of the mighty truths of eternity and immortality, both are silent on the presumptions of liberty and equality, and both devour themselves in solitary lassitude.' This is not so much an indictment of Tennyson (though it has some shrewd hits) as a definition of his own kind of poetry, which is the new American poetry, by contrasting it with what it is *not*. No account of Whitman's view of poetry would be complete without some reference to his descriptions of poetry such as Tennyson's.

Finally, there is Whitman's interest in language, as evidenced by his article on 'Slang in America' and his notes for *An American Primer*. 'Language', he wrote in the former, 'is not an abstract construction of the learn'd, or of dictionary-makers, but is something arising out of the work, needs, ties, joys, tastes, of long generations of humanity, and has its bases broad and low, close to the ground.' Whitman was aware that language was not simply a medium of expression that happened to be available for use: it was bound up with human history and psychology. The jottings in *An American Primer* are fascinating, ranging with lively curiosity over a wide area of questions concerned with language —words deriving from different trades and professions, changes in the meaning of words as a result of social or other changes, the varieties and significance of place names, words deriving from national character, and so on. And always there is an exultation in the rich expressiveness of the English language and at the same time an insistence that Americans should develop the language in their own way. 'American writers', the notes conclude, 'are to show far more freedom in the use of words—Ten thousand native idiomatic words are growing, or are today already grown, out of which vast numbers could be used by American writers, with meaning and effect—words that would be welcomed by the nation, being of the national blood—words that would taste of identity and locality which is so dear to literature.' 'Identity and locality': even in his discussion of language Whitman comes back in the end to this essential feature of his vision.

I have tried to say something about Whitman's view of the self, society and nature, and the relation between the three; the relation of all this to his view of American democracy; his attitude to America and to other countries; his notion of the Dance of Life; his concept of the poet and the poet's function; and his view of language. I must insist again, as I did at the beginning, that to abstract these points from the way they appear in his own writing is both misleading and unfair; yet the procedure is inevitable if we are to discuss the philosophy of a poet at all. I hope at least that I have succeeded in making clear my own view that in spite of contradictions, absurdities, pretentious and affected termin-ology, and other obvious faults, Whitman had a vision, and a true poetic one, and in his best poetry that vision comes through, not as a philosophic system, but as a series of symbolic gestures, moving, exciting, illuminating. To that, and to the lively poetic prose of the prefaces, we return. Perhaps the best conclusion to any account of Whitman's philosophy would be Whitman's own words from the poem beginning 'Myself and mine' in *Birds of Passage*:

> I call to the world to distrust the accounts of my friends, but listen to
> my enemies, as I myself do,
> I charge you forever reject those who would expound me, for I
> cannot expound myself,
> I charge that there be no theory or school founded out of me,
> I charge you to leave all free, as I have left all free.

We return in the end, not to grandiose theories of mankind, but to the concrete projection of the living individual; from this, the true poetic vision stems:

> Behold a woman!
> She looks out from her quaker cap,
>   her face is clearer and more beautiful than the sky.
>
> She sits in an armchair under the faded porch of the farmhouse,
> The sun just shines on her old white head.
>
> Her ample gown is of cream-hued linen,
> Her grandsons raised the flax, and her grand-daughters spun it with
>   the distaff and the wheel.
>
> The melodious character of the earth,
> The finish beyond which philosophy cannot go and does not wish
>   to go,
> The justified mother of men.

SCOTT'S ACHIEVEMENT AS A NOVELIST[1]

IN THE MINDS of too many teachers of English and in the pages of too many histories of English literature, Scott is an ultra-romantic figure who began his literary career under the influence of a rather extravagant German romanticism, moved from there to a general passion for antiquities, ballads and everything that was old, quaint, 'gothic' or picturesque, and then proceeded to embody this passion in a series of historical novels full of scenes of heroism, chivalry and general 'tushery'. In justice to those who present this distorted picture, it must be admitted that there is an element of truth in it: in his youth Scott *was* inclined to be romantic in this sense, in his narrative poems he does illustrate something of this attitude, and in later life, when inspiration flagged, he fell back on 'tushery' more often than his admirers would like to admit. But Scott's best and characteristic novels are a very different matter. They might with justice be called 'antiromantic' fiction. They attempt to show that heroic action, as the typical romantic writer would like to think of it, is, in the last analysis, neither heroic nor useful, and that man's destiny, at least in the modern world, is to find his testing time not amid the sound of trumpets but in the daily struggles and recurring crises of personal and social life. The courageous and passionate Jacobite rebel of *Redgauntlet* is dismissed at the end of the novel with a smile and a shake of the head, all his heroics reduced to a kind of posturing that one pities rather than admires; but humble Jeanie Deans in *The Heart of Midlothian*, who has led her life among simple folk and walks to London to try to get a reprieve for a sister whose offence, after all, was both common-place and sordid, *is* granted her heroic moment, her 'crowded hour of glorious life', and she finds it when, against all the laws of romance and chivalry, she pours out her heart in her humble

[1] First published in *Nineteenth Century Fiction*, September 1951.

Scots diction before a queen who is less a queen than a normally sensitive woman. And when Jeanie tries to find out how she can repay the kindness of the noble duke who had helped her to her interview with the queen, she asks: 'Does your honour like cheese?' *That* is the real Scott touch.

It is worth noting that the heroine of the novel considered by most critics to be Scott's best is a humble Scottish working girl. If Scott is to be classed as a romantic (though it is time we abandoned such indefinite and overworked terms), he must be regarded as at least as close to Wordsworth as to Coleridge. In the well-known fourteenth chapter of *Biographia Literaria*, Coleridge described the different parts he and Wordsworth had agreed to play in the production of *Lyrical Ballads*:

> It was agreed that my endeavours should be directed to persons and characters supernatural, or at least romantic; yet so as to transfer from our inward nature a human interest and a semblance of truth sufficient to procure for these shadows of imagination that willing suspension of disbelief for the moment which constitutes poetic faith. Mr Wordsworth, on the other hand, was to propose to himself as his object, to give the charm of novelty to things of every day, and to excite a feeling analogous to the supernatural, by awakening the mind's attention to the lethargy of custom. . . .

If we forget the tapestry figures of Scott's later novels and think of those which we cannot but remember most vividly—Jeanie Deans, Andrew Fairservice, Bailie Nicol Jarvie, Dugald Dalgetty, Saunders Fairford, Caleb Balderstone, Baron Bradwardine, Edie Ochiltree, and a host of others who live in the minds long after the plots of the novels in which they appear are forgotten—we realize that he is at least as successful in 'giving the charm of novelty to things of every day' as in the task assigned to Coleridge. It is a well-known fact that the titular heroes of Scott's novels are generally less real than the minor characters who abound in his works. It is, as a rule, the unheroic characters who have the most vitality: the pusillanimous gardener, Andrew Fairservice, is a more real and, fundamentally, a more important character in *Rob Roy* than the theatrical Helen Macgregor.

What does this mean? Are we to conclude that Scott had skill in creating lively minor characters, but failed in the general plan and structure of his novels? The answer to this and other questions lies in an examination of the *kind* of historical novel that Scott wrote, of the part played by the historical element in those novels and its relation to the other elements.

To identify Scott as a historical novelist is to place him in a category too wide to be helpful. A historical novel can be primarily an adventure story, in which the historical elements merely add interest and a sense of importance to the actions described; or it can be essentially an attempt to illustrate those aspects of the life of a previous age which most sharply distinguish it from our own; or it can be an attempt to use a historical situation to illustrate some aspect of man's fate which has importance and meaning quite apart from that historical situation. Stevenson's *Kidnapped* comes into the first category, and here, too, are many of the novels of Dumas; the eighteenth-century 'gothic' romance comes into the second; and the best of Scott's novels come into the third. Obviously, the least important kind is the second, for it considers the past simply as picturesque, and picturesqueness is merely a measure of the ignorance of the beholder. Cowboys are doubtless picturesque to New Yorkers, but they are not so to themselves or to their immediate associates. Mexicans may be picturesque to North American tourists, and Scottish fishwives to English artists, but their picturesqueness is obviously not an intrinsic quality. It is no exaggeration to say that to treat history as picturesque is the most superficial and least significant way of treating it. Scott did so occasionally, when he was tired or too hard pressed, and occasionally, too, he mingled the first of my two categories with the second and produced a picturesque historical adventure story, as in *The Talisman*, which is reasonably good of its kind but the kind does not stand very high in the hierarchy of literary forms. The work by which he must be judged—for it is only fair to judge a writer by his most characteristic achievement—avoids the picturesque and seeks rather to bring the past nearer than to exploit its remoteness.

The novels on which Scott's reputation as a novelist must stand or fall are his 'Scotch novels'—those that deal with Scottish history and manners—and not even all of those. *Waverley, Guy Mannering, The Antiquary, Old Mortality, The Heart of Midlothian, Rob Roy, The Bride of Lammermoor, A Legend of Montrose* and *Redgauntlet*—all, except *Redgauntlet*, earlier novels—constitute Scott's list of masterpieces. There are others of the Waverley Novels of which no novelist need be ashamed, many with excellent incidental scenes and memorable character studies, but this group of Scottish novels all possess Scott's characteristic virtues, and they represent his particular kind of fiction at its very best.

The fact that these novels are all concerned with Scottish history and manners is intimately bound up with the reasons for their being his best novels. For Scott's attitude to life was derived from his response to the fate of his own country: it was the complex of feelings with which he contemplated the phase of Scottish history immediately preceding his own time that provided the point of view which gave life—often a predominantly tragic life—to these novels. Underlying most of these novels is a tragic sense of the inevitability of a drab but necessary progress, a sense of the impotence of the traditional kind of heroism, a passionately regretful awareness of the fact that the Good Old Cause was lost forever and the glory of Scotland must give way to her interest.

Scott's attitude to Scotland, as Edwin Muir pointed out some years ago in a thoughtful and provocative study,[1] was a mixture of regret for the old days when Scotland was an independent but turbulent and distracted country, and of satisfaction at the peace, prosperity and progress which he felt had been assured by the Union with England in 1707 and the successful establishment of the Hanoverian dynasty on the British throne. His problem, in one form or another, was the problem of every Scottish writer after Scotland ceased to have an independent culture of her own: how to reconcile his country's traditions with what appeared to be its interest. Scott was always strongly moved by everything that reminded him of Scotland's past, of the days of the country's

---

[1] *Scott and Scotland*, Routledge, London, 1936.

independence and the relatively recent days when the Jacobites were appealing to that very emotion to gain support for their cause. He grew up as the Jacobite tradition was finally ebbing away, amid the first generation of Scotsmen committed once and for all to the association with England and the Hanoverian dynasty. He felt strongly that that association was inevitable and right and advantageous—he exerted himself greatly to make George IV popular in Scotland—yet there were strong emotions on the other side too, and it was these emotions that made him Tory in politics and that provided the greater blessing of leading him to literature and history.

Scott was two men: he was Edward Waverley and Baron Bradwardine, Francis Osbaldistone and (say) Mr Justice Inglewood, Darsie Latimer and, if not Redgauntlet himself, some one more disposed to his side than Darsie was. He was both the prudent Briton and the passionate Scot. And in many of his novels he introduces the loyal and respectable Englishman, allows him to be temporarily seduced by the claims of Scottish nationalism in one form or another, and then, reluctantly, sends him back to his respectable way of life again. So Edward Waverley leaves the Highlands and shakes off his associations with the Jacobite Rebellion, and Francis Osbaldistone leaves Rob Roy and returns to his father's London countinghouse.

This conflict within Scott gave life and passion to his Scottish novels, for it led him to construct plots and invent characters which, far from being devices in an adventure story or means to make history look picturesque, illustrated what to him was the central paradox of modern life. And that paradox admitted of the widest application, for it was an aspect of all commercial and industrial civilizations. Civilization must be paid for by the cessation of the old kind of individual heroic action. Scott welcomed civilization, but he also sighed after the old kind of individual heroic action. Scott's theme is a modification of that of Cervantes, and, specifically, *Redgauntlet* is Scott's *Don Quixote*.

Many of Scott's novels take the form of a sort of pilgrim's progress: an Englishman or a Lowland Scot goes north into the

Highlands of Scotland at a time when Scottish feeling is running high, becomes involved in the passions and activities of the Scots partly by accident and partly by sympathy, and eventually extricates himself—physically altogether but emotionally not quite wholly—and returns whence he came. The character who makes the journey is the more deliberate side of Scott's character, the disinterested observer. His duty is to observe, to register the proper responses, and in the end to accept, however reluctantly, the proper solution. It is not this character but what he becomes involved in that matters: his function is merely to observe, react, and withdraw. To censure Scott for the woodenness of his heroes—characters like Edward Waverley, Francis Osbaldistone, and many others—is to misunderstand their function. They are not heroes in the ordinary sense, but symbolic observers. Their love affairs are of no significance whatsoever except to indicate the nature of the observer's final withdrawal from the seductive scenes of heroic, nationalist passion. Waverley does not marry the passionate Jacobite Flora MacIvor but the douce and colourless Rose Bradwardine; Waverley's affair with these two girls is not presented as a serious love interest, but as a symbolic indication of the nature of his final withdrawal from the heroic emotions of the past. That withdrawal is never quite one hundred per cent: Waverley does marry the daughter of a Jacobite, but of one who has given up the struggle, and Francis Osbaldistone does (we are told in an epilogue, though we are not shown how it happens) marry Di Vernon, but only after she has dissociated herself from her violently Jacobite father and after Francis himself has, for all his earlier rebellion against a life of commerce, returned to his father's business. These pilgrims into Scotland carry back something of older attitudes that must be discarded, but only as a vague and regretful sentiment. Even Rob Roy tells Francis that the wild and heroic life may be all very well for himself, but it won't do for his children—they will have to come to terms with the new world.

The Jacobite movement for Scott was not simply a picturesque historical event: it was the last attempt to restore to Scotland

something of the old heroic way of life. This is not the place for
a discussion of the real historical meaning of Jacobitism—I am
concerned at present only with how Scott saw it and how he used
it in his novels. He used it, and its aftermath, to symbolize at
once the attractiveness and the futility of the old Scotland. *That*
Scotland was doomed after the Union of Parliaments of 1707 and
doubly doomed after the Battle of Culloden in 1746; the aftermath of 1707 is shown in *The Heart of Midlothian* and of 1746 in
Redgauntlet. In both novels, explicitly in the latter and murmuring
in an undertone in the former, there is indicated the tragic theme
(for it *is* tragic) that the grand old causes are all lost causes, and
the old heroic action is no longer even fatal—it is merely useless
and silly. One thinks of the conclusion of Bishop Hurd's *Letters
on Chivalry and Romance*: 'What we have gotten by this revolution, you will say, is a great deal of good sense. What we have
lost is a world of fine fabling.' But to Scott it was more than a
world of fine fabling that was lost; it was a world of heroic
ideals, which he could not help believing should still be worth
something. He knew, however, even before it was brought
home to him by Constable's failure and his consequent own bank-
ruptcy, that in the reign of George IV it was not worth much—
certainly not as much as novels about it.

Scott has often been presented as a lover of the past, but that is
a partial portrait. He was a lover of the past combined with a
believer in the present, and the mating of these incompatible
characters produced that tension which accounted for his greatest
novels. Writers on Scott have often quoted that passage in the
second volume of Lockhart's *Life* describing Scott's outburst to
Jeffrey on the question of legal reforms: 'He exclaimed, "No, no
—'tis no laughing matter; little by little, whatever your wishes
may be, you will destroy and undermine, until nothing of what
makes Scotland Scotland shall remain." And so saying, he turned
round to conceal his agitation—but not until Mr Jeffrey saw tears
gushing down his cheek.' One might put beside this Scott's
description of his purpose in his introduction to the *Minstrelsy of
the Scottish Border*: 'By such efforts, feeble as they are, I may con-

tribute somewhat to the history of my native country; the peculiar features of whose manners and character are daily melting and dissolving into those of her sister and ally. And, trivial as may appear such an offering, to the manes of a kingdom, once proud and independent, I hang it upon her altar with a mixture of feelings, which I shall not attempt to describe.'

But we must remember that this lover of old traditions engaged heavily in financial speculations with publishers and printers and spent a great deal of his life poring over balance sheets and estimates of probable profit. One might contrast with the above quotations not only many of Scott's own practical activities but such remarks as the one he made in his Journal after dining with George IV: 'He is, in many respects, the model of a British monarch. . . . I am sure such a character is fitter for us than a man who would long to head armies, or be perpetually intermeddling with *la grande politique*.' He did not seem much worried there about ancient traditions.

It is this ambivalence in Scott's approach to the history of his country—combined, of course, with certain remarkable talents which I shall discuss later—that accounts for the unique quality of his Scottish novels. He was able to take an *odi et amo* attitude to some of the most exciting crises of Scottish history. If Scott's desire to set himself up as an old-time landed gentleman in a large country estate was romantic, the activities by which he financed —or endeavoured to finance—his schemes were the reverse, and there is nothing romantic in James Glen's account of Scott's financial transactions prefixed to the centenary edition of his letters. He filled Abbotsford with historical relics, but they were relics, and they gave Abbotsford something of the appearance of a museum. He thus tried to resolve the conflict in his way of life by making modern finance pay for a house filled with antiquities. This resolution could not, however, eliminate the basic ambivalence in his approach to recent Scottish history: that remained, to enrich his fiction.

This double attitude on Scott's part prevented him from taking sides in his historical fiction, and Sir Herbert Grierson has complained, though mildly, of this refusal to commit himself. 'Of the historical events which he chooses for the setting of his story,' writes Sir Herbert, 'his judgment is always that of the good sense and moderated feeling of his own age. He will not take sides out and out with either Jacobite or Hanoverian, Puritan or Cavalier; nor does he attempt to transcend either the prejudices or the conventional judgment of his contemporaries, he makes no effort to attain to a fresh and deeper reading of the events.' Sir Herbert partly answers his own criticism later on, when he concedes that Shakespeare likewise concealed his own views and did not stand clearly for this or that cause. But there are two questions at issue here. One is whether Scott's seeing both sides of an historical situation is an advantage or a disadvantage to him as a novelist; the other is whether, as Sir Herbert charges, he accepts the prejudices or the conventional judgment of his contemporaries and 'makes no effort to attain to a fresh and deeper reading of the events'. I should maintain that his seeing both sides is a great advantage, and, as to the second point, that, in terms of his art, Scott *does* attain to a fresh and deeper reading of the events. I say in terms of his art, because I of course agree that there is no overt philosophizing about the meaning of history in Scott's novels. But the stories as told by Scott not only 'attain to a fresh and deeper reading of the events', but also, I submit, do so in such a way as to illuminate aspects of life in general. As this is the crux of the matter, it requires demonstration in some detail.

Let us consider first *Waverley*, Scott's initial essay in prose fiction, and a much better novel, I venture to believe, than most critics generally concede it to be. I have already pointed out that the plot is built around an Englishman's journey into Scotland and his becoming temporarily involved in the Jacobite Rebellion on the Jacobite side. How does he become so involved and how are the claims of the Jacobite cause presented? First he becomes angry with his own side as a result of a series of accidents and misunderstandings (undelivered letters and so on) for which neither side is to blame. In this mood, he is willing to consider the possibility of identifying himself with the other side—the

Jacobite side—and does so all the more readily because he is in-volved in friendly relations with many of its representatives. He admires the heroism and the clan spirit of the Highlanders, and their primitive vigour (as compared with the more disciplined and conventional behaviour of the Hanoverian troops with whom he formerly served) strikes his imagination. He becomes tem-porarily a Jacobite, then, not so much because he has been persuaded of the justice of the cause, or because he believes that a Jacobite victory would really improve the state of Britain, but because his emotions have become involved. It has become a personal, not a national, matter.

It should be noted further that Waverley goes into the High-lands in the first place simply in order to satisfy a romantic curiosity about the nature of the Highlanders, and it is only after arriving there that he succumbs to the attractions of clan life. Not that his reason ever fully succumbs: though he comes to realize the grievances of the Highland Jacobites, he has no illusions about their disinterestedness or their political sagacity, and even when he does surrender emotionally he remains critical of many aspects of their behaviour. Thus it is emotion against reason, the past against the present, the claims of a dying heroic world against the colder but ultimately more convincing claims of modern urban civilization.

The essence of the novel is the way in which these conflicting claims impinge on Waverley. It is worth noting that Waverley, though he began his progress as a soldier in the army of King George, did not set out completely free of any feeling for the other side. Though his father had deserted the traditions of his family and gone over completely to the Government, his uncle, who brought him up, was an old Jacobite, and his tutor, too, though an impossible pedant who had little influence on Waver-ley, supported the old régime in both Church and State. Waver-ley thus belonged to the first generation of his family to begin his career under the auspices of the new world—specifically, to be-come a soldier of King George as a young man. That new world was not yet as firmly established in Scotland as it came to be during Scott's own youth: there was still a possibility of successful rebellion in Waverley's day, but none in Scott's. It was too late for Scott to become a Jacobite, even temporarily, except in his imagination, so he let Waverley do it for him. The claims of the two sides are a little more evenly balanced for Waverley than for Scott, yet even in the earlier period the issue is never really in doubt, and Waverley's part in the Jacobite rebellion must be small, and must be explained away and forgiven by the Government in the end. Above all, it must be a part entered into by his emotions on personal grounds rather than by his reason on grounds of national interest.

I have said that the essence of *Waverley* is the way in which the conflicting claims of the two worlds impinge on the titular hero. The most significant action there cannot concern the hero, but involves the world in which he finds himself. It is important, of course, that the hero should be presented as someone sensitive to the environment in which he finds himself; otherwise his function as the responsive observer could not be sustained. To ensure that his hero is seen by the reader as having the proper sensitivity, Scott gives us at the opening of the book several chapters describing in detail Waverley's education and the development of his state of mind. Waverley's education, as described in Chapter Three, is precisely that of Scott himself. By his undisciplined reading of old chronicles, Italian and Spanish romances, Elizabethan poetry and drama, and 'the earlier literature of the northern nations', young Waverley was fitted to sympathize with the romantic appeal of the Jacobite cause and its Highland supporters. This, as we know from Lockhart and from Scott's own account, was Scott's own literary equipment, and it qualified Waverley to act for him in his relations with the Scottish Jacobites.

Waverley became involved in the affairs of the Highlands through a visit to his uncle's old friend, Baron Bradwardine, the first in Scott's magnificent gallery of eccentric pedants. The baron remains a sort of halfway house between the two sides: a Jacobite who takes the field in '45, he is nevertheless not as completely committed to the cause as such characters as Fergus Mac-

Ivor and his sister Flora, and at the end he is pardoned and restored to his estate. Bradwardine is a Jacobite more from his love of ancient traditions than out of any political feeling, and it is therefore proper that he should survive to indulge his love of the past harmlessly in antiquarian studies and pedantic conversation. Scott can afford to relax with such a character, as with other minor characters who do not serve to symbolize the extremes of one side or the other: and that is why we find so many of Scott's minor characters more real than some of the principals—their function is to live in the story and represent the more realistic, tolerant life of more ordinary folk whose destinies are less affected by changes of dynasty than those of higher rank. This is particularly true of such minor characters as Davie Gellatley and Duncan Macwheeble. Their function is similar to that of Justice Shallow and Master Silence in Shakespeare's *Henry IV*: they illustrate a kind of life that adapts itself easily to changes and is not really implicated in the civil conflicts surrounding it.

The characters in *Waverley* are marshalled with great skill. First we have the protagonists on either side: Fergus and Flora MacIvor represent different aspects of the Jacobite cause, Fergus displaying that mixture of ambition and loyalty which Scott regarded as an important characteristic of Highland chiefs, Flora embodying a purer and more disinterested passion for the cause; and on the other side is Colonel Talbot, the perfect English gentleman, despising the uncouth ways of the wild Highlanders and representing civilized man as Scott thought of him. In between the two sides stands Baron Bradwardine, the nonpolitical Jacobite, who does not have to die for his faith but is content to be left in the end with his antiquities and old-fashioned code of behaviour. Then there are the minor characters on either side, who represent either life persisting in ordinary human forms in spite of everything, or, as in the case of Evan Dhu Maccombich, the humble follower who does what he considers his duty out of simple loyalty to his ideals and without any understanding of the issues at stake. And in the centre is Edward Waverley, registering his creator's reactions to what goes on around him. He admires courage, honours

loyalty on either side, welcomes the victory of the Hanoverians
yet sorrows over the fate of the fallen—and then returns for good
to the victorious side, taking with him a wife from among the
less fanatical of the Jacobites. His attitude to Fergus MacIvor is
not unlike that of Brutus to Caesar—'there is tears for his love;
joy for his fortune; honour for his valour; and death for his
ambition'.

If there is no new historical interpretation of the Jacobite Rebellion in this novel, there is certainly a profound interpretation
of what it meant in terms of human ambitions and interests and
in terms of that conflict between the old world of heroic action
and the new world of commercial progress which, as we have
seen, was so central to Scott. It is the same kind of interpretation
that we find in Shakespeare's *Henry IV*: while accepting the most
enlightened contemporary view of the history involved, it uses
that history as a means of commenting on certain aspects of life
which, in one form or another, exist in every age. This is surely
the highest function of the historical novel as of the history play.

The high-ranking characters in the novels are often the most
symbolical, and they cannot therefore easily step out of their
symbolic rôle in order to act freely and provide that sense of
abundant life which is so essential to a good novel. This is therefore achieved by the minor characters (and here again the comparison with Shakespeare suggests itself). The 'humours' of
Baron Bradwardine, the complacent professional zeal of Bailie
Macwheeble, the simple and eloquent loyalty of Evan Dhu—
these give *Waverley* its essential vitality, though I think it is a
fault in the novel (one which Scott corrected in his subsequent
work) that they play too small a part while too large a part is
played by the more rigid actions of the major figures. The tragic
sense that romantic man must compromise with his heroic ideals
if he is to survive in the modern world gives way as the book
comes to a close to the less elevated sentiments of the realistic
common man. Waverley, leaving Carlisle after the execution of
Fergus MacIvor, makes a motion as though to look back and see
his friend's head adorning the battlements, but—here, significantly,

that whole episode ends—he is prevented by his Lowland Scots servant Alick Polwarth, who tells him that the heads of the executed men are on the gate at the other side of the town: 'They're no there. . . . The heads are ower the Scotch yate, as they ca' it. It's a great pity of Evan Dhu, who was a very well-meaning, good-natured man, to be a Hielandman; and indeed so was the Laird o' Glennaquoich too, for that matter, when he wasna in ane o' his tirrivies.' Similarly, when Waverley, now heir to a fortune, communicates to Bailie Duncan Macwheeble his plans to marry Rose Bradwardine, the worthy legal man brings the level of the action effectively down to that of ordinary professional success.

'Lady Wauverley?—ten thousand a-year, the least penny!—Lord preserve my poor understanding!'
'Amen with all my heart,' said Waverley, 'but now, Mr Macwheeble, let us proceed to business.' This word had a somewhat sedative effect, but the Bailie's head, as he expressed himself, was still 'in the bees'. He mended his pen, however, marked half a dozen sheets of paper with an ample marginal fold, whipped down Dallas of St. Martin's Styles from a shelf, where that venerable work roosted with Stair's Institutions, Direleton's Doubts, Balfour's Pratiques, and a parcel of old account books—opened the volume at the article Contract of Marriage, and prepared to make what he called a 'sma' minute, to prevent parties frae resiling'.

Thus the marriage of the heir to the Waverley estates to the daughter of the pardoned Jacobite is made real by a lawyer's jotting down a 'sma' minute, to prevent parties frae resiling'. Though we may have to abandon our dreams, the author seems to be saying, life goes on in spite of us, with its small daily matters for tears or laughter, of which, in spite of all alarums and excursions, human existence largely consists. It was because, at bottom, Scott had a tremendous feeling for this kind of ordinary daily life that he was able to suppress the implicit tragic note in so many (but not in all) of his novels and leave the reader at the end to put heroic ideals behind him with a sigh and turn with a smile to the foibles of ordinary humanity. And I should add that that smile is always one of tolerant fellow-feeling, never of condescension. The subtitle of *Waverley* is "Tis Sixty Years Since', and the phrase is repeated many times throughout the book. It deals, that

H

is to say, with a period which, while distant enough to have a historical interest, was not altogether out of the ken of Scott's own generation. In the preface to the first edition of *The Antiquary* his third novel, Scott wrote: 'The present work completes a series of fictitious narratives, intended to illustrate the manners of Scotland at three different periods. *Waverley* embraced the age of our fathers, *Guy Mannering* that of our youth, and the *Antiquary* refers to the last years of the eighteenth century.' (Scott, it will be remembered, was born in 1771.) As Scott comes closer to his own day, the possibilities for heroic action recede and the theme of the lost heir is introduced as a sort of substitute. It was with recent Scottish history that Scott was most concerned, for the conflict within himself was the result of relatively recent history. The Jacobite Rebellion of 1745 was the watershed, as it were, dividing once and for all the old from the new, and Scott therefore began his novels with a study of the relation between the two worlds at that critical time. It was not that the old Scotland had wholly disappeared, but that it was slowly yet inevitably disappearing that upset Scott. Its disappearance is progressively more inevitable in each of the next two novels after *Waverley*.

Guy Mannering is not in the obvious sense a historical novel at all. It is a study of aspects of the Scottish situation in the days of the author's youth, where the plot is simply an excuse for bringing certain characters into relation with each other. Once again we have an Englishman—Colonel Mannering, who, like Edward Waverley, shares many of his creator's characteristics—coming into Scotland and surrendering to the charm of the country. Scott has to get him mixed up in the affairs of the Bertrams in order to keep him where he wants him. Round Guy Mannering move gypsies, smugglers, lairds, dominies, lawyers and farmers, and it is to be noted that none of these characters, from Meg Merrilies to Dandie Dinmont, belongs to the new world: they are all essentially either relics of an earlier age, like the gypsies, or the kind of person who does not substantially change with the times, like that admirable farmer Dandie. These people are made to move around the Bertram family, or at least are brought into the story through some direct or indirect association with that family, and the family is decayed and impoverished. The lost heir is found and restored, and, largely through the benevolent offices of an English colonel, a Scottish landed gentleman is settled again on his ancestral acres. That is how things happen in the days of Scott's youth: no clash of arms or open conflict of two worlds, but the prophecies of gypsies, the intrigues of smugglers, the hearty activities of farmers, all set against the decay of an ancient family and all put to right in the end with the help of a gypsy, an English officer, and a Scottish lawyer. If the heroic element is less than in *Waverley*, the element of common life is greater, and the two virtues of honesty (in Dinmont) and urbanity (in Counsellor Pleydell) eventually emerge as those most worth while.

Counsellor Pleydell is a particularly interesting character because he represents that combination of good sense and humanity which Scott so often thought of as mediating between extremes and enabling the new world to preserve, in a very different context, something of the high generosity of the old. Pleydell is a lawyer, essentially middle class and respectable, but he is drawn with such sympathy that he threatens to remove most of the interest from the rather artificial main plot and share with Dandie Dinmont the reader's chief attention. If the gypsy Meg Merrilies provides something of the old-world romantic note—and she does so with great vigour and effectiveness—the lawyer and the farmer between them represent the ordinary man providing comfort for the future. The bluff courage and honesty of the farmer and the kindly intelligence of the lawyer dominate the story at the end.

Scott knew much of rural superstitions from the ballads, and he saw them as part of the ancient Scotland no less than Jacobitism or the feudal system. The gypsy prophetess Meg Merrilies is thus in a way the counterpart in this novel of Fergus MacIvor in *Waverley*. She, too, dies a violent death at the end of the book, and the stage is left to the representatives of the less spectacular virtues. The different strata of dialogue here are as clear as in the earlier novel. First listen to the simple yet eloquent speech of the gypsy:

'Ride your ways,' said the gypsy, 'ride your ways, Laird of Ellangowan—ride your ways, Godfrey Bertram!—This day have ye quenched seven smoking hearths—see if the fire in your ain parlour burn the blyther for that. Ye have riven the thack off seven cottar houses—look if your ain roof-tree stand the faster.—Ye may stable your stirks in the shealings at Derncleugh—see that the hare does not couch on the hearthstane at Ellangowan.—Ride your ways, Godfrey Bertram—what do you glower after our folk for?—There's thirty hearts there, that wad hae wanted bread ere ye had wanted sunkets, and spent their life-blood ere ye had scratched your finger. Yes—there's thirty yonder, from the auld wife of an hundred to the babe that was born last week, that ye have turned out o' their bits o' bields, to sleep with the tod and the black-cock in the muirs!—Ride your ways, Ellangowan.—Our bairns are hinging at our weary backs—look that your braw cradle at hame be the fairer spread up—not that I am wishing ill to little Harry, or to the babe that's yet to be born—God forbid—and make them kind to the poor, and better folk than their father!—And now, ride e'en your ways; for these are the last words ye'll ever hear Meg Merrilies speak, and this is the last reise that I'll ever cut in the bonny woods of Ellangowan.'

This is the high note, popular yet passionate, the note that Scott learned from the Border ballads. If one puts beside this the conversation between Counsellor Pleydell and Dandie Dinmont in Chapter Thirty-six and compares again with that the magnificent domestic scene at the Dinmont farm of Charlies-hope in Chapter Twenty-four (both unfortunately too long for quotation), one gets a view of the range of Scott's dialogue—from the passionate outburst of the gypsy to the humorous realism of the talk between Pleydell and Dinmont and the sympathetic domestic scene at Charlies-hope. These three passages illustrate Scott's basic equipment as a realistic 'social' novelist.

Finally, one should note a brief remark of Mr Pleydell's which illustrates perfectly his position as a sensible but sensitive man who had made a proper adjustment between his emotions and his way of life. Colonel Mannering has asked him what he thinks of the points of difference between the passionate old Covenanting clergy and the modern moderates, and this is his reply:

'Why, I hope, Colonel, a plain man may go to heaven without thinking about them at all—besides, *inter nos*, I am a member of the suffering and Episcopal Church of Scotland—the shadow of a shade now, and fortunately so—but I love to pray where my fathers prayed before me, without thinking worse of the Presbyterian forms, because they do not affect me with the same associations.'

I cannot attempt, in the space at my disposal, to give an account of the action of *Guy Mannering* or to illustrate how Scott manipulates his characters in order to produce the required picture of the Scotland of his youth. Nor can any account of the richness and vitality of the novels be given by a few brief quotations. But I must note that here, as so often in Scott, the formal plot is merely a device for bringing the necessary characters and situations into the novel: it is not a plot in the Aristotelian sense at all, but merely a stage contrived to accommodate the appropriate actors. Yet the action is not episodic: it all contributes to a central pattern, which is not, however, that laid down by the external plot.

One further point before I leave *Guy Mannering*. The nearer to the present Scott moves the more likely he is to present men of noble birth simply as fools. Those who think of Scott as the passionate defender of aristocratic privilege should note that the most highly born character in *Guy Mannering* is Sir Robert Hazlewood, whom Scott represents as a pompous ass, so obsessed by the dignity of his ancient lineage that he can talk of little else, and in other respects a selfish and foolish nonentity. Similarly, Sir Arthur Wardour of *The Antiquary*, equally obsessed by his noble ancestry, is shown as a gullible fool, and much less sympathetic than the antiquary himself, who, it should be noted, is of humble origin and a Whig.

The scene of *The Antiquary* is the Scotland of Scott's own day. The external plot, which is once again that of the lost heir, is, as usual, not to be taken seriously: its function is to bring the faintly drawn Englishman Lovel into Scotland and so set the appropriate characters into motion. In three successive novels Scott begins by bringing an Englishman into Scotland, by sending forth an observer to note the state of the country at the time represented by the novel's action. Lovel, of course, is no more the hero of *The Antiquary* than Christopher Sly is the hero of *The Taming of the Shrew*, and his turning out at the end to be the lost heir of Glenallan is the merest routine drawing down of the curtain. The life of the novel—and it has abundant life—centres in the Scottish characters whom the plot enables Scott to bring together, and in their reactions to each other. Jonathan Oldbuck, the antiquary (and it should be noted that there are antiquaries of one kind or another in a great many of Scott's novels) represents one kind of compromise between the old world and the new that is possible in the modern world. A descendant of German printers, a man of no family in the aristocratic sense, and a Whig in politics to boot, Oldbuck is yet fascinated by Scotland's past and spends his life in antiquarian studies. In the modern world the past becomes the preserve of the interested historian, whatever his birth or politics, while those who attempt to live in the past in any other way become, as Sir Arthur Wardour becomes, ridiculous and insufferable. Sir Arthur, continually lording it over the antiquary because of his superior birth, nevertheless knows less of Scottish history and traditions than the antiquary and is so vain and stupid that he falls a prey to the designing arts of an imposter who swindles him out of his remaining money, so that he has to be rescued through the influence of his friends. Sir Arthur is the comic counterpart of the tragic hero of *Redgauntlet*: both illustrate the impossibility of seriously living in the past after 1746. In *The Antiquary* the prevailing atmosphere is comic. This is unusual in Scott, however often he may end his novels with a formal 'happy ending' so far as the superficial plot is concerned. The melo-dramatic Glenallan episode in this novel and the drowning of the young fisherman Steenie Mucklebackit give a sense of depth and implication to the action, but they do not alter its essential atmosphere. In this novel, too, the hero is the character who plays the dominant part—the antiquary himself, the good-humoured, pedantic, self-opinionated, essentially kindly gentleman who is in many respects a latter-day version of Baron Bradwardine. Round him move Edie Ochiltree, the wandering beggar; the humble fishing family of the Mucklebackits; Caxon, the comic barber who deplores the passing of powdered wigs but takes comfort in the three yet left to him; the foreign imposter Dousterswiver; and other characters illustrative of the kind of life the east coast of Scotland (apart from the big cities) had settled down to by the end of the eighteenth century.

The plot of *The Antiquary* is even less important than that of *Guy Mannering*. It is essentially a static novel, in a sense a novel of manners, and the parts that stand out in the memory are such scenes as the gathering in the Fairport post office when the mail comes in, the antiquary holding forth at dinner or at a visit to a neighbouring priory, Sir Arthur and his daughter trapped by the tide and rescued by Edie Ochiltree and Lovel, the interior of the humble fishing cottage after Steenie's drowning, and similar pictures, many of them admirable genre portraits in the Flemish style. And as always in Scott, the novel lives by its dialogue, the magnificent pedantic monologues of Oldbuck, the racy Scots speech of Edie Ochiltree, the chattering of gossips in the post office, the naïve babbling of Caxon. No action, in these early novels of Scott, ever comes to life until somebody talks about it, whether in the sardonic tones of Andrew Fairservice, the vernacular declamations of Meg Merrilies, or the shrewd observations of Edie Ochiltree. And it is to be noticed that the dialogue is at its best when it is the speech of humble people: Scott could make them live by simply opening their mouths.

The characteristic tension of Scott's novels is scarcely perceptible in *The Antiquary*, though I think it can be discerned by those who look carefully for it. In *Old Mortality* it is present continuously and is in a sense the theme of the story. In this novel Scott goes back to the latter part of the seventeenth century to deal with the conflict between the desperate and embittered Covenanters and the royal armies intent on stamping out a religious disaffection which was bound up with political disagreements. Though this was an aspect of Scottish history which, in its most acute phases at least, was settled by the Revolution of 1689, it represented a type of conflict which is characteristic of much Scottish history and which Scott saw as a struggle between an exaggerated royalism and a fanatical religion. It should be said at the outset that as a historical novel in the most literal sense of the word—as an accurate picture of the state of affairs at the time—this is clearly Scott's best work. Generations of subsequent research have only confirmed the essential justice and fairness of Scott's picture of both sides. The only scholar ever seriously to challenge Scott on this was the contemporary divine, Thomas McCrie, who made an attack on the accuracy of Scott's portrait of the Covenanters, but posterity has thoroughly vindicated Scott and shown McCrie's attack to have been the result of plain prejudice.

But we do not read *Old Mortality* for its history, though we could do worse. We read it, as Scott wrote it, as a study of the kinds of mentality which faced each other in this conflict, a study of how a few extremists on each side managed, as they so often do, to split the country into warring camps with increasing bitterness on the one side and increasing cruelty on the other. Scott's interest, of course, would lie in the possibilities for compromise, in the technique of adjustment, in the kind of character who can construct a bridge between the two factions. And just as Edward Waverley, the loyal Englishman, became involved in spite of himself on the Jacobite side in 1745, so Harry Morton, the sensible, moderate, good-hearted Scot, becomes involved in similar circumstances on the side of the Covenanters. The Fergus MacIvor of the Covenanters is the magnificently drawn fanatic, Balfour of Burley. The leader of the other side, the famous Claverhouse, 'Bonnie Dundee', is introduced in person, and a convincing and powerful portrait it is. Between these extremes are all those whom varying degrees of zeal or loyalty brought into one camp or the other. The novel contains one of Scott's finest portrait galleries. On the Government side there is Claverhouse himself, his nephew Cornet Grahame, the proud Bothwell, descendant of kings, that perfect gentleman Lord Evandale, Major Bellenden, the veteran campaigner, and some minor figures. On the Covenanting side there is a whole array of clergymen, from the fanatical Macbriar to the more accommodating Poundtext, each presented with an individuality and with an insight into the motives and minds of men more profound than anything Scott had yet shown. The realistic, commonsense Cuddie Headrigg

trying, in the interests of their common safety, to put a curb on
the tongue of his enthusiastic Covenanting mother produces some
of the finest tragicomedy (if one may call it that) in English
literature: there are many passages here that would be worth
quoting if space did not forbid. The pious and kindly Bessie
Maclure shows the Covenanting side at its best, while the generous
Lord Evandale plays the same part for the other side. It is in the
gradations of the characters on either side that Scott shows his
greatest insight into the causes of civil conflict. Total conviction
is comparatively rare on either side, and when it is, it is either
bitter and passionate, as in Balfour of Burley, or nonchalantly
self-assured, as in Claverhouse.

If Scotland had not torn itself in two before the issues presented
in the eighteenth century were ever thought of, the fate of the
country might have been different, and Scott's study of the last of
the Scottish civil wars before the Jacobite Rebellions is thus linked
with his major preoccupation—the destiny of modern Scotland.
If moderate men on both sides could have won, the future would
have been very different. But, though there were moderate men
on both sides and Scott delighted to draw them, their advice in
the moments of crisis was never taken. There is no more moving
passage in the novel than the description of Morton's vain attempt
to make his fanatical colleagues behave sensibly before the Battle
of Bothwell Brig. There is a passion behind the telling of much
of this story that is very different from the predominantly sunny
mood of *The Antiquary*. The extremists prevail, the Covenanting
army is destroyed, and a victorious Government takes a cruel
revenge on embittered and resolute opponents. This is one novel
of Scott's where the moderate men do not remain at the end to
point the way to the future. Morton goes into exile and can
return to Scotland only after the Revolution. Lord Evandale
meets his death at the hands of a desperate man. And if the leaders
on both sides—the ruthless fanatic Burley and the equally ruthless
but gay cavalier Claverhouse—both go to their death before the
novel ends, there is no particular hope implied by their elimination.

Morton returns to marry his love, and the prudent Cuddie

settles down to be a douce henpecked husband, but the life has gone out of the novel by this time. The dominating figure, Balfour of Burley, may have been an impossible fanatic, but he represented a kind of energy possessed by none of the wiser characters. Harry Morton, the observer, the man who sees something good on both sides and is roped into the Covenanting side by a series of accidents, represents the humane, intelligent liberal in a world of extremists. *Old Mortality* is a study of a society which had no place for such a character: it is essentially a tragedy, and one with a very modern ring.

If *Old Mortality* is, from one point of view, Scott's study of the earlier errors which made the later cleavage between Scotland and her past inevitable (for it is true to say that after the Covenanting wars the English saw no way but a union of the two countries to ensure the perpetual agreement of the Scots to the king chosen by England and to prevent the succession question from being a constant bugbear), *Rob Roy* is a return to his earlier theme, a study of eighteenth-century Highland grievances and their relation to Scotland's destiny. It is, in a sense, a rewriting of *Waverley* and the main theme is less baldly presented. The compromise character here is the ever-delightful Bailie Nicol Jarvie, the Glasgow merchant who is nevertheless related to Rob Roy himself and, for all his love of peace and his commercial interests, can on occasion cross the Highland line into his cousin's country and become involved in scenes of violence in which, for a douce citizen of Glasgow, he acquits himself very honourably.

Rob Roy represents the old heroic Scotland, while the worthy Bailie represents the new. The Union of 1707 may have been a sad thing for those who prized Scotland's independence, but to the Bailie and his like it opened up new fields for foreign trade, and brought increased wealth. 'Whisht, sir!—whisht!' he cried to Andrew Fairservice when the latter complained of the Union. 'It's ill-scraped tongues like yours that make mischief between neighbourhoods and nations. There's naething sae gude on this side o' time but it might have been better, and that may be said o' the Union. Nane were keener against it than the Glasgow folk, wi' their rabblings and their risings, and their mobs, as they ca' them nowadays. But it's an ill wind that blaws naebody gude— let ilka ane roose the ford as they find it.—I say, let Glasgow flourish! whilk is judiciously and elegantly putten round the town's arms by way of by word. Now, since St. Mungo catched herrings in the Clyde, what was ever like to gar us flourish like the sugar and tobacco trade? Will anybody tell me that, and grumble at a treaty that opened us a road west-awa' yonder?' Rob Roy is courageous and sympathetic, and Helen Macgregor, his wife, is noble to the verge of melodrama, but they represent a confused and divided Highlands and are, after all, nothing but glorified freebooters. Scott, in the person of Francis Osbaldistone, pities their wrongs and feels for their present state, but he knows that they and what they stand for are doomed—indeed, they admit it themselves—and throws in his lot with the prudent Bailie.

It is, of course, grossly to simplify a novel of this kind to present its main theme in such terms. For Scott's sympathy with both sides leads him to produce scene after scene in which one group of characters after another moves to the front of the stage and presents itself in the most lively fashion. And the dialogue is some of the best Scott ever wrote. The Bailie is a perpetual delight, with his garrulity, prudence and essential generosity. The scene in the Glasgow prison, where he encounters his Highland relative; the episode at the clachan at Aberfoyle where he defends himself in a fierce tavern brawl with a red-hot poker; and his dialogue with the proud Helen Macgregor when she threatens him with instant death—no reader of *Rob Roy* can fail to feel the vitality and, what is more, the essential preoccupation with those aspects of human character which make men interesting and diverse enough to be worth contemplating at all which are manifest in these chapters. And the humour—for the book abounds in humour—is the rich humour of character, not mere superadded wit or cleverness. When the Bailie stands before the melodramatic Helen in imminent danger of being bundled into the lake on her hysterical orders, his conversation is absolutely central to his character:

'Kinswoman,' said the Bailie, 'nae man willingly wad cut short his thread of life before the end o' his pirn was fairly measured off on the yard-winles— And I hae muckle to do, an I be spared, in this warld—public and private business, as well that belanging to the magistracy as to my ain particular— and nae doubt I hae some to depend on me, as puir Mattie, wha is an orphan— She's a farawa' cousin o' the Laird o' Limmerfield—Sae that, laying a' this thegither—skin for skin, yea all that a man hath will he give for his life.'

That is the Bailie in danger; and here he is in the comfort of his own home, explaining the virtues of his brandy punch:

'The limes,' he assured us, 'were from his own little farm yonder-awa' (indicating the West Indies with a knowing shrug of his shoulders), 'and he had learned the art of composing the liquor from auld Captain Coffinkey, who acquired it,' he added in a whisper, 'as maist folks thought, amang the Buc-caniers. But it's excellent liquor,' said he, helping us round; 'and good ware has often come frae a wicket market. And as for Captain Coffinkey, he was a decent man when I kent him, only he used to swear awfully—but he's dead, and gaen to his account, and I trust he's accepted—I trust he's accepted.'

The Bailie dominates the book, and Andrew Fairservice, the dour Lowland gardener, comes a close second. One of Scott's most unattractive characters (he is the degenerate scion of the Covenanting tradition, while the Bailie is its more attractive heir: Calvinism and commerce often went together), Andrew has a flow of insolent, complaining and generally irritating conver-sation which is nevertheless irresistible. As Lord Tweedsmuir has said, 'he never opens his mouth but there flows from it a beautiful rhythmic Scots'. He is a constant irritant to the nominal hero, whose servant he is, and a constant joy to the reader. That ability to make an offensive character attractive through the sheer literary quality of his offensiveness, as it were, is surely the mark of the skilful artist. And such, I would maintain, Scott at his best, and in spite of certain obvious faults, always is.

There are two pivots to this novel; one is the relations between Francis Osbaldistone and his friends with Rob Roy and *his* friends, and the other is Francis's relations with his uncle and cousins. It is, I believe, a mistake to regard the family compli-cations in *Rob Roy* as mere machinery designed to provide a reason for young Osbaldistone's journey into Scotland: they loom much too largely in the novel for that. They represent, in fact, a statement of the theme on which the Rob Roy scenes are a variation—the impossibility of the old life in the new world. Francis's uncle is an old-fashioned Tory Jacobite squire, completely gone to seed, and his sons are either fools or villains. This is what has become of the knights of old—they are either freebooters like Rob Roy, shabby remnants of landed gentry like Sir Hildebrand, or complete villains like Rashleigh. Francis's father had escaped from this environment to embrace the new world wholeheartedly and become a prosperous London merchant. He is at one extreme, Bailie Nicol Jarvie is the middle figure, and Rob Roy is at the other extreme. But the pattern is more complicated than this, for the novel contains many variations on each type of character, so much so, in fact, that it is an illuminating and accurate picture of Scottish types in the early eighteenth century. And through it all runs the sense of the necessity of sacrificing heroism to prudence, even though heroism is so much more attractive.

It is interesting to observe that Scott tends to lavish most of his affection on the middle figures, those who manage to make themselves at home in the new world without altogether repudiating the old. Such characters—Jonathan Oldbuck, Counsellor Pleydell, Bailie Nicol Jarvie—are always the most lively and the most attractive in the novels in which they occur. They represent, in one way or another, the kind of compromise which most satisfied Scott.

Of *The Heart of Midlothian*, which most critics consider the best of Scott's works, I shall say nothing, since I have analysed it in accordance with the view of Scott here developed in the introduction to my edition of the novel.[1]

The Bride of Lammermoor, which followed *The Heart of Midlothian*, presents the conflict between the old and the new in naked, almost melodramatic terms: the decayed representative of an ancient family comes face to face with the modern purchaser of his estates. The book is stark tragedy, for the attempted com-

[1] Rinehart, New York, 1948.

promise—the marriage between the old family and the new—is too much for circumstances, and the final death of hero and heroine emphasizes that no such direct solution of the problem is possible. Too few critics have observed the note of grim irony in this novel, which goes far to neutralize the melodrama. The portrait of the Master of Ravenswood is bitterly ironical, and there is irony too in the character of his faithful servant, Caleb Balderstone. The pride of both master and servant, which has no justification in their present circumstances or achievements, is a grim mockery of that heroic pride which motivated the knights of old. Ravenswood is a tragic counterpart of Sir Arthur Wardour of *The Antiquary*: both retain nothing of value from the past except an unjustified pride.

A Legend of Montrose—the companion piece of *The Bride of Lammermoor* in the third series of 'Tales of My Landlord'—is a slighter novel than those I have been discussing: it lives through one character only, Captain Dugald Dalgetty, the only military figure in English literature beside whom Fluellen looks rather thin. But this one character is sufficient to illuminate the whole story, since, in a tale concerning the Civil War of the 1640s, he represents the most complete compromise figure—the mercenary soldier, trained in the religious wars of the Continent, willing to fight on and be loyal to any side which pays him adequately and regularly. This is another novel of a divided Scotland—divided on an issue foreshadowing that which divides the two camps in *Old Mortality*. Here again we have Highland heroism presented as something magnificent but impossible, and the main burden of the novel falls on Dugald Dalgetty, mercenary and pedant (a most instructive combination to those interested in Scott's mind), the man of the future who, ridiculous and vulgar though he may be, has a firm code of honour of his own and performs his hired service scrupulously and courageously.

After *The Bride of Lammermoor* and *A Legend of Montrose* Scott turned to other fields than relatively recent Scottish history, and in *Ivanhoe* he wrote a straight novel of the age of chivalry without any attempt to relate it to what had hitherto been the principal theme of his prose fiction—the relations between the old heroic Scotland and the new Anglicized, commercial Britain. A novel like *Ivanhoe*, though it has qualities of its own, is much more superficial than any of the Scottish novels, and is written throughout on a much lower plane. Scott did not, in fact, know the Middle Ages well and he had little understanding of its social or religious life. But he returned later to the theme which was always in his mind, and in *Redgauntlet* produced if not certainly the best, then the most illuminating of his novels.

Redgauntlet is the story of a young Edinburgh man who becomes involved against his will in a belated Jacobite conspiracy some twenty years after the defeat of Prince Charlie at Culloden. The moving spirit of the conspiracy turns out to be the young man's own uncle (for, like so many of Scott's heroes, young Darsie Latimer is brought up in ignorance of his true parentage), who kidnaps him in order that, as the long-lost heir to the house of Redgauntlet, he may return to the ways of his ancestors and fight for the Pretender as his father had done before him. Darsie, of course, has no liking for this rôle so suddenly thrust upon him, and is saved from having to undertake it by the complete collapse of the conspiracy. That is the barest outline of the plot, which is enriched, as so often in Scott, with a galaxy of characters each of whom takes his place in the complex pattern of late eighteenth-century Scottish life which the novel creates.

As with most of the Scottish novels, the story moves between two extremes. On the one hand, there is the conscientious lawyer Saunders Fairford, his son Alan, who is Darsie's bosom friend and with whom Darsie has been living for some time before the story opens, and other characters representing respectable and professional Edinburgh. Saunders Fairford is Scott's portrait of his own father, and the figure is typical of all that is conventional, hard-working, middle-class, unromantic. At the other extreme is Darsie's uncle, a stern fanatical figure reminiscent of Balfour of Burley. Between the two worlds—that of respectable citizens who are completely reconciled to the new Scotland and that of fanatical Jacobites engaged in the vain task of trying to recreate the old—Scott places his usual assortment of mediating figures, from the blind fiddler, Wandering Willie, to that typical compromise character, the half-Jacobite Provost Crosbie. This is the Scotland in which Scott himself grew up and in which he recognized all the signs of the final death of the old order. For most of the characters Jacobitism is now possible only as a sentiment, not as a plan of action. But to Redgauntlet, who has dedicated his life to the restoration of the Stuarts, it is a plan of action, and the tragedy—for the novel is essentially a tragedy—lies in the manner of his disillusion.

The story opens with the usual pilgrim's progress. Darsie, tired of his law studies and happily possessed of an independent income, decides to leave the Fairfords', where he has been staying, and take a trip to south-west Scotland for diversion. We are presented first with a series of letters between Darsie and his friend Alan Fairford, the former on his travels, the latter at home in his law studies preparing himself to be called to the Bar. These letters are written with a speed and deftness and with a lively fidelity to character that carry the reader easily into the story. Darsie becomes involved in a series of adventures which bring him into contact with a number of characters whom Scott needs to present in order to round out his picture, then is kidnapped by his uncle, and finally discovers his real birth and the destiny his uncle intends for him. The story, opened by letters, is continued in Scott's own person, with the help of the journal Darsie keeps while held in confinement by his uncle. This technique is not in the least clumsy, but keeps the emphasis at each point just where Scott needs it. Alan goes off to rescue his friend, but not before Scott has given us a brilliant picture of Scottish legal life, a perfect epitome of the professional activity which then was and to a certain extent still is the basis of Edinburgh's existence. Edinburgh and its worthy citizens are in no danger of losing their heads over an impossible and reactionary ideal. We move from there to Darsie and his uncle, and gradually the two sets of characters get nearer each other, until the climax, which is the end of the novel. Nowhere else (as Mr Edwin Muir has pointed out) did Scott express so

explicitly and so vigorously his sense of the doom of the old
heroic life. In the modern world such ideals were not even
dangerous, they were only silly, and though Scott accepted this,
it was with the deepest reluctance and with all his instincts outraged. Consider the climax of *Redgauntlet*, after the pathetic little
conspiracy has been discovered and the Government representative enters the room where the conspirators are arguing among
themselves. As General Campbell, the Government emissary,
enters, Redgauntlet challenges him in the old style:

'In one word, General Campbell,' said Redgauntlet, 'is it to be peace or
war?—You are a man of honour and we can trust you.'

'I thank you, sir,' said the General; 'and I reply that the answer to your
question rests with yourself. Come, do not be fools, gentlemen; there was
perhaps no great harm meant or intended by your gathering together in this
obscure corner, for a bear-bait or a cock-fight, or whatever other amusement
you may have intended, but it was a little imprudent, considering how you
stand with government, and it has occasioned some anxiety. Exaggerated
reports of your purpose have been laid before government by the information
of a traitor in your councils; and I was sent down to take command of a
sufficient number of troops, in case these calumnies should be found to have
any real foundation. I have come here, of course, sufficiently supported both
with cavalry and infantry, to do whatever may be necessary; but my commands
are—and I am sure they agree with my inclination—to make no arrests, nay, to
make no further inquiries of any kind, if this good assembly will consider their
own interests so far as to give up their immediate purpose, and return quietly
home to their own houses.'

'What!—all?' exclaimed Sir Richard Glendale—'all, without exception?'

'ALL, without one single exception,' said the General; 'such are my orders.
If you accept my terms, say so, and make haste; for things may happen to
interfere with his Majesty's kind purposes towards you all.'

'His Majesty's kind purposes!' said the Wanderer [i.e., Charles Edward, the
Pretender, himself]. 'Do I hear you aright, sir?'

'I speak the King's very words, from his very lips,' replied the General. '"I
will," said his Majesty, "deserve the confidence of my subjects by reposing my
security in the fidelity of the millions who acknowledge my title—in the good
sense and prudence of the few who continue, from the errors of education, to
disown it." His Majesty will not even believe that the most zealous Jacobites
who yet remain can nourish a thought of exciting a civil war, which must be
fatal to their families and themselves, besides spreading bloodshed and ruin
through a peaceful land. He cannot even believe of his kinsman, that he would

I

engage brave and generous, though mistaken men, in an attempt which must ruin all who have escaped former calamities; and he is convinced, that, did curiosity or any other motive lead that person to visit this country, he would soon see it was his wisest course to return to the continent; and his Majesty compassionates his situation too much to offer any obstacle to his doing so.'

'Is this real?' said Redgauntlet. 'Can you mean this?—Am I—are all, are any of these gentlemen at liberty, without interference, to embark in yonder brig . . . ?'

'You, sir—all—any of the gentlemen present,' said the General. . . .

'Then, gentlemen,' said Redgauntlet, clasping his hands together as the words burst from him, 'the cause is lost for ever.'

It is important for a proper understanding of Redgauntlet's character to note that his zeal is not only for the restoration of the Stuarts; it is, in some vague way, for the restoration of an independent Scotland, and his dominant emotion is Scottish nationalism rather than royalism. Scott made him a symbol of all that the old, independent Scotland stood for, and that is why his fate was of so much concern to his creator. No reader can mistake the passion of the scene from which I have just quoted: Scott, who burst into tears when he heard of old Scottish customs being abolished and who protested in horror when, at the uncovering of the long-hidden crown jewels of Scotland, one of the commissioners made as though to place the old Scottish crown on the head of one of the girls who were present—the Scott who, in his heart, had never really reconciled himself to the Union of 1707 (though he never dared say so, not even in his novels), was portraying in the character of Redgauntlet something of himself, something, perhaps, of what in spite of everything he wished to be. But as Darsie Latimer—who is clearly a self-portrait, though a partial one—he only touched the fringe of that tragedy, without becoming involved in it.

There are other characters and episodes in *Redgauntlet* worth dwelling on—the character of the Quaker, the episode of the attack on the fishing nets in the Solway, and that admirable short story, 'Wandering Willie's Tale'. One might, too, elaborate on the structure of the novel, which is perfectly tied together, and there is the recurring dialogue, which, as always in

Scott's Scottish novels, keeps abundant life continually bubbling.

Basing Scott's claim on these Scottish novels, what then was his achievement and what is his place among British novelists? It might be said, in the first place, that Scott put his knowledge of history at the service of his understanding of certain basic paradoxes in human society and produced a series of novels which both illuminates a particular period and throws light on human character in general. His imagination, his abundant sense of life, his ear for vivid dialogue, his feeling for the striking incident, and that central, healthy sense of the humour of character, added, of course, essential qualities to his fiction. But it was his tendency to look at history through character and at character through the history that had worked on it that provided the foundation of his art. Scott's might be called a 'normal' sensibility, if such a thing exists. He has no interest in aberrations, exceptions or perversions, or in the minutiae of self-analysis—not unless they have played a substantial part in human history. Fanaticism, superstition, pedantry—these and qualities such as these are always with us, and Scott handles them again and again. But he handles them always from the point of view of the ordinary sensitive man looking on, not from their *own* point of view. We see Balfour of Burley through Morton's eyes, and Redgauntlet through Darsie Latimer's. We feel for them, understand them even, but never live with them. That is what I mean when I talk of Scott's *central* vision: his characters and situations are always observed by some one standing in a middle-of-the-road position. That position is the position of the humane, tolerant, informed and essentially happy man. It is fundamentally the position of a sane man. Scott was never the obsessed artist, but the happy writer.

Scott's abundant experience of law courts, both in Edinburgh and in his own sheriffdom, gave him a fund of knowledge of ordinary human psychology, and he had besides both historical knowledge and imagination. His eccentrics are never as fundamentally odd as Dicken's eccentrics: they are essentially ordinary people, people he had known in one form or another. Most important of all, Scott *enjoyed* people, in the way that Shakespeare must have done. They live and move in his novels with a Fal-staffian gusto. There is indeed something of Shakespeare in Scott —not the Shakespeare of *Hamlet* or *Othello*, but the Shakespeare of *Henry IV* or *Twelfth Night*, and perhaps also of *Macbeth*. His gift for dialogue was tremendous, and his use of Scottish dialect to give it authenticity and conviction is unequalled by any other Scottish novelist except very occasionally John Galt, Stevenson in *Weir of Hermiston*, and perhaps Lewis Grassic Gibbon in our own century. In spite of all the tragic undertones in so many of his novels, most of them are redeemed into affirmations of life through the sheer vitality of the characters as they talk to each other. Scott's gallery of memorable characters—characters who live in the mind with their own individual idiom—cannot be beaten by any other British novelist, even if we restrict the selection to some eight of Scott's novels and ignore all the rest. But they are not merely characters in a pageant: they play their parts in an interpretation of modern life. I say of 'modern life' to emphasize the paradox: Scott, the historical novelist, was at his best when he wrote either about his own time or about the recent past which had produced those aspects of his own time about which he was chiefly concerned.

Of course Scott was often careless. He wrote fast, and employed broad brush strokes. Sometimes we feel that he wholly lacked an artistic conscience, for he could do the most preposterous things to fill up space or tie up a plot. His method of drawing up the curtain is often clumsy, but once the curtain is up, the life that is revealed is (in his best novels) abundant and true. Scott can be pompous in his own way when his inspiration flags, but he never fools himself into mistaking his pomposity for anything else. Above all, though he is concerned about life he is never worried about it. We read his best novels, therefore, with a feeling of immense ease and satisfaction. We may be moved or amused or excited, but we are never worried by them. His best novels are always anchored in earth, and when we think of Helen Macgregor standing dramatically on the top of a cliff we cannot help thinking at the same time of the worthy Bailie,

garrulous and kindly and self-important; Counsellor Pleydell is
the perfect antidote to Meg Merrilies, and even Redgauntlet must
give way before Wandering Willie and Provost Crosbie. The
ordinary folk win in the end, and—paradox again—the Wizard
of the North finally emerges as a novelist of manners.

CHRISTOPHER NORTH[1]

IN THE SUMMER OF 1802 a seventeen-year-old student at the
University of Glasgow read with enthusiasm the new edition
of *Lyrical Ballads* and then sat down and wrote Wordsworth
a long letter. 'To you, sir,' he told the poet, 'mankind are in-
debted for a species of poetry which will continue to afford
pleasure while respect is paid to virtuous feelings, and while
sensibility continues to pour forth tears of rapture.' The writer
of the letter was John Wilson, a tall, handsome young man from
Paisley who was entering on a phase of orgiastic cultivation of
sensibility from which he never fully recovered. The following
year he left Glasgow for Oxford, where he divided his time
between the writing of sentimental verses, fierce but brief bouts
of reading, and the more robust activities of wrestling and cock-
fighting. For Wilson was a man of great physical strength and
immense energy, a tremendous walker and a keen fighter, and
he strode about Oxford like a giant.

This combination of gush and energy is the clue to his character
and career. The moral earnestness of the early Romantic Movement worked on his native tendency to emotional self-indulgence
to develop a taste for lachrymose sentimentalities of the most
embarrassing kind; but at the same time his enormous vitality,
his relish of sensation and of physical exertion, gave him a gusto
that often enabled him to carry off his emotional debauches with
dash and even splendour. In another age he might have written
Rabelaisian stories or been a revivalist or run a one-man radio
show. As it was, he became a journalist and a professor of moral
philosophy. The journalist was Christopher North, the fluent,
lively, unpredictable, reckless, self-contradictory, flamboyant,
mischievous and wholly preposterous contributor to *Blackwood's
Magazine*; the professor held the Chair of Moral Philosophy at

---

[1] A talk broadcast in the Third Programme on 8th August 1954.

Edinburgh from 1820 until 1851, an absolute impostor, dependent for his lectures on material supplied to him regularly by a friend, a fraud, a windbag, who declaimed high sounding platitudes in a magnificent voice to cheering students.

On leaving Oxford, Wilson decided that he wanted to be a Lake Poet, like Wordsworth; having a respectable private fortune, he settled at Elleray on Windermere, where he led a strenuous outdoor life, climbing, riding, walking, fishing, swimming and sailing, and also writing poetry which showed a certain emotional and verbal facility and a taste for a melodramatic plot. Wilson is now very properly forgotten as a poet, though he wrote poetry sporadically all his life.

At Elleray Wilson got to know Wordsworth and De Quincey, and began to fancy himself as a literary man. He married in 1811, and this seems to have inspired him to read for the Scottish Bar. The next three years found him often in Edinburgh, but his centre was still Elleray and his ambitions combined those of country gentleman and man of letters when in 1815 his fortune disappeared through the dishonesty of an uncle and he was forced to change his way of life. He moved with his family to Edinburgh to live with his mother, with the aim of making his literary reputation in the Athens of the North.

The Scottish Bar in the eighteenth and much of the nineteenth century was often the road to a literary life, as the careers of Sir Walter Scott and his son-in-law J. G. Lockhart clearly show. Wilson never practised law, but, much more important for his career, he got to know Lockhart and the circle of lively young advocates in which Lockhart moved. This led eventually to his joining Lockhart in writing for *Blackwood's Magazine*, which was founded as a Tory rival to Jeffrey's *Edinburgh Review* in 1817 by William Blackwood, a shrewd, energetic and ambitious publisher with a flair for publicity and a total lack of scruple. Wilson's vigour and his ability to write about anything in a tone of exalted conviction made him just the man for the new magazine. *Blackwood's* made Wilson and Wilson made *Blackwood's*. Or perhaps it would be truer to say that Blackwood's made Christopher North, for that was the name by which he became familiar to the readers of 'Maga', as everyone in Edinburgh called it.

With Wilson, Lockhart and James Hogg, 'the Ettrick Shepherd', behind him, Blackwood was convinced that he could challenge the Whigs with a formidable rival periodical, and he was right. 'Maga' opened with a bang in October 1817, with three highly controversial articles, all of course anonymous. The first was a violent and unscrupulous attack on Coleridge, in the guise of a review of *Biographia Literaria*; the second (first of the notorious series on 'The Cockney School of Poetry') blasted the morals of Leigh Hunt; and the third, which excited the good citizens of Edinburgh to frenzy, was a mock biblical story entitled 'The Chaldee Manuscript', purporting to be a translation of a recently recovered ancient manuscript but in fact telling with thin disguise the story of the conflict between Whig and Tory literary characters in Edinburgh with a juicy revelling in personalities. In the words of Professor Ferrier, Wilson's son-in-law, who later edited his father-in-law's works: 'The Chaldee Manuscript was the first trumpet-note which dissolved the trance of Edinburgh, and broke the spell of Whig domination. . . . It fell on Edinburgh like a thunderbolt. . . . The satellites of the [Whig] party were scandalized. They protested lustily against the outrageous personalities and profanities of the Chaldee. . . . Friends and foes were alike confounded: the Tories were perplexed; the Whigs were furious.'

'The Chaldee Manuscript' was a joint composition by Wilson, Lockhart and Hogg. Hogg's was the original idea, but Wilson and Lockhart did most of the writing, sitting up to do it one night until eight the next morning, with a bowl of punch, and Blackwood beside them egging them on. The story begins with an account of Edinburgh and of Blackwood and goes on to tell of the founding of 'Maga':

And I saw in my dream, and behold one like the messenger of a King came toward me from the east, and he took me up and carried me into the midst of the great city that looketh toward the north and toward the east, and ruleth over every people, and kindred, and tongue, that handle the pen of the writer.

And he said unto me, Take heed what thou seest, for great things shall come of it; the moving of a straw shall be as the whirlwind, and the shaking of a reed as the great tempest.

And I looked, and behold a man clothed in plain apparel stood in the door of his house: and I saw his name, and the number of his name; and his name was as it had been the colour of ebony, and his number was the number of a maiden, when the days of the years of her virginity have expired.

The ebony name is of course Blackwood, and the number refers to his shop at 17 Princes Street.

Quite apart from the personalities involved, the element of biblical parody in the story gave strong offence to the orthodox. Scott disapproved, as he continued to disapprove of 'Maga's' personal violence. 'I trust you have had enough of certain pranks with your friend Ebony,' he said to Wilson and Lockhart at Abbotsford the following autumn. But they hadn't: there was much more scandal to come. *Blackwood's*, in fact, soon established a reputation for outrageous anonymous personal attacks on all sorts of people, and Wilson was responsible for some of the most violent.

Whether the attack on Coleridge was by Wilson is not certain. His friendship for Coleridge need not have stopped him, for he regarded these attacks as enormous jokes which could be perpetrated on friend and foe alike. But they were always anonymous and though he wrote them with immense gusto he would sweat with fear and anguish if it looked as though his authorship was going to be revealed. In 1825, in the character of Christopher North, he wrote that 'Wordsworth often writes like an idiot. . . . He is, in all things, the reverse of Milton, a good man, and a bad poet. . . . Not one single character has he created—not one incident—not one tragical catastrophe. He has thrown light on no man's estate here below; and Crabbe, with all his defects, stands immeasurably above Wordsworth as the Poet of the Poor. . . . I confess that the "Excursion" is the worst poem, of any character, in the English language.' This was written just after Wilson had returned from being entertained by Wordsworth at Rydal Mount, where he had protested his friendship and admira-

tion for the poet. In the same essay he attacked Scott, who had
always befriended him, as 'a tame and feeble writer'. Then, when
a threat of litigation by an Irishman named Martin, whom he had
fiercely attacked in the same piece, made it look as though Blackwood might be forced to reveal that Wilson was the author,
Wilson took to his bed in despair and wrote to Blackwood that,
on learning of the matter, 'I was seized with a trembling and
shivering fit, and was deadly sick for some hours. . . . To own
that article is for a thousand reasons impossible. It would involve
me in lies abhorrent to my nature. I would rather die this evening.'

Others on 'Maga' were motivated by political bias, but Wilson
was an utterly irresponsible critic, liable to be carried away by his
own verve and gusto and precipitated into saying the most
outrageous things. Yet by the same token his critical essays for
'Maga' had a splendid energy, especially after he had assumed the
character of Christopher North. That pseudonym was not at
first reserved for any individual contributor, and was liable to be
used by any of the regulars, but by degrees it became established
as Wilson's property, and it was certainly his invention. To write
as Christopher North seemed to precipitate the extrovert side of
his nature and to eliminate, at least for long periods, the moralizing
sentimentalist. This is particularly true of the series called *Noctes
Ambrosianae*, which again were not at first all written by Wilson
but which eventually became his sole property. These are dia-
logues, himself as Christopher North and James Hogg as the
Ettrick Shepherd being the most regular participants. The Ettrick
Shepherd represents a happy idealization of Hogg, who is presented in the *Noctes* as a true pastoral poet, simple, active, generous
and master of a fine Scots prose. The *Noctes* might be anecdotal,
jocular, convivial, critical, or any or all of these together. Incidental songs and poems might be included, sometimes a genuine
poem of Hogg's. Here is an example of the dialogue. The characters are North, the Ettrick Shepherd and a friend called Tickler.
As always, the Shepherd gets the best speeches:

North: I wish you would review these four volumes, James, for next
Number.

Shepherd: Tuts—what's the use o' reviewin? Naething like a skreed o' extracts into a magazeen taken in the kintra. When I fa' on, tooth and nail, on an article about some new wark, oh, Mr North, but I'm wud when I see the cretur that undertaken to review't, setting himsel wi' clenched teeth to compose a philosophic creecticism, about the genius of an owther that every man kens as weel as his ain face in the glass—and then comparing him wi' this, and contrastin him wi' that—and informin you which o' his warks are best, and which warst, and which middlin—balancin a genius against himsel, and settin his verra merits against his character and achievements—instead o' telling you at aince what the plot is about, and how it begins, and gangs on, and is wunded up; in short, pithy hints o' the characters that feegur throughout the story, and a maisterly abridgement o' facts and incidents, wi' noo and then an elucidatory observation, and a glowing panegyric; but, aboon a' things else, lang, lang, lang extracts, judiciously seleckit, and lettin you ken at ance if the owther has equalled or excelled himsel, or if he has struck out a new path, or followed the auld ane into some unsuspeckit scenery o' bonny underwood, or lofty standards —or whether—but I'm out of breath, and maun hae a drink.—Thank you, Mr North—that's the best bowl you've made yet.

Tickler: I never had any professed feeling of the *super-* or *preter-* natural in a printed book. Very early in life I discovered that a ghost, who had kept me in a cold sweat during a whole winter's midnight, was a tailor who haunted the house, partly through love, and partly through hunger, being enamoured of my nurse, and of the fat of ham which she gave him with mustard, between two thick shaves of a quartern loaf, and afterwards a bottle of small-beer to wash it down, before she yielded him the parting kiss. After that I slept soundly, and had a contempt for ghosts, which I retain to this day.

Shepherd: Weel, it's verra different wi' me. I should be feared yet even for the ninth pairt o' a ghost, and I fancy a tailor has nae mair;—but I'm no muckle affeckit by reading about them—an oral tradition out o' the mouth o' an auld grey-headed man or woman is far best, for then you canna dout the truth o' the tale, unless ye dout a' history thegither, and then, to be sure, you'll end in universal skepticism.

North: Don't you admire the romances of the Enchantress of Udolpho?

Shepherd: I hae nae doubt, sir, that had I read *Udolpho* and her ither romances in my boyish days, that my hair would hae stood on end like that o' ither folk, for, by nature and education baith, ye ken, I'm just excessive superstitious. But afore her volumes fell into may haunds, my soul had been frichtened by a' kinds of traditionary terrors, and mony hunder times hae I maist swarfed wi' fear in lonesome spats in muirs and woods, at midnicht, when no a leevin thing was movin but mysel and the great moon. Indeed, I canna say that I ever fan' mysel alane in the hush o' darkened nature, without a beatin at my heart; for a sort o' spiritual presence aye hovered about me—a presence o' something like and unlike my ain being—at times felt to be solemn and nae mair—at times sae awfu' that I wushed mysel nearer ingle-licht—and ance or twice in my life-time, sae terrible that I could have prayed to sink down into the moss, sae that I micht be saved frae the quaking o' that ghostly wilderness o' a world that wasna for flesh and bluid!

 North: Look—James—look—what a sky!

 Shepherd: There'll be thunder the morn. . . .

The greatest joke in Wilson's life was his appointment to the Chair of Moral Philosophy at Edinburgh in 1820. It was an unashamedly political appointment. By far and away the best available candidate for the position was Sir William Hamilton, but Hamilton was a Whig, and the Town Council, which made the appointment, had a large Tory majority. The Whigs did not give up without a fight. 'The Chaldee Manuscript' and other indiscretions of *Blackwood's* were cast up against him and his moral character impugned, much to Wilson's anguish, for, fierce though his own critical attacks could be, he could not bear the slightest touch of adverse criticism himself. Scott and other influential Tories bestirred themselves on his behalf. In the end, Wilson won easily, by twenty-one votes to nine. Christopher North became Professor Wilson, or, rather, the split in Wilson's personality became permanent, and Christopher North and John Wilson went different ways. The contributions to 'Maga' continued, and Christopher North's journalistic career went on its spirited way undeterred by the moral obligations of the professor.

 When Wilson learned that he had got the Chair, jubilation soon gave way to panic. He had now to give regular lectures on moral philosophy, and what did he know of moral philosophy? He sat down and wrote an impassioned plea to his old college friend Alexander Blair, a critic and philosopher who later became Professor of Rhetoric and Belles Lettres at University College, London, but who was now working at his father's soap factory near Birmingham. After telling Blair of his appointment, and describing the anguish he had suffered during the campaign of defamation against him, he went on: 'God only knows what is to be the ultimate issue. One thing is certain, that if I can get through the *first course of Lectures* with reputation, my future life may glide on usefully and respectably. I therefore, my best friend, conjure you by all that is holy beneath the heavens to listen, now, to my words—and, if you can do what I now implore, you will confer upon me the greatest blessing one human being ever conferred upon another, and, ultimately, be no sufferer in anything yourself.'

Wilson went on to implore Blair to come to Edinburgh for three months and help him prepare his lectures. When Blair delayed, the appeals became more and more frenzied. 'Till I hear that you are coming, I cannot rest—nor begin to do anything. Though when I hear a detailed account from you of the first part of the course, and of what things in it you wish me to try—I will make the attempt before you come. Whatever subjects you propose to me, let them be tolerably easy. . . . I am terrified to lie down each night and know that another day has gone by uselessly.'

Blair could not come to stay with Wilson in Edinburgh, but he helped his friend by writing a series of long impersonal letters which contained the substance of a course in moral philosophy. This set the pattern that was to continue for years. Wilson depended absolutely on Blair's letters, and could not lecture at all without them. Sometimes the expected letter did not arrive until the morning of the lecture, and he read it on his way to the university. Wilson's appeals to Blair make the most extraordinary reading. When a student asks a question or proposes an objection, Wilson has him put it in writing and forwards it to Blair for his answer. Here is a typical extract from a letter to Blair: 'I enclose a letter from one of my students. If the objections in it appear good and worthy of answer I wish you to state them as general objections to our Theory, and to refute them.' Or this: 'Could you send me a good letter-full on the effects of passion on association? Any thing you chuse bold and eloquent.'

On 24th March 1826 he appealed for a suitable concluding lecture: 'Last day it would greatly injure me not to have a good lecture. . . . The subject I propose is "General Education". . . .

It is for the 12th of April. Think for a day or two before you begin—treat the subject according to your own views— send it off to me in letters, writing off-hand and vigorously, but not disturbing me for God's sake.'

What sort of professor did this second-hand philosopher make? He was a roaring success from first to last. His impressive bearing, his tremendous voice, his gift for impromptu rhetoric of the most luscious kind, enabled him to take off from Blair's material and soar into vague, impassioned eloquence. Few remembered what he said, but all agreed that he was wonderful. Trembling with anxiety and apprehension a few moments before, he would brace himself, stride into the lecture hall, prop a number of Blair's letters up in front of him—the students thought he was improvising from random notes jotted on the backs of old envelopes— and thunder away. David Masson, who later became Professor of English at Edinburgh, attended Wilson's lectures as a young man, and gave this account of them:

As far as ever I could ascertain, it was nothing that could in any conventional sense be called a systematic course of Moral Philosophy that Wilson administered to his students, but a rich poetico-philosophic medley in all the styles of Christopher North, with the speculative made to predominate as much as possible. His way was to come in from his ante-room with a large bundle of ragged papers of all sorts and sizes . . . and, throwing these down on the desk before him, either to begin reading from them, or sometimes, having apparently failed to find what he wanted uppermost, and having also felt in vain in his waistcoat pockets for something likely to answer the purpose, to gaze wildly for a moment or two at a side-window, and then, having caught some thread or hint from the Tron Church steeple, to begin evolving what seemed an extempore discourse.

The first time that I heard him, the effect of these preliminaries, and of his generally wild and yellow-haired appearance, so much stranger than anything I had been prepared for, almost overcame my gravity, and I had to conceal my face for some time behind a hat to recover sufficient composure to look at him steadily. The voice and mode of delivery were also singular. It was not so much reading or speaking as a kind of continuous musical chaunt, beginning in a low hollow tone, and swelling out wonderfully in passages of eloquence, but still always with a certain sepulchral quality in it—a moaning sough as of a wind from the timbs, partly blowing along and partly muffling the purely intellectual meaning. From my recollections of him, . . . I should say that the chief peculiarities of his elocution, in addition to this main one, were, in the first place, a predominance of *u* among his vowel-sounds, or a tendency of most of his other vowels, and especially the *o*, to pass more or less into one of the sounds of *u*; and, in the second place, the breaking up of his sentences in the act of uttering them by short pants or breathings, like *ugh!* interjected at intervals. . . . In speaking in one of his lectures of the endurance of remorse, and in illustrating this by the fancy of the state of mind of a criminal between his condemnation and his execution, he wound up, I remember distinctly, with a phrase uttered, as regards the longer interjected breathings, exactly thus: 'Ay! and there may be a throb of remorse (*ugh!*) even at that last moment— when the head—tumbles—into the basket—of the executioner (*ugh!*)', the last *ugh!* being much the most emphatic.

Habitually eloquent, after a manner which these and other peculiarities rendered unlike the eloquence of any one else, Wilson was sometimes so deeply and suddenly moved by the feeling of what he was saying or describing that he rose to unusual heights of impassioned and poetical oratory. In particular, there were certain lectures, the time of the coming round of which was always duly known, when his class-room was crowded by professors and strangers in addition to his students, in expectation of one of his great outbursts. . . .

But though his students cheered him, we do not remember John Wilson as a moral philosopher today. Nor do any of us look into the twelve-volume collected edition of his works as critic, essayist, short-story writer and poet. His ultra-sentimental tales of Scottish village life anticipate the worst of the Kailyard school; his poetry is facile and derivative; his criticism is unprincipled and erratic. But at his best Christopher North had the kind of brilliance that comes from sheer energy. The *Noctes Ambrosianae*, self-consciously picturesque, exaggerated, preposterous, as they often are, nevertheless are above all *living*: they project the man's own image of himself with brilliant clarity, as well as with a boisterous kind of wit that is like nothing else in English —or Scottish—literature. He played up to his own notion of romanticism, and produced a unique brand of it.

THE WRITING OF SCOTTISH LITERARY HISTORY[1]

WE LIVE IN AN AGE of handbooks and digests, and textbooks of literary history, as of almost everything else, have for some time been commonplaces of the schoolroom. Yet Scottish literature has, even in Scotland, escaped this treatment. Neither T. F. Henderson's informative and methodical *Scottish Vernacular Literature, A History*, published at the end of the last century, nor J. H. Millar's discursive and opinionated *Literary History of Scotland*, which appeared at the beginning of this one, nor Agnes Mure Mackenzie's breathless and idiosyncratic *Historical Survey of Scottish Literature to 1714*, now some twenty years old, nor John Speirs' scrappy and intermittently perceptive little book on *The Scots Literary Tradition* which came out in 1940, has either established itself as a textbook or succeeded in imposing an accepted pattern on the Scottish literary scene. In the minds of most people who think at all about Scottish literature, there lies a picture in four sections: the first shows the so-called Scottish Chaucerians, mediaeval, vigorous, and at once Scottish and European; the second is of the eighteenth-century revival, with only the figures of Ramsay, Fergusson and Burns discernible, and the first two not very clearly; the third presents *Whistle Binkie* and the Kailyard and is generally agreed to be something that one shakes one's head over; and the fourth shows Hugh MacDiarmid, perhaps Lewis Grassic Gibbon, Sydney Goodsir Smith, and the whole controversy about the Scottish Renaissance and Lallans. A few may discern the figure of George Douglas Brown, flourishing his *House with the Green Shutters*, between the Kailyard and the Renaissance. The ballads are there somewhere, too, but nobody knows precisely where. Scott, Galt and the nineteenth century Scottish novel do not seem to be part of many people's

---

[1] Delivered before the Edinburgh Branch of the Saltire Society on 11th December 1954.

picture of Scottish literary history these days. And as for what happened between the Middle Scots poets and Allan Ramsay— well, there was the Reformation, and civil war, and between them Scottish literature somehow got lost until the stability of the eighteenth century made its rediscovery possible.

I do not think that this is an unfair picture of how even informed people think of Scottish literary history. Nor is this view alto- gether absurd; it is in many respects just, although, I would suggest, woefully inadequate and in parts somewhat distorted. That we need a new perspective on the history of Scottish litera- ture, a patterning of its material at once richer and subtler, is surely beyond dispute. The question to which I wish to address myself is this: How are we to look at Scottish literature in order to dis- cover that pattern, and what sort of pattern will it turn out to be? Which is tantamount to asking: How should Scottish literary history now be written?

I am not rash enough, or arrogant enough, to try to give a complete answer to this question. What I want to do rather is to present some of the material for an answer and show some of the preliminary questions that must be faced before that answer can be given. The first of such preliminary questions is the simple and fundamental one: What is literary history? History, we all know, is more than a list of names, events and dates; and literary history is more than a chronological list of authors with descriptions and summaries of their works. The literary historian must, of course, have the texts of previous literature available to him: literary history cannot be written before there are libraries and catalogues. But if his own work is to be more than a chronological catalogue he must have some ideas of causation and continuity, some sense of the cultural context, some insight into the way in which the arts are related to the civilization of which they are a part. His apparatus must be flexible: rigid theories of psychological or sociological causation only result in the torturing of the material until it fits the Procrustean bed of pre-conceived notions of cause and effect. On the other hand, it must not be so flexible as to provide a totally different kind of explanation for every new

K

phenomenon, explaining one writer by the tradition within which he worked, another by personal frustrations, a third by the region in which he was born and a fourth by the *Zeitgeist*. The true historian—the historian, that is, who wishes to provide new illumination and understanding by presenting his material in a historical way—must be able to manipulate a great number of different factors with tact and wisdom. There is the life of art itself, with its own traditions and its own laws of development; there are social, economic, political, religious, and psychological factors; there are accidents of time and place, and actions and reactions of every kind which help to condition the texture both of a culture in general and of the work of any given writer.

The literary historian must have a rich enough dialectic—if I may use that ugly term—to enable him to manipulate these various causal factors with reference to each movement and to each author that he takes up, emphasizing now one kind of cause, now another, but always remembering the complexity of causation which lies behind even the simplest cultural phenomenon. He should not, for example, employ a rigid opposition between a pair of mutually exclusive concepts such as faith and reason, or romantic and classical, explaining literary movements in terms of simple alternation between one and the other, for that is to do violence to the richness and variety of the life of the imagination out of which literature arises. We shall never understand, for example, the complex figure of Allan Ramsay, who is at the same time an Augustan character trying to introduce the idiom of London's Age of Elegance into Edinburgh and the exponent and practitioner of a colloquial Scots vernacular, if we try to fit him into a naïve classic-romantic antithesis. Nor can we properly see or explain Burns if we see him through the spectacles of the English literary historiographers as a pre-Romantic looking forward to Wordsworth and the English Romantic Movement. And the fatuousness of seeing Burns as a pre-Romantic and Scott as a Romantic—thus making 'Holy Willie's Prayer' a precursor of *Rob Roy*—is sufficiently evident. In the context of European literature Scott has appeared to some as the founder of a new romantic interest in the feudal glories of the mediaeval past; but if we accept this, what becomes of *The Heart of Midlothian*, *The Antiquary*, *Old Mortality* and *Redgauntlet*, among Scott's greatest and most characteristic novels, which record the transition from the heroic to the modern world and explore the relation between heroism and prudence, with the triumph always accorded in the end to the latter? It is not Rob Roy but Bailie Nicol Jarvie, not the knight at arms but the antiquary who researches into his exploits, not Balfour of Burley but the representative of moderation and compromise, not the spectacular prison-breaker but the humble Jeanie Deans, who evoke Scott's deepest sympathetic understanding; and Redgauntlet's hysterical and anachronistic knight-errantry is dismissed with a smile and a shake of the head. We must beware of importing into Scottish literary history the categories of the English literary historiographer.

The Scottish literary historian can, however, learn a great deal from his English colleague, if he knows when to see him as an example and when as a warning. The historical patterning of English literature began in the eighteenth century, and it is instructive to see what preparation was necessary before it was able to emerge. Bibliographical and biographical material came first. John Leland and John Bale in the sixteenth century first collected the names, and the titles of the works of all the English-born writers they could discover. In the seventeenth century a critical tradition began to emerge, enabling writers to discriminate between the good and the less good. In the same century began the tradition of writing 'Lives of the Poets' that culminated a century later with Dr Johnson. Libraries, too, were being built up and organized, so that older texts were available. The Bodleian was founded about 1600 and its first catalogue published in 1605. The manuscript riches of the Oxford and Cambridge colleges were catalogued by Edward Bernard in 1697. The great collection founded by Sir Robert Cotton (now part of the British Museum collection) remained in private hands throughout the seventeenth century but passed to the nation in 1700. The catalogue of the Harleian Collection was published by order of the Trustees of the

British Museum in 1759. Three years later we learn that Thomas Warton was thinking 'in earnest' about his history of English poetry, whose first volume appeared in 1774. By this time also theories about the nature of primitive poetry and the relation between poetry and civilization had been put forward by innumerable critics and philosophers. There was also a sufficient body of linguistic knowledge available, largely as a result of the Herculean labour of the great George Hickes at the end of the seventeenth century.

Libraries, catalogues, bibliographies, biographies, notions of causation and development, linguistic knowledge—these are some of the prerequisites for literary history, and their necessarily slow development explains why literary history is such a late kind of writing to appear in any culture. I have mentioned library catalogues more than once, and though this may seem a very minor tool for the literary historian, it is crucial nevertheless. Uncatalogued libraries, where the reader stumbles on older works without knowing what he is to expect in advance, produce antiquaries, not historians. It is no accident that it was only after the Harleian Collection, so rich in earlier English literature, had been catalogued, that Thomas Warton decided to write the first History of English Poetry. Scotland has tended to run to antiquaries rather than historians partly at least because so much material of prime importance for the writing of Scottish cultural history has lain so long uncatalogued in the basements and attics of both libraries and private houses. The history of the Scottish song-lyric in the sixteenth and seventeenth centuries, for example,—a matter of the first importance for our understanding of what really happened to Scottish poetry in the so-called 'gap' between the end of the Middle Ages and the eighteenth century—has remained so long unwritten because there were no public indications of where the relevant material might be found. The material exists; it is being patiently ferreted out by individual researchers; but history has been held up, and in some cases distorted, for lack of proper signposts to the material.

We in Scotland have the libraries, though they are not catalogued as well as they might be; we have the linguistic and textual scholarship; we have now, I think, the interest and perhaps even the zeal. Have we the critical tradition which is necessary to define the scope and perspective of a literary history? In spite of the many individual essays devoted to a revaluation of the Scottish literary tradition that have appeared during the last twenty years or so, I am not sure that we can say that we have the critical tradition. The spate of creative activity associated with the Scottish Renaissance has, it is true, been moved in some degree by a replacement of Burns by Dunbar as the Scottish poet who ought to be looked back to, as well as by a fierce repudiation of the Kailyard tradition, but this represents an emotional need rather than a clear critical perception. I do not think that we have had in Scotland a really lively critical tradition since the rhetorical school of Hugh Blair and Lord Kames in the eighteenth century. Careful critical studies of individual authors are now the great necessity. Perhaps I may be allowed to say that my own studies of Robert Burns and of Robert Louis Stevenson were intended as humble contributions to that kind of critical revaluation on which the new historian of Scottish literature must depend. I should like to see full-dress critical studies of all the major and many of the minor Scottish poets. We talk so much of Dunbar and his importance for the history of Scottish poetry. Where is the great new critical book on Dunbar, or on any of the Middle Scots poets? We are producing editions, yes, and biographies, but the full-dress book-length critical revaluations have still to come. And the significant new history of Scottish literature waits for them.

As for general theories of causation and continuity: there has been a considerable amount of controversy on such matters in Scotland during the last two decades, but far too much of it has been facile sloganizing. Dr Agnes Mure Mackenzie's lively rewriting of Scottish political history has many virtues, though not all will agree with her point of view, but her work is largely written in what I must pedantically call a two-term dialectic—Scotland versus England, the Presbyterian versus the Episcopalian, and so on—which, it seems to me, is neither rich nor flexible enough to enable a full and fair picture to be presented. We still need a great deal more exploration of the nature and the various metamorphoses of Scottish culture, and its relation not only to European culture and to English culture but to what might be called its own anti-self.

I said earlier that the English literary historiographers could present us with warnings as well as with examples. The chief of those warnings is provided by their tendency to slip into a simple-minded teleological kind of interpretation, what I call the hills-and-valleys method of writing literary history. We know that Shakespeare was the greatest Elizabethan dramatist, so we look for anticipations of his qualities in earlier dramatists and call them pre-Shakespearean. We know that Chaucer was the greatest mediaeval English poet, so we set him likewise on a peak and visualize earlier poets struggling up to the Chaucerian heights and later poets—Lydgate, Occleve, and so on—slipping down on the other side into the bog of late mediaeval dullness. Similarly, early Tudor lyrics are presented as movements towards the Elizabethan lyrical efflorescence, as though Wyatt and Surrey said to each other: 'The Golden Age of the Elizabethan lyric will be along soon; we'd better start practising for it.' There is, of course, some truth in this view (though it is a fact that the Tudor lyric is most successful when it is most mediaeval), but when such a method is used to discuss literary movements it can become intolerable. Certain early nineteenth century poets show a new kind of interest in Nature, a preference for introspective, personal, poetry, a love of the Middle Ages, and a kind of poetic idiom which differs sharply from that of Thomson and Gray. Very well then: we call these qualities—not all found in the same poets—the Romantic Movement and look for traces of them in earlier writers. When we find them, we call the writers who display them pre-Romantic. So we have Thomson—in diction poles apart from Wordsworth—showing an interest in Nature, and he is promptly labelled pre-Romantic because of it. 'Wordsworth will be along in a couple of generations; I'd better get this Nature thing prepared for', he mutters to himself as he writes 'The Sea-sons'. So Gray, because he could be wild and extravagant, is for very different reasons called a pre-Romantic. The fact that Johnson and Wordsworth both disliked Gray for the same reasons does not seem to have caused the literary historians to hesitate in applying this classification. And if, as so many of these historians did, you consider the Romantic Movement a Good Thing, a blessed return to freedom and spontaneity after neo-classic rigidity the one far-off divine event towards which all eighteenth century poetry steadily moves, you go down the waiting list of eighteenth century poets and give them marks according as they anticipate this glorious revolution. That this is a method calculated to distort beyond all recognition the true nature and achievement of the eighteenth century poets—and for that matter of the nine-teenth century poets too—hardly needs demonstration. We see the great Elizabethans waving across the arid gulf of the later seventeenth and the eighteenth century to the Romantics on *their* peak. And then a revolution in taste occurs. The Romantics are decried, the metaphysicals elevated as the height of English poetry; Pope is reinstated, Tennyson replaced by Hopkins; Mr Cleanth Brooks writes his *Modern Poetry and the Tradition*—and lo! every valley shall be exalted and every mountain and hill laid low; the valleys become hills and the hills valleys; the garment of the earlier literary historians is simply turned inside out.

Of course there are peaks in any literature; there are dull periods and new flowerings; but to see any period simply in the light of its falling away from an earlier kind of excellence or its anticipation of a future one is not to see it in itself as it really is. We must never allow the historical pattern to distort our vision of the individual literary figure. So, in Scottish literature, we must not undervalue Stevenson because he comes between *Whistle Binkie* and the final extremes of the Kailyard. Our task is, on the contrary, to understand how the virtues and the limitations of Stevenson's art are related to the texture of the Scottish culture of his day. Nor, to take another example, must we despise *The Gude and Godlie Ballatis*—which possess many real beauties, as well as some absurdities—because they represent a Puritan impulse which in other respects has done some harm to Scottish culture. Do not misunderstand me: I am not pleading for critical relativism. I am not saying that everything must be praised as good of its kind. Not at all: the ideal literary historian must never confuse explanation with evaluation and allow himself to praise something as literature merely because it is interesting as a symptom or an effect. What I do insist on is that he should not allow his historical pattern to distort his view of the individual work. And that means that the pattern should be rich and flexible enough to be really helpful, to illuminate rather than to smother. Simplification is of course inevitable in any kind of historical writing; one simplifies in order to see the total picture more clearly. Naïve over-simplification, on the other hand, only obscures the total picture.

So much for the pitfalls. Let me now turn to my original question: How should we look at Scottish literature in order to discover its historical pattern? There is, of course, no simple or single answer, certainly none that I should be prepared to give in a preliminary discussion of this kind. All I wish to do here is to present some considerations which are important to anyone concerned with this question. We need not expend overmuch ingenuity in distinguishing the origins of Scottish literature from other elements in Northumbrian writing: all nations have a beginning somewhere and at some time, and there is nothing unusual or upsetting to national pride about the fact that the Scots literary language was, at one stage of its development, identical with the Anglian speech of northern England or that Northumbria as a linguistic region straddled what were to become the national boundaries of England and Scotland. As Dr Agnes Mure Mackenzie has pointed out, Scotland has a long past but she is a new nation. The Scottish literary language developed as the nation developed, and to deny Scots its independent status as a national tongue on the grounds that at an early stage in its career it was part of a wider linguistic unity makes as much sense as to deny English its status as an independent language on the grounds that the Saxons brought their speech with them from the district later called Schleswig Holstein. If Scots, in the modern sense of the term, is the Scottish language which developed from the northern form of Anglian speech, the important question for the Scottish literary historian is not so much the implications of its origin—it is what it developed into, not what it arose from, that concerns him—as its relation to the two other literary languages of Scotland, Gaelic and Latin.

The Latin question is common to all European literatures in the Middle Ages, and it is a nice point whether historical treatment of a national literature should take equal account of the important material produced in Latin, or whether the national tradition should be defined strictly in terms of language. Is the history of English literature the history of literature written in English, or the history of all literature produced in England which, in any way at all, reflects English thought or sensibility? Most literary historians have taken it to be the former, and have omitted works written in Latin as they have omitted those in Anglo-Norman. One can argue for either procedure. I myself would be inclined to say that, while the historian of English literature should not give equal attention to Latin literature produced in England, he should take sufficient note of it to make clear that the country was employing an international literary medium at the same time as it was employing a national one, and some discussion of the relation between national and international elements in a literary culture would follow from this. In Scotland, always in many senses a more European country than England, the Latin literature is of considerable importance in defining the relation of Scottish to European culture, and should be given at least some consideration from that point of view: George Buchanan, for example, represented Scotland in Europe in a very special way.

The Scottish Gaelic tradition presents, in many ways, more formidable claims. It links Scottish culture, not with the Latin culture of mediaeval Europe, but with the Celtic culture of Ireland, always somewhat apart from what might be called the Mediterranean centre of mediaeval European influence. The

Mediterranean centre produced the great Rose tradition which is so important in European poetry; the garden of the love allegories is the standard setting for a whole literary *genre*. Dunbar is in touch with this tradition when he writes, at the beginning of 'The Golden Targe':

> Ryght as the stern of day begouth to schyne,
> Quhen gone to bed war Vesper and Lucyne,
>   I raise and by a rosere did me rest;
> Up sprang the goldyn candill matutyne,
> With clere depurit bemes cristallyne,
>   Glading the mery foulis in thair nest;
>   Or Phebus was in purpur cape revest
> Up raise the lark, the hevyns menstrale fyne
> In May, in till a morrow myrthfullest.

We know this rose garden and this May morning. It comes from the secular Mediterranean centre of mediaeval European poetry, just as the powerful poem 'Done is a battell on the dragon black' or 'Ane ballat of our Lady' represents the religious Latin tradition, deriving from the mediaeval Latin hymn. But when Henryson, towards the beginning of 'The Testament of Cresseid', writes:

> I mend the fyre and beikit me about,
> Then tuik ane drink my spreitis to comfort,
> And armit me weill fra the cauld thairout:
> To cut the winter nicht and mak it schort,
> I tuik ane Quair, . . .

or Dunbar writes his 'Tydings fra the Session', each has his eye on the local Scottish scene and derives his imagery and his attitude from a particular Scottish situation. That is one polarity—between the European (either secular or religious or both) and the purely Scottish. It is not difficult for the literary historian to come to terms with *that*. But turn from these poems to, say, this song by Mary MacLeod:

Ged a theid mi do m' leabaidh	Though I go to my bed
Chan e cadal as miannach leam	It is not sleep that I wish,
Aig ro mheud na tuile	For the flood is so great
Is mo mhuileann gun iarann air; . . .	And my mill is unshod. . . .

This is the opening of a poem addressed to Iain MacLeod on his presenting the poetess with a snuff-mull. In subject, in tone, in literary convention, it is worlds away from the Mediterranean centre, and in its mixture of formality and spontaneity equally far from the 'realistic' elements in Dunbar and Henryson. The difference is not to be explained by the fact that Mary MacLeod lived some two hundred years after the Middle Scots poets I have quoted, for the poem is equally different from anything produced in England or Lowland Scotland at this time. It represents a different poetic tradition and a different tradition of sensibility. The situation is complicated by the fact that Mary MacLeod's poetry stands between the older Gaelic poetry of the formal bardic schools and the more popular, less rhetorical verse of eighteenth century Scottish Gaelic poets: this is a polarity within Gaelic literature itself, and to consider it adequately would take us into the relation between the older Scottish Gaelic literature and the Gaelic literary language that was evolved chiefly in Munster. It was only in the seventeenth century that a Scottish Gaelic tradition, independent of the formal, rhetorical training of the Irish schools, began to develop, to produce in the eighteenth century, with the poetry of Alexander Macdonald, Duncan Ban Macintyre, Dugald Buchanan and Rob Donn Mackay, a minor Scottish Gaelic literary Renaissance. The first printed work by a Scottish writer written in what could be called Scottish Gaelic as distinct from Irish Gaelic was the small collection of poems published for Alexander Macdonald in Edinburgh in 1751 with the significant title *Ais-eiridh na Sean Chanain Albannaich*, or *Revival of the Old Scottish Tongue*.

What is the historian of Scottish literature to make of all this? How is he to handle the Gaelic tradition, how present it in relation to the Scots tradition? Does the turning away from the Irish bardic schools to produce a more purely Scottish poetry fit in to any total picture of the Scottish literary tradition? Does the outburst of Jacobite Gaelic poetry in eighteenth century Scotland arise from the same impulse which produced so much Jacobite Scots song and which, by providing a new folk emotion for the

Scottish people at a period in civilization when folk emotion was dying out, delayed so remarkably the sophistication of Scottish song? Scottish literary historiography must surely consider these matters, as it must consider the odd fact that Lowland Scotsmen fussed and flurried over Macpherson's *Ossian* while totally ignoring the contemporary Gaelic poetry being produced on their very doorstep. The pattern here is extraordinarily complex, and the historian's duty is to make sense of it without naïve over-simplification. There is a chronological line, with a tradition mutating according to its own laws; there are intersecting circles of cultural influence, Lowland, Highland, Irish, English, European; there are shifting relations between the writer and his audience; there are social, political and economic developments which produce special problems for the Scottish writer.

Coming to terms, then, with Scotland's three literary languages presents a challenging problem of organization and interpretation for the historian of Scottish literature. The problem is relatively simple as far as mediaeval literature is concerned, but when English develops as a fourth language (or rather replaces Latin as the third) the situation becomes much more complex, not to say confused. We all know about the political, religious and social reasons which sent Scottish writers more and more to English as their medium of expression, and we know something of the divided sensibility that resulted. But the transition has never been either fully explained or fully documented. We know that the prestige of Elizabethan English literature, the removal of the Scottish King to London to ascend the English throne, the natural turning of a Protestant Scotland towards a Protestant England, the growing English political influence, all tended to encourage Scotsmen to write in English, and that Puritan suspicion of secular love poetry sent much folk poetry underground, whence it partially re-emerged in unexpected ways in the eighteenth century. But how much really went underground? And how much of it was really folk poetry? What was the position of Scottish court poetry at the end of the sixteenth century, and how far are the popular songs that later came to the surface derived from these court poems? Has the migration of Scottish court poets, and musicians, in 1603 really been documented and examined? Have the *enclaves* of older Scots poetry and music which survived the Reformation at Aberdeen and elsewhere been properly investigated? Most historians of Scottish literature are content to jump across what they conceive to be the gap between the end of the Middle Ages and the eighteenth-century revival. But it is the sixteenth and seventeenth centuries that provide the clue to what really happened to Scottish culture and to the Scottish sense of nationality, and the literary historian must look at the relatively scanty data provided by this period very carefully indeed.

One of the most important phenomena demanding the investigation of the historian of Scottish literature is the mutation of the Scots literary language into a vernacular. Montgomerie, writing in the latter part of the sixteenth century, could produce a stanza like this:

> Like as the dumb solsequium, with care ourcome
>   Dois sorrow, when the sun goes out of sicht,
> Hings doun his head, and droops as dead, nor will not spread
>   But locks his leavis through langour all the nicht,
>   Till foolish Phaeton rise
>   With whip in hand,
>   To purge the crystal skyis
>   And licht the land.
> Birds in their bour waitis for that hour
>   And to their prince ane glaid good-morrow givis;
> Fra then, that flour list not till lour,
>   Bot laughs on Phoebus loosing out his leavis.

This shows art, gravity and a sensibility thoroughly at home in the convention it uses. Only some twenty years later, Sir Robert Aytoun was writing thus:

> Why did I wrong my judgement so
> As to affect where I did know
>   There was no hold for to be taken?
> That which her heart thirsts after most,
> If once of it her hope can boast,
>   Straight by her folly is forsaken.

There are three obvious ways in which this stanza (which, however, it must be remembered, was meant to be sung) differs from
Montgomerie's. First, it is written in English, not in Scots;
secondly it is derivative rather than traditional; thirdly, it belongs
to an exercise, an *étude*, rather than to a fully realized poem. At
this stage, at least, there is a loss involved in a Scottish poet's
moving from Scots to English.

Another comparison will take us a stage further. Going back
to Alexander Scott, we find a stanza like this:

> For nobillis hes not ay renown
> Nor gentillis ay the gayest goun,
> Thay cary victuallis to the toun
> 　　　That werst dois dyne:
> Sa blissely to the busk I boun,
> Ane uthir eitis the berry doun
> 　　　That suld be myne.

The opening of Sempill's 'Habbie Simson' is in the same stanza
form:

> Kilbarchan now may say alas!
> For she hath lost both game and grace,
> Both *Trixie* and *The Maiden Trace*;
> 　　　But what remead?
> For no man can supply his place:
> 　　　Hab Simson's dead.

There is a difference in weight here; though both Scott and
Sempill use images and expressions drawn from popular speech,
Scott's language is more highly charged, it has more gravity and
greater reverberation. 'Habbie Simson' is sprightly popular verse
written for amusement by a member of the landed gentry, and
written in a language which by this time few educated people
felt to be suitable for the highest kind of art. True, it draws on a
tradition of poetry of popular revelry which earlier had produced
such poems as 'Christ's Kirk on the Green' and 'Peblis to the Play',
but it is frivolous rather than truly humorous because it does not
grow out of that tradition but uses it in what might almost be
called a patronizing way. This is not to say that the 'Epitaph on

Habbie Simson' is not an important poem; it is indeed important historically, both for drawing attention to the possibilities of folk humour as a way of bringing the vernacular into current poetry and for reviving a stanza form which was to play such an important part in eighteenth century Scottish poetry, but it lacks a dimension. Between Sempill of Beltrees and Burns Scottish vernacular poetry had to learn how to be the product of the whole man, how to achieve scope and density—in short, how to recover that lost dimension. Where it did so, it was by transmuting antiquarian, patriotic and patronizing gestures towards the vernacular into something deeper, something with an organic connection with contemporary sensibility; and that transmutation was itself made possible by re-establishing living contact with certain important currents in Scottish literature and Scottish folk poetry.

The difference between a vernacular and a language is that in the latter case there is a literary tradition, arising out of the different forms of the spoken language and transcending them, which reflects back on the spoken language and gives it a steady relationship to the national culture. Once the literary tradition is broken, once there is no literary language growing out of the spoken language (however different from it it may be, and however many artificial elements may have been added), the spoken language is bound to disintegrate into a series of regional dialects. So, after the Norman Conquest of England, the central literary position of West Saxon was lost, since French replaced Anglo-Saxon as the literary language, and Middle English fell into a series of regional dialects. Only after the re-establishment of English as the literary language of England did a linguistic norm emerge and, while differences between spoken dialects persisted, the language was pulled together by the integrating force of a literary tradition. Similarly, in Scotland, Middle Scots (whatever its original relationship with Northumbrian English) had, in virtue of its literary tradition, been a language and not a vernacular; Scots became a vernacular only after the literary language of its serious writers had ceased to be Scots. How to use the *vernacular* as a *language* in serious literature (that is, in literature that was more than an antiquarian exercise, a jest, or a *tour de force*) was the problem faced by Ramsay, Fergusson and Burns. The problem was never permanently solved, for English remained the main language of serious expression; it was solved occasionally and temporarily, partly by happy accident, partly by the intervention of genius.

'Habbie Simson' is a vernacular squib; 'Holy Willie's Prayer' is a Scots poem, written in a literary language in which English and Scots reinforce each other. Yet the latter is not quite the same kind of thing that Alexander Scott or Montgomerie wrote. Burns only re-established contact with the Scots literary tradition by looking at it through the spectacles provided by folk song and other kinds of popular art, and as a result the tradition as he uses it is a composite one, in which the satiric boisterousness of Lyndsay's *Satire of the Three Estaitis*, the happy artifice of Montgomerie, the stark clarity of the ballads, the richness and warmth and earthiness of folk song, the pious beat of Scottish psalmody, combine to produce a precarious but—while it lasted—a brilliant unity. It was Burns' predecessors who made that synthesis possible; it was his own genius that made it brilliant; it was the cultural context of his time that made it precarious.

That cultural context requires the most careful examination. The nature of the Scottish poetic tradition which James Watson revived in 1706— the year before the incorporating union between England and Scotland was finally voted—with the publication of the first volume of his *Choice Collection of Comic and Serious Scots Poems both Ancient and Modern*, is of prime importance for an understanding of what happened to Scottish poetry in the eighteenth century. With its mixture of poems of popular revelry, laboured exercises in courtly English, macaronics, mock elegies, serious sixteenth century Scots poems, trivial epigrams and epitaphs, poems by Drummond and Montrose, flytings, laments, and miscellaneous patriotic pieces, it appears at first to represent the casual putting together of whatever Watson found to his hand. Yet (except for ballads, which it lacks, and songs, which are few, and the perhaps surprising lack of anything by Lyndsay) the collection represents with a fair degree of accuracy the different kinds of material available for the development or reconstruction of the Scottish poetic tradition in the eighteenth century. The tradition of the makars was represented by Montgomerie (we must wait until Ramsay to find the so-called Scottish Chaucerians made available); the courtly tradition in English by Drummond and Aytoun; the older popular tradition by 'Christ's Kirk on the Green' and the newer by 'Habbie Simson' and other pieces; various kinds of popular and semi-popular Scottish song were represented, some in Scots and some in English, though the collection was not strong here; the characteristic Scottish humour and Scottish violence are represented in several ways, as is the goliardic tradition as it developed in Scotland and the tradition of macaronic humour associated with it. What Watson printed represented things that were still going on in Scotland, though often not on the surface. In bringing them to the surface he prevented them from being obscured completely by the new face of Scottish culture and at the same time helped to divert patriotic attention from politics to literature. It is true that that attention was mixed up in many quarters with confused ideas about the vernacular and primitive poetry and the natural man, and this confusion made serious difficulties for Burns. But it also provided an environment which encouraged the production of an enriched vernacular poetry under certain circumstances and at certain levels, and that was decisive for the course of eighteenth century Scottish poetry.

Much has been written on the eighteenth century movement, but, it seems to me, its full complexity and significance for the literary historian has not yet been fully appreciated. Allan Ramsay's extraordinary mixture of vanity, coyness, genteel pretension, urban swagger, rustic colloquialism and Scottish patriotism, his split personality and basic uncertainty of taste, reflect the confusions and difficulties of the Scottish cultural scene of his day as well as his own psychology. Robert Fergusson's independence of the *literati*, resulting in part from the self-confidence that a formal education gave him—he had not the inferiority complex about

L

his small knowledge of the classics which both Ramsay and Burns had—and the quiet assurance which he manifested in the writing of his Scots poems, must also be considered as an illuminating product of the reaction of personal circumstance with the historical situation. That the Cape Club provided a better atmosphere for a poet than the self-conscious young would-be gentlemen of the Easy Club provided for Ramsay or the Tarbolton Bachelor's Club for Burns is an important fact for the historian of Scottish literature. While Ramsay declared with nervous defensiveness that he understood Horace but faintly in the original and Burns found it expedient to present himself to the genteel world as a remarkable example of the natural man, Fergusson wrote as he pleased and cheerfully thumbed his nose at Dr Johnson and his Scottish admirers. Fergusson's student days at St. Andrews had put him in touch with the old goliardic tradition; his language combined elements from his parents' Aberdeenshire, from the Fife of his university days, from the Edinburgh he was born and worked in, and from the older literary Scots of his reading. All this means that he was in a better position to face the problem of writing in the vernacular, and of raising the vernacular to the level of a literary language, than either Ramsay had been or Burns was to be; but his sadly early death ruined that prospect. If Fergusson had lived to meet Burns and discuss Scottish poetry with him, the story to be told by the Scottish literary historian today might be a very different one.

And what of the galaxy of eighteenth century Scottish philosophers, historians and scientists who wrote in English? How is the pattern of their activity to be woven together with that of the Ramsay-Fergusson-Burns movement? We must remember that David Hume was an ardently patriotic Scot as well as a good European, but his Scottish loyalties led him to acclaim as magnificent much worthless English poetry written by Scotsmen. This paradox deserves more exploration and explanation than it has so far received. Or again, what of the rhetorical critical tradition of the eighteenth century Scottish critics? The rôle which Burns played before the Edinburgh gentry (but fortunately played less

and less in his own poetry) and the critical reception of the Kil-
marnock volume in Edinburgh were alike determined by the
notions of primitive poetry which were being put forward by the
Edinburgh critics and which are related to the general excitement
about primitive poetry to be found in such various scholars and
poets as Bishop Lowth, Thomas Gray and Bishop Percy. This
concept of primitive poetry, which was taken to include everything from the Old Testament to Scottish folk song and from
the supposed oral literature of the American Indians to Ossian,
provided a back door, as it were, through which Scottish vernacular poetry could be smuggled into the drawing rooms of the
literati. Unless we understand this, we not only misunderstand
the relation of the vernacular to the genteel tradition in late
eighteenth century Scotland, but are also liable to underrate the
dangers and the temptations which threatened Burns. The degree
to which Burns escaped those dangers and resisted those temptations is astonishing.

These considerations far from exhaust the aspects of eighteenth
century Scottish literature demanding further investigation by
the potential historian of Scottish literature. The various forms
in which a frustrated Scottish national feeling expressed itself
culturally in the eighteenth century have never been fully examined, nor has the cultural significance of what Burns called
'sentimental Jacobitism' been properly explored. The relation
between national tradition and commercial progress as reflected
in the activities of Glasgow merchant princes and Edinburgh
lawyers is relevant here, and helps to explain Scott, whose greatest
novels, as I have suggested, record with reluctant approval the
modulation of a heroic into a commercial civilization. Scott, like
Cervantes, saw that in the modern world knight-errantry is at
best a splendid folly and at worst a brutal brigandage (Rob Roy
combined both), and *Redgauntlet* is Scott's *Don Quixote*. He
sighed for the Stuarts, and worked himself to exhaustion in order
to make George IV popular in Scotland. His best novels, like his
life, record the price of progress.

The nineteenth century has its own problems. The cultural

significance of the Edinburgh periodicals of the earlier part of the century; the fate of the Scottish novel; the significance of *Whistle Binkie*, which is not simply a sentimentalizing of Scottish life but the deliberate introduction of the Scot as what might be called a music hall figure, thus pointing the way to Harry Lauder and the twentieth-century Scotch comics (it has never been noted how many Irish comic poems there are in *Whistle Binkie*—the Irishman had already become a stock figure of comedy, the fate of oppressed groups everywhere); the enormous effects of industrialization on urban Scottish life and imagination; the strangling of Highland society and culture after the '45 Rebellion with all the sad results in Highland depopulation, urban overcrowding, and the destruction of communal life; the growth of the Kailyard; the various nineteenth century attempts at a Scottish literary renaissance; the significance of such figures as James Hogg (whose *Memoirs of a Justified Sinner* is one of the greatest pieces of imaginative prose produced in Scotland in modern times) and Robert Louis Stevenson; such phenomena as the popularity of Professor Wilson's (Christopher North's) flamboyant and sentimental lectures on moral philosophy at Edinburgh University or the character and pretensions of Professor John Stuart Blackie; the ideal of the lad of pairts and the part played in the formation of taste and character by the Scottish educational system—these are only a few of the many themes and problems which the future historian of Scottish literature must weave convincingly into his pattern.

And then the reaction; the anti-Kailyarders, the modern renaissance, the controversy about Lallans, the attempt to discover or create a new inclusive Scottish literary language; the re-emergence of Gaelic poetry. When he comes to modern Scotland the historian will, I think, do well to regard English as a medium for Scots writers comparable to Latin in the Middle Ages—a widely understood medium always available to the educated man and one means of linking the national with the universal, but never at the expense of a more purely indigenous Scots literary language. The attempts of those who have been striving to recreate such a Scots literary language must surely be seen against the relevant historical background. No literary language has ever been merely the spoken language; the language of Dunbar, like that of Chaucer and that of Shakespeare, goes down into the spoken language at the same time as it reaches far beyond it into a richer, and, if you like, an 'artificial', vocabulary. The modern Lallans movement, revolting against the conception of Scots as a number of regional dialects to be used in comic or sentimental verse, and going back to the golden age of Scottish poetry in the fifteenth century when Scots was used more richly and variously than it has ever been used since, must be seen as an attempt to bring together elements from Middle Scots, from modern Scottish dialects and from English in order to form again a rich and subtle literary language. Such a language is bound to be synthetic, but 'synthetic' is not a term of abuse: it is a term applicable to any literary language in the making. The historian will seek for the proper analogies to illuminate what has been going on; he may think of the language of Wyatt and Surrey and the English 'courtly makers' of the sixteenth century when the modern English poetic language was in the making. There is always a certain amount of wastage in such experimentation—think of all the ink-horn terms that went into and then out again from the English language in the sixteenth century; but at the end came Shakespeare.

My task is not, however, to defend the modern movement, still less to write any section of the new history of Scottish literature I am trying to point to. I have tried simply to suggest some lines of approach and indicate some important questions which remain to be answered before such a work can be profitably undertaken.

A CAMBRIDGE DIALOGUE[1]

SCENE: Over port in the Combination Room of —— College

CHARACTERS

The Master	*Professor Nuclear*
Mr. Brightly	*Mr. Penumbra*
Dr Mutation	*Dr Price*

Professor Elmer Dreibelbis (a Fulbright Fellow from America)

The dialogue opens in medias res:

Dr Price: ... And what, Penumbra, was the price of bread in London in 1340?

The Master: Dear me, what an odd question.

Mr Penumbra: The price of bread was what it always was in every healthy community—labour and faith.

Dr Price: That, my dear Penumbra, is sheer obfuscation. How the devil can you hope to understand the past if you ride rough-shod over facts in that way? What do you know about wool in Leicester in the thirteenth century? What was the effect on the ordinary citizens' lives of the practices of 'regrating' and 'fore-stalling'? What sort of underwear do you think Richard II wore, and where did he get it?

Mr Brightly: That were indeed to consider too curiously. I see no reason why we should extend the limits of our curiosity with respect to persons in the past beyond the limits we observe in considering those of the present. I neither know nor care what kind of underwear Sir Winston Churchill wears nor how many times a week—or a day—the Duke of Edinburgh changes his shirt. It has always seemed to me that the idlest of all speculations has been the perennial concern, among those dwelling outside Caledonia, as to what a Highlander wears under his kilt.

[1] First published in the Cambridge number of *The Twentieth Century*, February, 1955.

Dr Price: Ah, but did you know, Brightly, that Robert the Bruce's father fled from Yorkshire to Scotland because he was in debt to the Jews and was unable to pay? And that this Anglo-Norman gentleman, fleeing north out of the most strictly economic motives, founded the modern Scottish nation? No no, you can't dismiss the real facts of history so airily. Whisky was first invented by the Irish as an embrocation for sick mules, and came over from Ireland to Scotland in the baggage of a group of Scottish poets returning to their native land from one of the bardic schools of Munster. Having no mules, they used it on themselves, internally, with very agreeable effect. And now Scotch whisky is the greatest single dollar-earning export of the United Kingdom. Doesn't *that* make you think?

The Master (muttering to himself): Ah, but where will you find such men, and such mules?

Mr Penumbra: No one will deny that these facts are interesting, Price. But they are not important. Of course, they may be of temporary importance to a certain number of people at a certain time, but it would argue a grossly distorted scale of values to consider that they are of any ultimate importance. The most important thing to human beings is whether they are to be saved or damned. Yes, I know you think this sounds old-fashioned, and it *is* old-fashioned. The notion that because something is old-fashioned it is wrong is a very odd one indeed. I don't know what Chaucer paid for a loaf of bread or what Richard II wore next to his skin. But I do know that Chaucer and Richard and I all agree about Heaven and Hell, and I know, too, that Saint Thomas à Becket wore a hair shirt next to his skin.

The Master: Uncomfortable, my dear boy, damnably uncomfortable. I should hate to think that any of our young men went in for such an—er—unhygienic practice. The Greeks knew better than that. It was said of the Getan god Zalmoxis that he was born clad in a bear's skin (from which, indeed, he derives his name), and the Greeks believed that at one period of his life he was a slave to Pythagoras of Samos before being manumitted and returning to his own people. Thus even a god, if he wears hair next to his skin, becomes a slave of the philosopher. There are no hair shirts on Greek statues, Penumbra.

Mr Penumbra: No, Master: but there are often fig leaves. What more vivid testimony to the truth of the story in Genesis and the awful reality of the Fall of Man?

The Master: I can't say that I altogether approve of the fig leaf used for the purpose of concealment. I find the male anatomy attractive in all its features. Fig leaves in cooking, now, are another matter: I know a little Greek restaurant in Soho which does the most admirable things with them.

Mr Penumbra: I should be the last man to despise modern Greek cooking, or indeed any of the delights of the flesh. I don't want you to think that, because I believe that the only really important thing about a man is whether he is going to be saved or damned —and I mean by that quite literally whether he will go to Heaven or to Hell—I don't think that other things are worth attending to also. All I maintain is that these other things belong to a lower sphere, as it were. *Sub specie aeternitatis*, it doesn't matter a hoot what port I am drinking this evening. But in this world we do not pass our life *sub specie aeternitatis*; the world and the flesh must have their due. Chaucer had great fun with the *Canterbury Tales*, and then wrote his 'Retraction' saying in effect that all his lively satirical writing was but childish nonsense in the sight of Heaven. Price, the decanter stays with you.

Professor Dreibelbis: If I may break into this fascinating conversation, I should like to say, Professor, if you'll pardon me, that you seem to be having it both ways. You want your hair shirt *and* your bottle of wine.

Mr Penumbra: My dear Professor Dreibelbis (but you must not call *me* professor: I am but a humble lecturer), of course I want to have it both ways. And why not? Man is both body and spirit, has something of the animal and something of the divine in him. Animals and angels can have it one way: man, being fatally dualistic, must be content to indulge both sides of his nature. Doubtless if the Fall had not occurred, man would have become more and more spiritual and, as Milton suggested in

Paradise Lost, eventually reached a state even higher than the angels.

Professor Dreibelbis: So the Fall enables you to enjoy your liquor, eh, Dr Penumbra?—

[*Mr Penumbra* (muttering): I do not hold a doctor's degree.]

Professor Dreibelbis: I'm afraid I find it hard to see why you consider it a bad thing.

Mr Penumbra: It was Noah who discovered the uses of the grape. He sinned in so doing, but glory to him nevertheless. That is a paradox, Dreibelbis: we must be content to accept it as such.

Professor Dreibelbis: All I can say, Dr Penumbra, is that I don't fancy going to Heaven if they don't serve dry Martinis there.

Mr Penumbra: If you ever get to Heaven, Professor Dreibelbis, you won't *want* dry Martinis. Having once tasted the celestial liquor, you will wonder how you ever could have abided the earthly variety.

The Master: —and cocktails most of all. Ugh! Now my idea of nectar is of something light and dry, like a Montilla, an unfortified sherry. Or perhaps a hock. There are those who think of it as port, but surely nectar is not a dessert wine? The late Dr Variorum once confessed to me that he always thought of it as a white Montrachet; Professor Scholiast of Aberdeen once told me he thought of it as one of the lighter Highland malt whiskies—an Inchgower, say, or a Glen Grant, though he himself preferred the heavier Campbeltowns and Islays. On the other hand, old Textual of Magdalen has always insisted that it must be a Beaujolais—not a Burgundy, because he was certain that the *pinot noir* grape could not possibly be grown in the Islands of the Blessed (I forget his reason for this); but the Gamay, a grape which changes its quality marvellously according to the latitude in which it grows, he held to be the most probable source of the heavenly liquor. An odd view, I must confess, because, while I have drunk some excellent Beaujolais, it can hardly be compared to its Burgundian cousins in respect of nobility. Softness, yes; fruitiness, yes—but then if you want softness and fruitiness, what is wrong with a good Châteauneuf-du-Pape?

Rhône wines in Heaven! A strange thought! But I digress.

Mr Penumbra: None of these parallels really holds, Master. I admit it seems strange to us—I myself am very partial to a good claret, and would consider life the poorer without my daily bottle of Pontet Canet—but the fact is that in our fallen natures we cannot have the remotest conception of the food and drink consumed by the angels (and I agree with Milton and certain of the Fathers that angels both partake of nourishment and excrete). Allegory and symbol are our only resource. That is where the Middle Ages, superior to us here as in so many other respects, evoke our admiration and wonder: *they* knew that the only way to shadow forth the ultimate truths was to avoid the documentary and concentrate on the allegorical. But it is a habit of mind we have lost. We are the poorer for it.

Mr Brightly: Come come, Penumbra, do you really think we should be better off if all the poets of the last few hundred years had kept on writing things like *The Romance of the Rose* and *The Faerie Queene*? Surely the greatest thing that ever happened to literature was the liberation of the spirit of humane curiosity into the complexities of the human animal. That spirit—the spirit of Montaigne and of Shakespeare—is the source of the greatness of *King Lear* as well as of *Emma* and *Great Expectations* and *Middlemarch* and *Portrait of a Lady*, and of all that is best in English poetry from Chaucer to Dylan Thomas. You talk with a curious complacency about Chaucer's 'Retraction'. That, if you will forgive my saying so, Penumbra, is a typical piece of modern cant. Chaucer's humane, ironic gaze on the human scene owed nothing significant to his religious views, and all that the 'Retraction' meant was that he realized that great literature and mediaeval Christianity were incompatible, and as an act of prudence plumped for the latter in the end. It seems to me downright dishonest to glory in the brilliant humanist irony of, say, 'The Nun's Priest's Tale' and at the same time to hold that the mediaeval concentration on the next world and concern with saving one's grubby little soul was something wonderful, to be held up for our imitation.

Mr Penumbra: No soul is grubby or little in the eyes of its Maker, Brightly. But I am familiar with your argument. Indeed, I once thought that way myself, I can assure you that you labour in a wilderness of confusions. It would take too long to demonstrate all of them, and this is not, perhaps, the proper place to do so. All that I will say now is that you can't have truly great literature without a sense of man's place in the whole divine scheme of things and of the radical imperfection of human nature. The true 'modern cant'—if I may borrow your expressive term —is that man is self-sufficient and perfectible and human progress automatic and inevitable.

Mr Brightly: Such a view is hardly modern, Penumbra. Rousseau and Godwin and Shelley perhaps held it; I don't know anyone who holds it today. The great modern orthodoxy is that unless you revel in the total depravity of human nature and in the fact of human guilt, you cannot do anything decent at all. All this chat about literature and original sin, which started with T. E. Hulme and T. S. Eliot. Talk of confusion of thought! It's one thing to say that human nature is limited and imperfect— that is true enough in all conscience. But that has nothing to do with the theological dogma of original sin, which states that every person born in the world is morally culpable because Adam ate the apple in the garden. Even if one inherits imperfection, one cannot inherit guilt—surely a most diabolical doctrine. The fact is, of course, that man is capable both of appalling horrors and of incredible nobility and self-sacrifice, and history shows no correlation whatever between religious faith and the latter. Take a look at Runciman on the Crusades. The only consistent force for good in human conduct has been the humane, liberal imagination. It flashes forth rarely enough in human affairs, but when it does it works the only real miracles in both life and letters.

Mr Penumbra: I can understand someone believing that in 1913; it seems incredible to me that any thoughtful person can believe it today, having seen what the humane, liberal imagination, as you call it, has done to civilization—two world wars and numberless other horrors, including the hydrogen bomb.

Mr Brightly: That's an argument one hears so often today, but how wrong it is! Was Hitler a humane liberal? Was Stalin? It seems to me monstrous to blame modern wars and other horrors on the very people who alone protested against them. The humane, liberal imagination was not strong enough to stop these things, I grant you. It still operates in only a minority of men. And it was that minority that Hitler persecuted and all modern dictators have set out to destroy. You may not have had an ideal world if, say, Bertrand Russell had been guiding world affairs for the last fifty years, but you would have had a better world than the one we have had, and a lot better world than that of your precious Middle Ages.

The Master: We must not become heated, my dear boy. And it is a mistake to preach to one's colleagues. If you have anything to say, say it to the young men. They alone will never betray you.

Mr Brightly: The young men are all so busy genuflecting and contemplating the total depravity of their souls these days that there is no getting at them.

The Master: Fashions change, my dear boy, fashions change. And genuflection, if done with proper grace, can be a charming gesture.

Mr Penumbra: Never mind, Brightly. Though we disagree fundamentally, we can still talk to each other; so there is hope for us both.

Mr Brightly: Yes, we can still talk to each other, and neither of us need fear the Inquisition or the concentration camp. That's one victory, at least, for the agnostic liberal tradition you dislike so.

Professor Nuclear: These arguments fall strangely on the ears of a mere scientist. But I confess I was relieved not to hear the familiar charge that the modern scientist is to blame for all the troubles of the modern world.

The Master: I don't think anyone would blame you personally, Nuclear. You play a good hand at bridge and take an intelligent interest in the life of the College. In fact, my dear fellow, I don't know what we'd do without you. All the same, I do wish you chaps would stick to things like Archimedes' principle and perhaps a little dabbling in electric light and even wireless. I understand that it is quite likely that you will blow up the whole world by accident one of these days. I think that would be deplorable.

Professor Nuclear: Look, Master. What we physicists are doing is trying to find out things about the structure of the physical world. *We* didn't set out to make H-bombs. Our object has always been to find things out. What use is made of our knowledge—what we ourselves are asked to do with it—is society's responsibility, not ours.

Professor Dreibelbis: But isn't the scientist a member of society too?

Professor Nuclear: Of course he is. And he reads his newspaper and votes and does all the other things that a responsible citizen does. All this nonsense about scientists living in ivory towers! The scientist does his professional job like everybody else. His job is to find out as much as possible about the physical structure of the universe.

Professor Dreibelbis: And let the chips fall where they may?

Professor Nuclear: I don't know about chips: my point is simply that scientists are not responsible for what society decides to do with their knowledge.

Mr Brightly: But only scientists can make atom bombs, and if they refused to make them, they couldn't be made.

Professor Nuclear: True enough, Brightly. And I may tell you that such a thought has often crossed the minds of many of us who are working in this field. But who are we to set ourselves up against the rest of society? We are not expert politicians or strategists. We are scientists.

Mr Brightly: Yes, but you said a moment ago that you were also citizens. And in a democratic state, citizens make policy.

Dr Price: Don't you believe it, Brightly. In the kind of political democracy that we enjoy, citizens have the right to help to decide which among several self-chosen politicians should make policy for them. That is all. That is as far as democracy can go in a large modern industrial state. Had you

or I any vote in deciding whether Germany should re-arm?
Mr Brightly: No; I see your point of course, Price. It's a matter
of delegation. Our elected delegates decide for us, even on issues
which are not discussed at the time of election. I suppose the only
alternative would be a referendum whenever any issue of major
policy arose, or a General Election every few months.

The Master: The Greek city state was the only democracy, my
dear boy. The idea, like the word, is Greek. But how tawdry
the word has now become! The true democracy, as I see it, is
a state where everyone takes his wine like a gentleman. Have you
noticed the way the young men wolf their food in hall these days?
I deplore such lycanthropic dining.

Dr Mutation: If I may butt in with an irrelevant question: I
have been pondering the etymology of your name, Dreibelbis.
I thought at first it must be Pennsylvania Dutch, so-called, but
reflection has failed to yield any satisfactory etymology. 'Dreibel'
is, I believe, Low Dutch for 'trigger of a rifle', but I cannot
connect that with the element 'bis'.

Professor Dreibelbis: I don't blame you, Dr Mutation. As a
matter of fact, we all thought in our family that the name was
Pennsylvania Dutch—we've lived a long time in Pennsylvania—
until my elder brother was offered a partnership in a big Phila-
delphia law firm.

Dr Mutation: Offered a partnership —? I'm afraid I don't see
the connection.

Professor Dreibelbis: Well, it was like this, doctor. My brother
was offered a partnership in the big law firm—one of the biggest
in the country—of Antonelli, Murphy and Rabbinowitz. You
know how it is—one partner gets the Italian clientèle, another
the Irish, another the Jewish, and so on. Well, my brother was
offered a partnership, but they felt that Antonelli, Murphy,
Rabbinowitz and Dreibelbis was too heavy a mouthful, so to
speak. So he got in touch with an English professor at Penn
State—that's where he'd gone to school, though he had a scholarship at the University of Pennsylvania too—and asked him what
Dreibelbis meant in English. He was going to change his name

to the English equivalent. But the English professor couldn't figure out what Dreibelbis meant. So he told my brother to search among his family papers and try and find out where the family originally came from. Well, it sure was a crazy story. It turned out, from some papers a cousin of ours was able to turn up, that the family had originated in France, in a little village somewhere on the lower slopes of the Alps, and that the name was originally 'de ville basse'; that means 'of the low town'. Then they moved to the Rhine, where the name became Germanized into Dreibelbis. So the English professor suggested that my brother change his name to Lowton. And that's what he did. Antonelli, Murphy, Rabbinowitz and Lowton the law firm is now—sounds just right.

Dr Mutation: I see. Most interesting. But you didn't follow your brother's example?

Professor Dreibelbis: And change my name? No. I figured that what was good enough for my father and grandfather was good enough for me.

Mr Penumbra: I'm glad to see someone who doesn't believe in automatic progress and has some feeling for tradition.

Mr Brightly: What about the progress from De Ville Basse to Dreibelbis? Just the kind of textual corruption which enabled the Church to read irrelevant prophecies into the Hebrew prophets. That's tradition for you.

Professor Dreibelbis: But I *do* believe in progress, Dr Penumbra. I think you people are too easily put off by the horrors of the recent war. If you looked at civilization from further west, you'd get a different view, I think. Take a typical small town in the American Middle West, for example, the kind that produces the average American analysed by the sociologists. Healthy, well-fed children, all of them getting a decent education; comfortable homes, everyone in touch with the world through radio and TV; clean hygienic stores, with all perishable food kept under refrigeration; a high standard of living all round; workers in factories enjoying better working conditions and higher wages than ever before in history; farms run by the latest kinds of

machinery, and the farm worker no longer the illiterate clod he
was in European countries not so long ago; and everyone with a
chance, real freedom of opportunity—oh, I know it's the fashion
for intellectuals to sneer at America's material progress, but
believe me, Dr Penumbra, these are things to be proud of. I know
that American TV isn't the great cultural force that it might be
and that we've no third programme on our radio, and I know
about horror comics and the Kinsey report and McCarthyism.
We're far from perfect, Dr Penumbra, but we've got one hell of
a lot that no other country has had before, and I guess that's
progress sure enough.

Mr Penumbra: It's a question of the price you pay for such
material progress, Professor.

Dr Price: The economy of a modern industrial state forces its
own cultural pattern. There is, of course, a certain levelling
down. Education is free and universal, but watered. Commercial
wireless and television are forced to play down to the most certain
(that is, the lowest) responses of the largest number of people,
because the broadcasting companies are selling guaranteed audiences as well as time. Differences in native endowment between
people are denied or minimized. Advertising exploits people's
fear of being different. In America we see the culture of the
modern industrial state more clearly than here, but it is essentially
the same picture as here. We are on the same road. It is silly to
attack these features of modern civilization as American wickedness. We should welcome America as the mirror in which we
can see ourselves larger than life-size.

Mr Penumbra: You enjoy the spectacle?

Dr Price: As an economic historian, I appreciate it. I ask myself
how it is related to the price of a Ford car in 1920. The answer
satisfies my sense of the fitness of things.

Mr Brightly: The modern economist is the last survivor of the
species of disinterested scholar; the man who loves knowledge
for it's own sake like Browning's Grammarian. I salute you, Price.

Dr Price: My dear Brightly, if the prevision of a former bursar
of this college had not resulted in the laying down of some

extraordinarily good port, purchased at a very reasonable price shortly before the war, you would not now feel like saluting me.

The Master: Ah, you mean that that was Dionysus speaking not Clio? It has always struck me as odd that the libations offered to the Muses consisted of water or milk, and honey. Now, honey I understand, is used in the preparation of Drambuie, a Scottish liqueur derived from whisky, and perhaps the Muses were partial to some kind of Drambuie. I can't understand the milk—though perhaps Calliope, being the Muse of epic poetry, required a sustaining diet of milk stout; you need stamina to complete an epic. But what a vulgar drink! Water of course, has its uses. ''Αριστον μὲν ὕδωρ, as Pindar sang, 'water is best'; and I like to think that by some proleptic feat of the imagination, not un-common in poets, he was telling us that, in the words of my old friend Professor Scholiast, an authority on Scotch whisky, soda should be avoided like the plague in drinking a true Highland malt whisky, and a few drops of pure spring water—five drops of water per half gill of whisky, to be exact—should be added to release the natural oils. The natural oils of genius are, however, seldom released by water.

Professor Nuclear (rising): Well, Master, I must be off. My genius, such as it is, is oiled enough, and I must get back to the lab.

The Master: Back to the —! At this time of night! My dear boy, surely this is carrying your zeal for scientific discovery rather far? I know that the great Euclides (he of Alexandria, I mean; Euclides of Megara, though a dialectician of no mean order, had lesser claims to fame)—the great Euclides did say that there was no royal road to geometry; but Archimedes, who was a physicist like yourself, made his greatest discovery in his bath. Is there not a moral there?

Professor Nuclear: I have no doubt that you could extract several, Master. But the college bathrooms are hardly fitted for scientific research. And I have an experiment set up at the lab. which I must take a look at.

The Master: Well well, goodnight, my boy. I commend your zeal. But don't go and blow us all up.

M

Professor Dreibelbis (rising): And I must go too, Master. I have to finish writing my report for the Fulbright people tonight.

The Master: You mean, you are required to report on us?

Professor Dreibelbis: Not on you, Master, on myself and what I've been doing. I suppose they want to know whether I've made good use of my year here.

The Master: And have you?

Professor Dreibelbis: It's been a wonderful year, Master. Cambridge has something which no other university has got. I know there are plenty of crazy people here, but you'll find them in any academic community. What I like best about it is the variety of people's interests. Why, I've heard physicists discussing T. S. Eliot and linguists talking about the philosophy of history. The other day I met a man who was writing a book on Rudyard Kipling, and I discovered that he was in history, not in English at all! Now that's a very remarkable thing, Master, and it's something we don't have in America. When I see the Master of one of your colleges writing to the London *Times* about the weather or the migration of birds, I know that I'm in the presence of a very precious feature of English civilization.

The Master: Greek, Dreibelbis, Greek. When Sophocles wrote the *Antigone*, the Athenians were so impressed that they appointed him a general in the war against Samos. Cambridge still preserves something of the Greek view of the whole man; there is, I think, a freer meeting of different disciplines here than at most other places. Of course, you Americans elect your generals as Presidents, but then you have a constitution that keeps them from carrying out their policies.

Mr Penumbra: Was it not here at Cambridge that psychology was first joined with literary criticism and anthropology with the study of religion? I fear these mis-matings, Master.

The Master: Fear of where the intellect leads is improper in Cambridge, my dear Penumbra, a city where, like Socrates, we are taught to follow whithersoever the argument leads us. Good night, Dreibelbis: speak kindly of us in your report.

THE 'NEW CRITICISM': SOME QUALIFICATIONS[1]

MR WILLIAM O'CONNOR'S article on the 'new criticism' provides an interesting conspectus of some of the main trends in modern critical thought, written by one who is in substantial agreement with the whole modern movement. It seems to me, however, that it shows an insufficient awareness of possible alternatives to that 'new' approach which regards the primary problem in the critical examination of a work as the demonstration of its 'internal consistency'. The only alternatives he actually mentions are 'scholarship' (he points out early in his essay 'the chief differences between the new criticism and scholarship') and the method which employs 'the old dichotomy of content and form'. Now, in the first place, 'the chief difference between the new criticism and scholarship' as explained by Mr O'Connor is the difference between *any* criticism and scholarship. Scholarship throws light on the social and biographical origins of a work, on the cultural environment out of which it sprang, and on the transmission of the text, and thus often enables the critic to understand in some degree how the work came to be written and to see more clearly the meanings of certain parts of the text; but his job as a critic, whether his brand of criticism be old or new, remains the assessment of the literary worth of the work in question. The new criticism has no monopoly in this perception. As for the escape from the dichotomy of content and form, this has been sought by generations of critics and has been achieved in one fashion or another by many who take wholly different positions from those taken by any representative of the new movement—by R. L. Stevenson and John Middleton Murry, to mention only two, who are as different from each other as from any of

---

[1] This essay was written in 1950 in reply to an article explaining and defending the new movement in literary criticism (especially American literary criticism) which appeared in the American periodical, *College English*.

those mentioned by Mr O'Connor. I think it is not unfair to say that many who appreciate and have profited from the achievements of the new critics (and I consider myself one of those) nevertheless resent the assumption of some of their spokesmen that they alone are really critics, all others being mere scholars, historians, *Einfluss*-hunters, 'positivists', or unprincipled impressionists.

One can see, of course, what it is that leads them to such a view. The new critics have taken criticism more seriously—grimly, even —than representatives of other schools of thought, and, at least from Dr Leavis on, have seen the function of the critic as central to a civilization. Not only have they taken every opportunity to differentiate between criticism and other kinds of literary investigation, but they have also, unlike the more traditional critic, refused to start by a consideration of the impact of the work on the ordinary cultivated reader and then proceed to explain that impact in terms of the work's qualities. Instead, they have made critical analysis a tool for the total reassessment of the impact. They have striven by every possible means to widen the breach between amateur and professional criticism: even their vocabulary helps to serve this purpose, so that when Mr John Crowe Ransom writes an essay on the nature of poetry, he does not call it, as critics of other schools would, 'The Nature of Poetry', but 'Poetry: A Note in Ontology'.

There is both good and bad in this, just as there is both good and bad in the criticism of criticism which the new critics encourage (and of which the present discussion is an example). Criticism of criticism is, after all, an intellectual luxury and may lead to an inability to enjoy more nourishing fare. 'It is the chief penalty of becoming a professional literary man,' Mr T. S. Eliot once remarked to Mr William Empson, 'that one can no longer read anything with pleasure.' The phrase 'curl up with a good book' has been cheerfully abandoned to the Philistines, and people who take literature seriously are supposed to have more rigorous methods of dealing with the work of poets and novelists.

Of course, there is much gain in this rigour. The scrutinizing of literary theories is not only a valuable philosophical activity calculated to throw light on the differentiating characteristics of the literary work of art but it also sometimes helps us to approach individual works with a clearer understanding of what they are and so of how to read them with greater understanding and satisfaction. These are two separate, though related, functions of criticism—one might call them roughly the 'philosophical' and the 'appreciative'—and when their separate nature is not realized much confusion may result. It would be absurd to maintain that no Greek appreciated Sophocles until Aristotle had written the *Poetics*, or that English playgoers had to wait for A.C. Bradley or Professor Heilman before they could understand and enjoy *King Lear*. Appreciation can be independent of critical theory—a proposition which the new critics do not explicitly deny but a denial of which seems to be implicit in much of their writing. But if we do not concede that it is possible to enjoy art without formal training in criticism and without possessing general ideas about aesthetics, we are flying in the face of experience, setting up a priestly critical profession to mediate between artists and their public, and encouraging the growth of the most barren kind of academicism in matters artistic and literary.

We all agree that criticism is valuable, but we must be clear about its kind of value. Eliot has defined criticism in the sense in which we are using the term as 'the commentation and exposition of works of art by means of written words'—a reasonable, if inelegant, definition; but it should be noted that the definition itself says nothing of what this 'commentation and exposition' is supposed to achieve. In the same essay, as Mr O'Connor has reminded us, Eliot denies that criticism is 'autotelic' (it should be said that this essay was written in 1923, before Eliot had rid himself of that pontifical pretentiousness in manner and vocabulary which mars some of his early prose) and specifically asserts that it must always profess an end in view, which he roughly defines as 'the elucidation of works of art and the correction of taste'. But we must go further than this. 'Elucidation' is an ambiguous word, and 'the correction of taste' an even more ambiguous phrase.

Elucidation itself will vary according to the purpose of the eluci-
dator. Miss Lily Campbell's elucidation of Shakespeare's historical
plays is very different in nature and purpose from the elucidation
supplied by, say, John Palmer in his *Political Characters of Shakespeare*, a fact which Mr O'Connor sees but which he might have
explored further. A poem or a play or a novel can be very many
things at the same time—a reflection of the cultural climate of its
age, a document in the mental history of its author, a carefully
patterned arrangement of words, ideas, images and situations, a
fable, a piece of rhetoric, and the communication of a unique
insight into an aspect of human experience through one or several
of these means. We may choose to elucidate the work as any one
of these things, or as any two, or as so many as we think we can
handle.

But our new critic, with his awareness of the difference between
criticism and scholarship, has his answer at once: 'There is no real
difficulty here,' he will reply. 'What the literary critic should
concern himself with is the work qua work of art. He should
ignore it as a document in the history of ideas, as an expression of
the writer's personality, or as anything but a poem or a play or a
novel, and the problem is to find out what a poem or a play or a
novel really is, what it is *uniquely*, what it is that no other form of
written expression is. Having done this, he can proceed to demonstrate its special formal qualities and exhibit it as a literary
work of art.' He then proceeds to find a formula which will
define the *quiddity* of a literary form and goes on to the analysis
of individual texts which demonstrates that any given example
conforms to this definition.

This is all very appealing. The human mind has a fondness for
definitions and categories, for contrasts and exclusions, for analytic
demonstrations. Nevertheless, a sense that the true quality of a
poem somehow escapes this sort of defining and categorizing and
demonstrating has persisted throughout the history of criticism
and has given rise to every kind of evasive impressionism in order
to avoid coming to grips with the basic question of whether and
why a given poem is good. 'It were as wise to cast a violet into

a crucible that you might discover the formal principle of its colour and odour, as seek to transfuse from one language into another the creations of a poet,' wrote Shelley; but the modern critic, in spite of his awareness of the uniqueness of a given work of art, is made uncomfortable by such statements because they open the door to autobiographical chatter masquerading as criticism. And there again we can understand and sympathize with this insistence that without a stern formal discipline real criticism is impossible.

But in a sense 'real criticism' *is* impossible. This is not by any means to say that there are no standards of value, that we must fall back on personal taste, or vague impressionism, or on mere gush. We do, however, mean that no critical statement about a work of literary art—least of all, about a poem—can be a complete statement of what it is and why it is good. On the level of aesthetic theory, it may be possible to construct a set of valid general principles, but practical criticism, criticism designed to demonstrate the nature and quality of a work and so to increase understanding and appreciation, must always be fragmentary, indirect, approximate, and can never be a complete and wholly satisfactory description of what in fact takes place in the work of art.

It is not difficult to see why this should be so. A poem is an immense complex of meaning which is nevertheless simple and immediate in its impact, and it is impossible to describe that complex and simultaneously to account for its impact. To resolve the poem into mere complexity by analytic discussion is often useful and helpful, but it hardly begins to explain the reasons for its total impact on the experienced and sensitive reader, nor does it necessarily increase appreciation for the inexperienced. The richness and uniqueness of poetic statement, so rightly insisted on by the new critics, is far too often underestimated in their practice, for in their desire to concern themselves only with literary criteria they are liable to narrow their analysis so as to exclude all elements that are not exclusively related to those criteria. But the fact is that there is no such thing as a purely literary work of literature.

A work of literary art is necessarily a mixed form. It produces its effect by being several things at once—not by mere complexity but by operating simultaneously on several different levels not only of meaning but of existence.

Our search for 'criteria that make possible judgments about literary worth', in Mr O'Connor's phrase, if pursued with a disinterested desire to find out what a work of literary art really is rather than with a desire to find merely a consistent method, will eventually turn up the fact that literary discourse is by its very nature several kinds of discourse at once. A poem is a structure with 'internal consistency', but it is also often a fascinating record of the poet's mind, a period-piece reflecting with moving brilliance the climate of an age, and a story. We may differentiate uses of language in a poem which are not to be found in other ways of writing, but this does not mean that the full impact of a poem can be determined by examining only its differentiating qualities. Who can hear Mozart played on the harpsichord without enjoying, as part of his reaction to the actual music, the poignant feeling of listening to the gaiety of a lost civilization? Is this reaction 'impure', sentimental, irrelevant? If, in seeing *Hamlet*, we appreciate its dramatic structure and its poetic magnificence while, at the same time, seeing it as the work of Shakespeare the Elizabethan, are we being aesthetically wicked? A work of literary art, which, because of its richness, its use of so many elements of expression, can be so many things at once, is often, also, a work of history and of autobiography and of moral philosophy; and its impact on us is the more profound because it is all these things. In appreciating a work of art, we have only one ear cocked for 'internal consistency', for the purely 'formal' aspect. And often when such consistency has been demonstrated we do not read the work with any richer enjoyment.

The new critics, of course, have their answer here. Messrs Wimsatt and Beardsley, in a widely discussed article (duly cited by Mr O'Connor), have in their very title boldly stigmatized as a 'fallacy' the consideration by the critic of the impact of a work on the reader. Their concern with what a literary work *is*, uniquely and formally, rather than with the reasons for which it is enjoyed, logically leads them to dismiss the testimony of those who enjoy literature as irrelevant. The new criticism tends, in fact, to be impatient with the testimony of readers. A poem, the argument seems to run, *should* be enjoyed for those of its aspects which differentiate it from other forms of discourse; whether it is ever so enjoyed is considered an irrelevant question. This is a seductively tidy way of looking at things—as though we were to enjoy people only for such of their attributes as distinguished them from all other kinds of living creatures and not for their total selves—but it leads, in criticism as in morality, to a puritanism which does violence to the values found in experience.

Why, it might be asked, is the 'affective fallacy' in any sense a fallacy? The value of literature surely lies in its actual or potential effect on readers—admittedly, on experienced and sensitive readers, on readers who have had sufficient exposure to this kind of thing to have developed a proper responsiveness and discrimination. To deny this is to fall into the 'ontological fallacy' of believing that a work of art fulfils its purpose and achieves its value simply by *being*, so that the critic becomes concerned only to demonstrate the mode of its being by descriptive analysis. This is comparable to saying that a body of moral laws exists in order to have an internal logical structure and that to consider the effect of obeying any given law would be to move from questions of moral philosophy to questions of social or individual behaviour. Literature is a phenomenon produced by men in order to communicate in a certain way with their fellows. In the last analysis, the test of its value can be judged only by the receiver, and judged by him on some kind of 'affective' theory. Of course the critic must consider the means by which this special kind of communication—in virtue of which literary discourse differs from other kinds of discourse—is achieved, and this in turn leads him to an examination of internal consistency as one among many characteristics of a work of art. (The new critics generally talk as though it were the only essential characteristic.) But we must distinguish between means and ends. Poetry, in the largest sense of the word, is a unique method of making a unique kind of communication, and it is the real or potential effectiveness of the communication which justifies the method, not vice versa.

There is, of course, the question of communication *to whom*. Who is the ideal reader whose reactions are to be taken as the norm? We must not take a purely pragmatic view and send out pollsters to find out who are most affected by which works—to that extent Messrs Wimsatt and Beardsley are right. The ability to discriminate between more and less effective uses of the medium of poetry is achieved by deep and wide experience in reading. The most brilliant literary mind, if faced only by the poems of Eddie Guest, might believe that they represented the height of poetic expression; but, given the opportunity to read widely and richly, he will change his views. Deep and wide reading provides a better training in critical appreciation than a thousand ingenious analyses of poems. If critical analysis be provided as well, the process can be speeded up, and the reader may be made aware of how the effects which he appreciates are achieved—and that in itself increases appreciation.

The best 'appreciative' criticism is that which enables the reader to get a glimpse of the real life in a work: having glimpsed it, he can proceed to enter into all its rich vitality. No critical method is absolute, foolproof, or 'true'. I have known students who have been more effectively brought to see the essential life in a poem by hearing it read aloud slowly than by the most careful analysis of its structure. Art is meant to be experienced, and the function of criticism is to assist that experience.[1] After reading some of the new criticism, one might imagine that an effective stage performance would achieve less towards an understanding of *Hamlet* than an analysis of its internal consistency made in the study. Criticism of any work of art is a kind of performance, a sort of substitute for performance. Part of the true glory of a scene in *Hamlet* may be brought out for students by having them act it out. There are, of course, other ways, and the careful discussion of

---

[1] 'Be minute,' wrote Coleridge to Sotheby, 'and assign your reasons often, *and your first impressions always*' (my italics).

structure, imagery and similar points can be of immense help. But to say that what matters about a work of art is not its communicative potential but its internal consistency is to put the cart before the horse completely.

One must not forget the pedagogical aspect of criticism. As far as its classroom use is concerned, the function of criticism is to increase awareness of what a work of literary art really is and by so doing to increase appreciation of it. To teach a student that criticism always and necessarily involves demonstration of internal consistency, or of paradox, or of ambivalent meanings, or what have you, *may* be useful but is often fatal. If the student does not learn that such devices are means to achieve a communicative effect and that the reader remains dead to the work so long as that communicative effect remains unachieved, then he has learned only to be a pedant. How often have I seen a student who has got it into his head that ingenuity of analysis is the mark of the good critic proceed to make a pretentious fool of himself by demonstrating with misguided ingenuity the existence of manifestly absurd meanings in some poem or story. There is such a thing as a 'feeling' for a work and its period which can save one from such barren stupidities. Our new critics generally have this feeling, because they are men of wide reading and historical knowledge. They have assimilated a whole historical tradition, and they know, before they approach *Hamlet* as professional critics, to what area of human sensibility and significance it belongs. In their demand that all works should be treated as though they were contemporary and anonymous they are in effect requiring the student of today to do without tools which they themselves are continually using, though often not consciously. There is, in fact, no limit to what ingenious analysis can achieve by way of demonstrating complexity and consistency of structure in any work at all, good or bad: how far you can go is taught you by your 'taste'—and taste is the sum of what you have learned about art by willing and interested exposure to it. It necessarily includes an element of historical discrimination, since wide reading experience is bound to produce in a reader of any native sensitivity at all some awareness of the difference between the cultural points of reference of, say, Milton and Matthew Prior. This does not mean that there may not be even greater differences between two contemporary writers.

It is not wise to give the student the impression that the end-product of literary activity is the critical analysis of the work and not the work itself. I do not suggest for a moment that the new criticism would maintain such a preposterous position, but its practitioners often implicitly suggest this attitude. Literature exists to be read and enjoyed, and criticism, at least in its peda-gogical aspect, exists in order to increase awareness and so increase enjoyment. The purely philosophical critic may entertain himself by trying to isolate the quiddity of poetry (but I should maintain that the quiddity of poetry is that, unlike all other forms of communication, it has no single quiddity), but the 'appreciative' critic will use any means at his disposal—analytic, descriptive, histrionic, yes, even historical—to arouse alert interest, to produce that communicative impact without which all further critical discussion is useless.

Another objection might be brought against much (but not all) of the new criticism. Even if we agree that it is possible to isolate and define the differentiating qualities of a work of literary art, we may not agree that those qualities are to be discussed in terms of structure. To many of the new critics all criticism is analysis of structure, and demonstration of value is demonstration of structural complexity and coherence. There are, however, many valuable kinds of literature whose value does not reside in their structural effectiveness. There is not even a single poetic use of language. Good verse can consist of propositional statements neatly phrased, with an agreeable rhythm and pleasantly chiming rhymes serving more or less as pleasing decoration (as in John Pomfret's 'The Choice', for example), or, at the other end of the scale of poetic expression, it may be like a poem of Donne's or of the later Yeats, a flaming organic unity in which every element in the expression contributes equally to the total communication. To place a poem in this scale is not necessarily to pass any value-judgment on it, for there can be good poems at any place in the scale. We may with some justice hold, however, that the potentialities for really impressive poetic expression are less likely to exist at the lower end of the scale and that the most effective poems are those which come in the middle or higher parts of the range. Such questions can only be resolved by reading poems and considering what each achieves. One might say that at the lower end of the scale of poetic expression the handling of language is nearer to that of prose or perhaps to that of non-artistic literary expression and that it makes less use of the characteristically poetic ways of handling language. But is this necessarily a value-judgment? Is the best poetry the most poetical poetry, poetry which uses most of those aspects of language which differentiate the poet's use of it from other kinds of use? And, anyway, is this difference to be explained in terms of structure? The point is, to say the least, arguable.

By concentrating on what they deem to be the differentiating qualities of poetic expression (in the widest sense of 'poetic') and by seeing these qualities in terms of complexity and coherence of structure, many of the new critics often find themselves unable to cope with such simpler forms of literature as the verse-essay or the song-lyric. The new criticism is incapable, for example, of demonstrating the magnificence of Burns's songs (which I have recently seen dismissed with something very like contempt by a young critic). The devices by which Burns, in 'Auld Lang Syne', sublimates nostalgia for the past in present good fellowship to close with a formal social gesture which holds past and present together for one tenuous moment by ritual, man's way of marking permanently the fleeting meanings of things—this sort of thing cannot be handled or even discussed by the new criticism without embarrassment. And what of the devices by which lyrics are fitted to music? These are some of the areas in which modern criticism, largely because of its persistence in considering every 'affective' theory as a 'fallacy' and thus clinging to what I have called the 'ontological fallacy', is seriously inadequate.

This has an effect on the vocabulary of the new criticism and, indeed, on its prose style, which as a rule is ugly and clotted. There seems to be a tendency to equate grace and clarity with superficiality and a preference for a technical jargon which is not, in fact, necessary in order to communicate adequately. Some of the results of this—for example, the comical 'Glossary of the New Criticism' which appeared in *Poetry* some time ago—are likely to encourage the worst kind of verbal exhibitionism and, among the hangers-on of the movement, have often done so.

But it would be unjust to judge the new criticism by its more ragged camp followers. All I am concerned to do here is to point to some limitations and inadequacies of its characteristic method. I certainly recognize its great achievement in helping to abolish from our colleges the mumbling survey course consisting of biographical facts combined with lists of adjectives appropriate to each writer and in insisting on the close reading of individual texts. But the alternative is not necessarily to throw out all that Mr Ransom, for example, or Mr Wimsatt would like to throw out, to remove from our critical vocabulary all adjectives designed to point to the nature of the work's impact on the qualified reader, to manipulate a few pretentious technical terms. We can learn from the new critics without using their jargon, adopting their puritanism, or employing their Procrustean method of forcing every literary work into a pattern of complex coherence or ambivalence or paradox or some such criterion. We can learn to read carefully, sensitively, critically, without losing sight of the richness and essential 'impurity' of all effective literary art and without forgetting that, as the rejected Saintsbury once remarked, 'in the house of poetry are many mansions'. What we want is a richer, not a narrower, aesthetic than the traditional combination of autobiographical impressionism and description. Catholicity of taste does not mean the abandonment of standards, nor does the recognition that different kinds of value may legitimately be called 'literary' imply the loss of critical principles. In the last analysis, the characteristic method of the new criticism—immensely helpful though it has been, and brilliantly as it is often employed—is inadequate because it is too easy. Its tendency towards what Professor Crane has called 'critical monism' leads to a drastic oversimplification of what in fact a work of literary art is, what kind of pleasure it gives, and why it is valuable. It is the invention of ardent but simple minds and, too often, of minds that are really happier talking about literature than reading and enjoying it.

THE CRITICISM OF FICTION: SOME SECOND THOUGHTS[1]

FICTION IS TODAY, as it has been for some time, the dominant literary form, and one might suppose, therefore, that modern criticism would have devoted itself particularly to the novel and the short story. The modern critic, however, has preferred to concentrate on poetry, for reasons which are not difficult to see. The abundance and variety of fiction makes the establishment of critical norms for that art a very difficult business; ideals of complexity and consistency of structure can be applied to lyrical poetry without too much strain, but the novel is often a more discursive form and rarely one in which the readers' main interest lies in the appreciation of structural artfulness. Not that structural artfulness is lacking in a good novel, but it is not often what the reader is primarily interested in seeing.

One can, of course, develop an ideal definition of a good novel which would recognize that, in the artistic handling of prose narrative, the total significance flowers cumulatively out of the handling of each unit of meaning at each point. If I may be allowed to quote from one of my own earlier attempts to grapple with this problem, I might give the following ideal definition: 'Fiction as an art form is the narration of a series of situations that are so related to each other that a significant unity of meaning is achieved; the situations are presented in language such that at each point in the progress of the narrative the kind of relation between retrospect and anticipation is set up that continually and cumulatively reinforces the desired implications of the plot, so that plot becomes symbolic as well as literal in its meaning.' And I added: 'One definition of a "bad novel" would therefore be a novel in which no adequate complex of meaning has been achieved, where the devices of style, structure, etc., which the

[1] A lecture delivered at the University of Rochester, N.Y., in 1950.

author has employed have not been adequate to shape the work into an illuminating unity.'[1] Symbolization, the development of new meanings out of situations by the way in which they are arranged, ordered and presented, would thus depend equally on style and structure—style being the handling of the presentation at each particular point, and plot the larger aspects of the same thing. On this definition, style would become a function of plot, and expression and structure would be part of a single complex of effective artistic communication.

The fact is, however, that such a definition, though useful as indicating an ideal towards which the art of fiction *tends*, is rarely if ever an accurate account of what goes on in a novel. Even in lyric poetry, where intensity of expression is at its maximum and the fusion of the different elements that make up the poem can almost achieve a unity which gets beyond chronological sequence to lie in the mind as a single instantaneous pattern, this kind of unity is never wholly achieved, and the fact that the expression takes place in units that are deployed in a chronological sequence makes it impossible for the whole poem to burst into total meaning outside time, as it were. Indeed, it might be maintained that if a poem could achieve this kind of simultaneity it would cease to be a poem; for, after all, its medium is language and language depends on time, on the arrangement of a sequence, in order to communicate at all. One might say that lyrical poetry *tends towards* the escape from the time dimension, approaching ever nearer to this ideal as the poem becomes more finely wrought, but that if it were ever fully to achieve this ideal it would cease to exist.

With fiction, the unreality of the ideal definition is more clearly demonstrable. It can be applied with profit, though never wholly literally, to Flaubert, to some of James, to some of Stevenson; but what of Scott and Dickens and Trollope? A great deal of English fiction is much more muddied with life, much more crowded with boisterous irrelevancies, than any Flaubertian or Jamesian or

[1] *A Study of Literature*, Cornell University Press and Oxford University Press, 1948, p. 55.

N

Stevensonian definition of the art of fiction would allow. 'Most people suppose,' wrote Stevenson to James in 1884, '... that striking situations, or good dialogue, are got by studying life; they will not rise to understand that they are prepared by deliberate artifice and set off by painful suppressions.' By what is the relation between 'deliberate artifice' and the knowledge of life in a novel of Dickens? Where did Scott get the vernacular dialogue which is what provides the true vitality in all his Scottish novels? The English tradition is rich in novels whose whole glory is their wealth of shouting and jostling characters who are brought vividly to the reader's eye by means of a superficial and not very craftsmanlike plot, and who are dismissed only when their creator has become exhausted. Dryden's famous remark on the *Canterbury Tales*—'Here is God's plenty'—has nothing to do with structure or pattern, yet it is a remark peculiarly applicable to the work of English novelists from Defoe to Joyce Carey.

Let us put the question another way. Few critics would deny that Willa Cather's *Alexander's Bridge*, a finely constructed but lifeless novel written under the influence of James, is much inferior to the same writer's *The Song of the Lark*, which is crowded with details that have no proper place in the plot, is structurally defective, and comes to an end only when the author has nothing more to say. In spite of its formal defects, *The Song of the Lark* is a rich and satisfying novel, pulsing with life, creating its own universe as it moves, picking out and presenting vividly freshly remembered incidents from the author's childhood. Language here has been made to *hold* life, and though there are moments in the novel which irritate or offend, the work as a whole has force and vitality and can be read with satisfaction by the most sophisticated reader.

Are there, then, two criteria, one drawn from art and one drawn from life? Must we distinguish between the kind of novelist who achieves an artful disposition of the pattern, and the kind who, disregarding the more purely aesthetic aspects of his work, creates a convincing and lively world of action? To do so would represent a complete abdication of the critic's function. The distinction here is surely not between the artful and the lively, but between different kinds of artfulness. James himself talked about the necessity of 'the sense of felt life' in a novel, and it would never have occurred to him to sacrifice this to superficial neatness of form. To achieve the illusion of a living and pulsing world is not the work of the man who merely knows life and feels strongly about it; it is the work of the writer who can handle language in such a way that what he knows and feels can be carried alive into the reader's imagination. We most adequately face our problem by realizing that form manifests itself in a variety of ways, that an episodic novel may have an adequate form of its own even though its structure is neither complex nor consistent, that, in fact, the novel fulfils itself in many and various ways and no single definition of a good novel will do.

The richness of a Dickens novel has its own means of communicating itself, and it is not artless. The fact that Dickens wrote many of his novels for serial publication, that he did not always know what he was going to do with his characters once he had created them, that he sometimes had no notion of how he was going to end a novel until he had written a substantial part of it, would all mean eventual failure if he were writing *The Portrait of a Lady* or even *Treasure Island*. There are, of course, some Dickens novels—*Great Expectations*, for example—where structural unity does exist and is of the greatest importance in achieving the total effect; but *The Pickwick Papers* in one way and *Nicholas Nickleby* in another illustrate how a novel can move along in no particular direction once it has set up a world for it to move in, and what we enjoy here is not the movement but what it brings us to.

The universe of each of these two Dickens novels is both rich and consistent, even though the structure may not be consistent. The universe is created by character, not by plot, the only function of plot being to deploy the characters. (Character itself is created by art, working with the raw materials supplied by observation and imagination.) The death of little Nell in *The Old Curiosity Shop* is preposterously sentimental; it is a bad scene, and offends most of us, but it does not kill the novel, as it would kill another kind of novel, for as an ending it is not necessary to complete the novel's meaning, and as an episode it exists by itself, to be taken or left.

We turn to Trollope, not a great novelist but an agreeable one, and ask ourselves what is the 'peculiar pleasure' we derive from his works. He, too, creates a fictional world, but it exists not so much in virtue of the fascinating and lively characters who inhabit it as in virtue of its concreteness and inclusiveness. Trollope's world is a 'probable' world, and we enjoy living in it in a relaxed and even escapist way because it is easy to enter, pleasant to walk about in, and adequately credible. It is, of course, dangerous to generalise about Trollope, who wrote so many different kinds of novels: but at least it might be said that he is read today (and he is read surprisingly widely) because his world of muted crises, of human situations presented and worked out against a stable background, is both valid and self-contained. There are no passionate glimpses into the well-springs of human nature, nor do the plots build up cumulatively a unique insight which depends for its adequate presentation on the continuous relation between style and structure; there is little 'symbolization' and clearly no searching for *le mot juste*. Trollope makes language carry conviction; the pressure is low and the craftsmanship is only adequate, but the fictional world does emerge, convincing, logical, argeeable and interesting to contemplate. This is doubtless a minor kind of art, but it is civilized and pleasant.

A very different kind of self-contained world is that created by Joyce's *Ulysses*. Here the structure *is* important, but not in the way that the structure of, say, *Madame Bovary* is important. More accurately, one might say that the structure of *Ulysses* is important the way it is in Flaubert, but it has a still more important function—to emphasize the completeness and logicality of the world which the novel creates as it moves. The more I read *Ulysses*, the less interested I am in the working out of the Homeric theme or in the organization of the plot as organization. I find myself more and more fascinated by the completeness of the world presented, by the fact that an incident on page 25 is explained and illuminated by another incident on page 300, that an unexplained gesture of Leopold Bloom in the fourth episode is given logic and meaning with reference to something that happens or is explained twenty episodes further on. This is a novel which cannot possibly be appreciated on first reading, not because we lack the Homeric clues (which are quite unimportant and can in fact be totally ignored by the reader without much loss) but because a great deal of the pleasure we get out of the book derives from our recognition when reading a passage on, say, page 20 that what is said here has richer meaning with reference to a fragment of conversation on page 200, an incident on page 250, or a character's recollection on page 300. This is not what we normally mean by adequacy of structure, for that kind of structure is cumulative, and builds up its meanings in chronological sequence, taking account of the fact that our memory of early incidents fades as we get further into the book. But *Ulysses* makes no concessions to memory; its effects are not achieved cumulatively but simultaneously; to enjoy the book fully we must have it all lying in our mind at once and see as we read any given part all the other parts which support and explain it and which in turn are supported and explained by this part. The simultaneity (which, as I have noted in discussing lyric poetry, can never be really achieved) is not, of course, present in the actual process of reading, which takes place in time, but if we know the book well and remember it in detail we can compensate for chronology by memory.

The richness of *Ulysses* is thus very different from that of *The Pickwick Papers*. It is not the gusto and vitality of Joyce's novel which impress us (as they so often do in Dickens) so much as the sheer completeness and self-consistency of the world in which the characters move. It all fits together; everything has a satisfying meaning if we are familiar enough with the novel to keep in mind all the relevant passages simultaneously. This is a kind of effect difficult to parallel elsewhere in fiction. The enjoyment to be derived from this savouring of the interrelationships between the different parts of the world created by the novel does not come from the appreciation of form as such, but from the pleasure of inhabiting a fictional universe so much more totally known to us in its interrelated parts than anything can be in real life. As far as I know, this kind of effect and value in fiction has not been recognized by critics.

The very completeness of Joyce's world prevents us from being overcome by a sense of its abundance, for a sense of abundance arises when we get glimpses of more characters than we can properly account for. Quaint or lively characters who emerge out of a dim background to reveal themselves as comic or picturesque and then return to the unknown from whence they came can add immensely to the sense of life in a work; one might consider the function of minor characters in Scott, for example. Scott's handling of minor characters, particularly of the dialogue he puts into their mouths, does have real relevance to the over-all structure of the novel, but we appreciate this aspect of his work not because we appreciate this relevance but because these characters help to make the world in which they dwell both more interesting and more human. *Interestingness* is a criterion no serious critic has dared to apply to art, but I can see no reason why it should not be applied. We must, of course, distinguish it from suspense and other ways of holding attention, which may be quite meretricious. By interestingness I mean the ability to intrigue and fascinate the reader the more he reads—not simply the ability to make him read on in order to find out what happens next, but the power to keep him absorbed in the individual incident. Mere truth is no more valid a criterion for art than for philosophy. What is obviously true is liable to be trite: what *might* be true and is at the same time suggestive, intriguing, attention-compelling, is a better criterion to apply to both philosophy and art. Devices for increasing the interestingness of a work of fiction may be quite independent of the conventionally accepted formal properties and may be successfully practised independently of them.

Aristotle, we all know, said that plot was the 'soul' of drama, and in a sense this is certainly true for Greek drama and for much subsequent drama and fiction. But is plot the 'soul' of Shakespeare's *Henry IV*, Part I? The story of that play is important; the patterning of events, with their causal connections, helps to give the play its meaning, to make the whole thing pleasingly comprehensive as a unit. But does the 'peculiar pleasure' we derive from the play really derive from the manner in which the various incidents are arranged with respect to each other? There could be no play without the plot, true enough, but the richness of dialogue and incident, the bubbling vitality which is conveyed not by the *order* in which things happen but by the *way* in which they happen, by the life which springs from the characters in operation—this is what we most enjoy the play for, and this is achieved not by structural artfulness but by artfulness in the use of language to present the given incident. What Levin Schücking called, in a somewhat different connection, Shakespeare's 'episodic intensification' can be usefully applied to any play or novel in which the life emerges through the energy and colour of the individual incident, and where the work as a whole is a series of such incidents linked by relatively flat passages whose function is to ensure that the nominal structure does not fall apart.

I am not trying to restore the old distinction between the novel of character and the novel of incident, though this has its uses, but I am maintaining that there are kinds of interest in fiction which do not depend on those qualities of organization which we like to think of as of basic significance in a work of art. Professor R. S. Crane, in a brilliant article in the *American Journal of General Education* for January 1950, has analysed the structure of *Tom Jones* in astonishing detail. He does not, however, raise the question of the part played by structure in the total impact of the novel. In what degree do the kinds of interest which we find in *Tom Jones* depend on this structure—a structure, it might be added, whose complexity nobody can see until Professor Crane has pointed it out? This is not a rhetorical question but one which deserves a careful and an honest answer.

I suppose that Professor Wimsatt of Yale would say that this line of argument is an example of the 'affective fallacy', and that the whole notion of interestingness as a criterion is based on the erroneous assumption that the way in which the work affects the reader (albeit the experienced and sensitive reader) is critically relevant. But the ontological fallacy, which is the name I give to what he and others profess, is even more misleading, for it assumes that the essence of a work of art is something different from its capacity for being properly perceived. If Berkeley's theory of knowledge had been applied to art, Dr Johnson could never have refuted him by kicking a stone: for the *esse* of a work of art *is* its *percipi*. That being so, what we perceive is of the first importance, and the quality of the perception depends directly on the original creator who arranged things in terms of their perceptive potentialities. The artist, like God, works in a communicative medium, and the test of his success is the reactions of the qualified receiver. In examining the reactions of the qualified receiver (reader, in the case of novels) the critic can determine the kinds of appeal different kinds of work possess, and he can then proceed to find out what it is in them which accounts for the appeal. The most fruitful criticism always operates in this way: it clarifies and explains effects with reference to their causes in the work.

There are more types of artfulness at work in fiction than are dreamed of in our philosophy. How does Jane Austen, for example, achieve that sublime clarity of presentation which is a source of perpetual wonder to the reader, and what is the relation of that clarity to her characteristic irony? The analysis of the relation of style to plot in her novels will go only a little way in answering these questions, and the mere analysis of structure will not begin to answer them. The wit of Huxley's *Antic Hay* is part of the texture of the dialogue, and that texture cannot be discussed with the same critical tools which can demonstrate the cunning of James's *The Turn of the Screw*. Fiction is, in fact, a blanket term which covers many different kinds of skills, many different ways of handling narrative in language, for many different purposes.

There are even important differences in what might be called the unit of artifice. In some novelists it is possible to examine each phrase, noting the effectiveness of the smallest unit of expression and its contribution to the sum of significance. We all know—we have the author's word for it—that this can be done for Flaubert, where the slightest alteration in the form of expression can be disastrous to the shape of the whole paragraph and so to the rhythm of the total work. But in, say, Hardy's *The Return of the Native* the unit of artifice is large: it is not the individual word or phrase, but the swell of the whole paragraph, and as long as that swell is maintained one could change phrases and even whole sentences without impairing the work in the least. This is equally true of Scott, though not where he is working with vernacular dialogue, and indeed it is true of most nineteenth century English novelists except (odd juxtaposition!) Emily Brontë and Stevenson. It is quite unrealistic to suggest that in Hardy's novels the expression at each point is so perfectly subdued to the total intention that the smallest alteration would be fatal. One could alter or omit large passages without the most perceptive critic being aware that anything was wrong. Hardy's massive, flinty style is based on a large unit of artifice, not, as with Flaubert, on a small one, and differences of this kind must be noted by the critic if he is not to make a fool of himself by applying analytic techniques indiscriminately whether or not they are appropriate to the kind of craftsmanship the artist employed.

We are inclined to be hypnotized by the word 'artist'. If the writer is an artist, we maintain, then he *must* be aware all the time of the precise relation of each individual stroke to the total effect he is aiming at. But two things should be remembered: one is that artists are men, and therefore fallible, and their works are thus no more perfect than the highest kind of human achievement in other categories; the other is that the term 'artist' covers a great many different ways of handling a communicative medium, and brilliant craftsmanship may be demonstrated by any one of an indefinite number of kinds of cunning. This is particularly true of the novel, which in English especially is an 'impure' art form—

or at least we have to consider it impure if we hold too narrow a definition of art. Our ideal definition of the novel is helpful if we consider it as an ideal towards which certain kinds of fiction tend; but if we allow it to determine in advance what we are going to see in a novel, it will end by obscuring the reasons why fiction is in fact enjoyed, and thus divorcing the critic wholly from the appreciative reader. A critic so divorced is engaged merely in a kind of pedantic play, which may be amusing to himself and his fellow professionals but has no further function. It is in order to avoid this that I have thought it worth while to emphasize certain distinctions between different kinds of novels and their 'peculiar pleasures'.

TRANSLATING THE HEBREW BIBLE

PERHAPS THE BEST-KNOWN PASSAGE from the Bible, to English-speaking people, is the Authorized Version rendering of the 23rd Psalm:

The Lord is my shepherd, I shall not want.

He maketh me to lie down in green pastures: he leadeth me beside the still waters.

He restoreth my soul: he leadeth me in the paths of righteousness for his name's sake.

Yea, though I walk through the valley of the shadow of death, I will fear no evil: for thou art with me; thy rod and thy staff they comfort me.

Thou preparest a table before me in the presence of mine enemies: thou annointest my head with oil: my cup runneth over.

Surely goodness and mercy shall follow me all the days of my life: and I will dwell in the house of the Lord for ever.

This is an English poem, grave and pellucid in style, and it has left a permanent influence on the imagery of English poetry and the rhythms of English prose. The tone, one might say, is Anglican, the same tone that we find in that great Church of England poet, George Herbert. A Hebrew psalm has in this version become an Anglican poem; it is a rendering of the original Hebrew, true enough, but the rendering is stamped with the temper of those who made it. Phrases such as 'green pastures' and 'still waters', which are so important in setting the tone of the whole poem, are not, in fact, literal renderings of the Hebrew '*binoth deshe*' and '*al mai m'nuchoth*', which mean, respectively, 'by pastures of tender grass' and 'by waters of quietness'. The Douay version, translating from the Latin Vulgate, renders the second verse: 'In place of pasture there he hath placed me. Upon the water of refection he hath brought me up', and though the literal meaning is similar, the lyric flow has disappeared.

The difference is not doctrinal. The Anglican calm of the Authorized Version rendering does not arise from the fact that the translators were drawing on the special features of their variety of Protestant Christianity, for many of the special features of their translation came originally from the Geneva translation of 1560, which was the work of Puritans who worked before the Anglican compromise and who would not have accepted it if they had known of it. The Geneva version begins: 'The Lord is my shepherd, I shall not want. He maketh me to rest in grene pasture, and leadeth me by the stil waters. He restoreth my soule, . . . ' The English psalter of 1530 begins the psalm: 'The lorde is my pastore and feader: wherfore I shal not wante. He made me to feade on a full plenteous batle grownde: and did dryve and retche me at layser by the swete ryvers.'

The personality of the psalm, as it were, differs in each rendering. In the Vulgate the notion of 'Shepherd' disappears completely, and instead of the psalm opening 'The Lord is my shepherd; I shall not want', it begins: '*Dominus regit me, et nihil mihi deerit*' (The Lord rules me, and nothing will be lacking to me). The 'green pastures' of the Geneva and Authorized versions are in the Vulgate the much more factual, even technical, '*in loco pascuae*', while '*super aquam refectionis*' ('upon the water of refection', as we have seen Douay translate it) stresses the reviving nature of the waters and says nothing about their stillness. The whole tone of the psalm is more businesslike and practical in the Vulgate.

Luther's German version has the greenness, but makes the water fresh rather than still: '*Er weidet mich auf einer grünen Aue, and führet mich zum frischen Wasser.*' This is not too far removed from the Authorized Version, though the first verse in Luther—'*Der Herr ist mein Hirte; mir wird nichts mangeln*'—has not the flow of the English, due largely to the accumulation of consonants. '*Mir wird nichts mangeln*' is a clumsy mouthful beside 'I shall not want', with its liquid 'll' and 'w'. And no European translation has the perfect simplicity of the Hebrew: '*Yahwe ro-i, lo echsor.*'

If you cannot achieve the simplicity of the Hebrew original, you can always try for a quite different effect. Here are the first two verses of the psalm in de Saci's French Bible (Paris, 1759):

C'est le Seigneur qui me conduit: rien ne pourra me manquer.

Il m'a établi dans un lieu abondant en pâturages: il m'a élevé près d'une eau fortifiante.

This is translated from the Vulgate, not the Hebrew, but it is equally removed in tone from both. Nor does it bear any resemblance to the efficient German or the limpid English. The first verse reads like a line from a neo-classic tragedy. One can almost imagine someone inquiring of the heroine—Phèdre, say,

> Ah Phèdre, who leads you yonder through the dark?

and Phèdre answering,

> *C'est le Seigneur qui me conduit: rien ne pourra me manquer.*
> ('Tis the noble lord himself: I can lack nothing now.)

Further, 'eau fortifiante' suggests smelling salts, and the 'lieu abondant en pâturages' suggests Marie Antoinette playing at being a milkmaid rather than the realities of pastoral life in Palestine.

Every language, and sometimes every age, produces its own Bible. The Authorized Version, with which English-speaking readers are most familiar, represents the final successful attempt, after nearly a hundred years of continuous effort, to put the Bible into an English which does no violence to the natural genius of the language: the Hebrew Bible is in this version a work of English literature, and has all the assurance of an original work. One can see this assurance developing through the earlier versions. Here is the Authorized Version rendering of Joshua 24.26: 'And Joshua wrote these words in the book of the law of God, and took a great stone, and set it up there under an oak, that was by the sanctuary of the Lord.' This is a simple enough sentence, done in workmanlike prose, flowing naturally with nothing forced or artificial about it. Compare it with the version in Matthew's Bible of 1537: 'And Josua wrotte these wordes in the boke of the law of God, and toke a great stonne and pitched it on ende in the sayde place euen vnder an ocke that stode in the sanctuary of the Lorde.' There is a verbosity here, arising from the translator's anxiety to get in all of his original, and as a result the tone is somewhat forced, the passage is not yet properly acclimatized in English.

The Hebrew Bible, when properly domiciled in seventeenth century English (and seventeenth century English, which Dr Johnson in his *Dictionary* drew on as the great standard of English vocabulary, has become the norm of English religious speech), has a quality, a tone, even a meaning, as different from that of the original as from that of any other translation. Luther's Bible, which is the German equivalent of the English Authorized Version, gives a very different feel to the passage from Joshua which I have just quoted: '*Und Josua schrieb dies alles ins Gesetzbuch Gottes; und nahm einen grossen Stein und richtete ihn auf daselbst einer Eiche, die bey dem Heiligthum des Herrn war.*' How different in essential meaning is '*ins Gesetzbuch Gottes*' from 'in the book of the law of God', and again how different both these renderings are from the three stark Hebrew words, '*b'sefer torath elohim*'. The German is stark in its own way, but with the starkness of a report written by an efficient civil servant. The English, with its long run of monosyllables, each a word of elemental significance ('book', 'law', 'God',) has certain overtones of familiarity, or at least of simple customariness, for all its dignity. Yet Hebrew, Authorized Version and Luther are more like each other than either is to the English version of Monsignor Knox, who renders the phrase 'in the book which contained the divine law', adding a verb and changing a noun phrase into an adjective and in so doing giving a sophisticated abstractness to the whole notion.

A good test of the intention of any translator, or group of translators, is their rendering of the very first verse of the Hebrew Bible. The Authorized Version translates: 'In the beginning God created the heaven and the earth', and you might think that that was the only possible way to translate a very straightforward original (unless, perhaps, you decided to make 'heaven' plural, because of the form '*shamayim*'). Monsignor Knox, however, renders the sentence: 'God, at the beginning of time, created heaven and earth', which is a very different idiom indeed, an idiom of didactic elegance rather than of primitive simplicity. The French has something of Monsignor Knox's tone: '*Au commencement Dieu créa le ciel et la terre*', which becomes even more pronounced in the following verse: '*La terre était informe et toute nue; les ténèbres couvraient la face de l'abîme; et l'Esprit de Dieu était porté sur les eaux.*' The difference between this and the Authorized Version—'And the earth was without form, and void; and darkness was upon the face of the earth. And the spirit of God moved upon the face of the waters',—is the difference between Virgil and Homer, between the artificial epic and the natural epic. Indeed, such a phrase as '*les ténèbres couvraient la face de l'abîme*' might have come out of Victor Hugo. Luther is much more like the Authorized Version: '*Am Anfang schuf Gott Himmel und Erde. Und die Erde war wüste und leer, und es war finster auf der Tiefe; und der Geist Gottes schwebete auf dem Wasser.*'

The interesting word in the German is '*schwebete*' (hung in suspense, hovered) as a rendering of the Hebrew '*merachepheth*'. Both the Authorized Version and Douay render simply 'moved', while the Vulgate has '*ferebatur*' (was borne), translated in the French version as '*était porté*'. There is a long exegetical tradition, both Jewish and Christian, attached to this word. The great eleventh century Jewish commentator Solomon ben Isaac (generally known as Rashi) explains that the Throne of Glory was suspended in the air and hovered over the face of the waters, sustained by the breath (the Hebrew '*ruach*' means both 'breath' and 'spirit') of God and God's command, like a dove hovering over the nest. Basil and other patristic commentators render '*incubabat*', which again has the notion of brooding and hatching. And in *Paradise Lost* Milton (who knew Hebrew) wrote of the Holy Spirit:

> Thou from the first
> Wast present, and with mighty wings outspread
> Dove-like satst brooding on the vast Abyss
> And mad'st it pregnant.

Sir Thomas Browne, in his *Religio Medici*, has the sentence: 'That is that gentle heat that brooded on the waters, and in six days hatched the world.' And Andrew Marvell, in his poem 'The Waterfall', has the following lines:

> Unless that spirit lead his mind
> Which first upon thy face did move,
> And hatch'd all with his quickning love.

In the face of this strong tradition in favour of the notion of brooding and hatching as implied in '*merachepheth*', the Authorized Version translators stuck to the simple 'moved'. The case is interesting, for as a rule the use of biblical ideas of this kind in English literature after 1611 came through the Authorized Version. There was, in fact, no word which would express in English the varied suggestions attached to the original, and rather than do violence to the language, the translators kept the simple and general word, 'moved'. It is testimony to the store they set by simple and idiomatic English.

Consider another example. Most of us know the opening of the 40th chapter of Isaiah from Handel's magnificent setting of 'Comfort ye, comfort ye, my people', in his *Messiah*. The whole of that passage in English has a grand cadence to it, rising to a climax on 'her iniquity is pardoned' and dying away immediately afterwards to a perfect close. (Handel, who wanted to end on the climax, left out the closing phrase.)

> Comfort ye, comfort ye my people, saith your God.
> Speak ye comfortably to Jerusalem, and cry unto her, that her warfare is accomplished, that her iniquity is pardoned: for she has received of the Lord's hand double for all her sins.

The meaning of the fine opening phrase is not clear. It seems to mean 'Comfort yourselves, my people', but in fact the 'ye' is not reflexive and the sense is, 'Comfort my people (says God to the prophet)'. The Authorized Version translators risked ambiguity, not this time in order to keep the individual words simple, but for the sake of the cadence. (There is even some reason for believing that they deliberately tried to imitate the rhythm of the original Hebrew, and put in the ambiguous 'ye' so that the phrase would correspond in its cadence with the Hebrew '*nachamu, nachamu ami*'.) The Vulgate does have the reflexive sense; there God is calling on the people to comfort themselves: '*Consolamini,*

consolamini popule meus, dicit Deus vester,' which the French renders: *'Consolez-vous, mon peuple, consolez-vous, dit votre Dieu.'* The ceremonial note of the English disappears in the utilitarian Vulgate (though the Latin has a sonority of its own) and, even more completely, in the elegant French. The French, indeed, sounds to English ears rather like a ticket agent announcing politely to a crowd of customers that all his tickets are sold out and they must comfort themselves as best they can. Luther (following the Hebrew meaning) renders: *'Tröstet, tröstet, mein Volk, spricht euer Gott'*, which is forceful and effective. The German continues: *'Redet mit Jerusalem freundlich und prediget ihr, dass ihre Ritterschaft ein Ende hat, denn ihre Missethat ist vergeben; denn sie hat zweyfältiges empfangen von der Hand des Herrn, um alle ihre Sünde.'* This sounds a bit like a list of instructions issued in triplicate to subordinate officials, but it has good prose rhythm and a fine solidity. Solidity is perhaps the characteristic quality of Luther's Bible. The English Bible, at least in the Authorized Version, has a flowing limpidity combined with occasional ritual overtones; the French Bible is elegant and polished and discreet; the German Bible has a solid middle-class ring about it: it is a book for substantial *bürgerliche* readers who stand no nonsense. A simple Bible, a polite Bible, a bourgeois Bible—and the Hebrew Bible is none of these.

Another test is the famous and difficult one from the last chapter of Ecclesiastes. The Authorized Version reads:

In the day when the keepers of the house shall tremble, and the strong men shall bow themselves, and the grinders cease because they are few, and those that look out of the windows be darkened,

And the doors shall be shut in the streets, when the sound of the grinding is low, and he shall rise up at the voice of the bird, and all the daughters of music shall be brought low;

Also when they shall be afraid of that which is high, and fears shall be in the way, and the almond tree shall flourish, and the grasshopper shall be a burden, and desire shall fail: because man goeth to his long home, and the mourners go about the streets:

Or ever the silver cord be loosed, or the golden bowl be broken, or the pitcher be broken at the fountain, or the wheel broken at the cistern.

o

Douay, rendering literally from the Vulgate, reads:

When the keepers of the house shall tremble, and the strong men shall stagger, and the grinders shall be idle in a small number, and they that look through the holes shall be darkened:

And they shall shut the doors in the street, when the grinder's voice shall be low, and they shall rise up at the voice of the bird, and all the daughters of music shall grow deaf.

And they shall fear high things, and they shall be afraid in the way, the almond tree shall flourish, the locust shall be made fat, and the caper-tree shall be destroyed: because man shall go into the house of his eternity, and the mourners shall go round about in the street.

Before the silver cord be broken, and the golden fillet shrink back, and the pitcher be crushed at the fountain, and the wheel be broken upon the cistern.

The obscurity is equal in both versions. The Authorized Version makes capital out of the obscurity by choosing words which, although simple in themselves, have overtones of vague suggestion. 'And all the daughters of music shall be brought low,' is more suggestive than the matter-of-fact 'shall grow deaf' of the Vulgate, and 'or ever the silver cord be loosed' more evocative than 'before the silver cord be broken'. Douay tries to bully the true sense out of the words by rendering each one with literal correctness; the Authorized Version, while as literal as it can be, chooses words which suggest meanings even when the precise significance is obscure. Thus in the Authorized Version Ecclesiastes is an English prose poem, and in the Douay translation Ecclesiastes is a very competent rendering of a difficult Vulgate text.

Dr Robert Gordis, in his edition and translation of Ecclesiastes published in New York in 1945, gives us the modern scholar's view of what the Hebrew really means:

In the day when the watchmen of the house tremble,
And the strong men are bent.
And the grinding maidens cease, for they are few,
And the ladies peering through the lattices grow dim.
When the doubled doors on the street are shut,
And the voice of the mill becomes low.
One wakes at the sound of a bird,

And all the daughters of song are laid low.
When one fears to climb a height,
And terrors lurk in a walk.

The hair grows white, like ripe almond-blossom,
The frame, bent like a grasshopper, becomes a burden,
And the caper-berry can no longer stimulate desire.

So man goes to his eternal home
While the hired mourners walk about in the street. . . .

This certainly clears up many obscurities. Much of the sug-
gestiveness is gone, but we really do know what the passage is all
about. To read this after reading the Authorized Version is like
looking at a distant mountain view after the mist has cleared and
the sun has come out; in the mist it seemed wonderful and
romantic, but we could not make out the individual features of
the scene at all. Clear and simple though the Authorized Version
so often is, readers respond more often than they think to the
vague thrills of the mist-enwrapped view rather than to the
details of the landscape. (One could go through the Book of
Job, for example, and point out scores of phrases which, in the
Authorized Version, have had an immense influence on the development of English religious thought—*every one of them mis-
understood*. But this is partly due to mistranslation of a difficult
text.)

But to return to Ecclesiastes. Consider now de Saci's French
translation of the passage I have been discussing:

*lorsque les gardes de la maison commenceront à trembler; que les hommes les plus
forts s'ebranleront; que celles qui avaient accoutumé de moudre, seront réduites en
petit nombre et deviendront oisives, et que ceux qui regardaient par les trous, seront
couverts de ténèbres;*
   *quand on fermera les portes de la rue, quand la voix de celle qui avait accoutumé de
moudre sera faible, qu'on se levera au chant de l'oiseau et que les filles de l'harmonie
deviendront sourdes; . . .*
   *avant que la chaine d'argent soit rompue, que la bandelette d'or se retire, que la
cruche se brise sur la fontaine, et que la roue se rompe sur la citerne.*

The rhythms here are not dissimilar from those of the Authorized Version—they derive from the grouping of the phrases in

the original Hebrew, and carry over in some degree into all translations—but there is a tone of secular elegance about the French which derives from some profound quality of the French literary language. And while the German retains the note of romantic suggestion, it seems more solidly grounded in physical occurrences than it does in the English:

> ... *Und die Thüren auf der Gasse geschlossen werden, dass die Stimme der Müllerin leise wird, und erwachet, wenn der Vogel singet, und sich bücken alle Töchter des Gesangs....*

There is something about '*Vogel*' that is lacking in 'bird', and a phrase such as '*und erwachet, wenn der Vogel singet*' suggests a characteristic phase of German romantic poetry, while 'and he shall rise up at the voice of the bird' (every word a monosyllable) has an elemental folk feeling. The whole German rendering of this passage is to the English of the Authorized Version rather what the heavy magic of Heine's '*Das ist der alte Märchenwald*' is to the less sophisticated mystery of one of Wordsworth's 'Lucy' poems:

> Rolled round in earth's diurnal course
> With rocks and stones and trees.

There are, of course, other translations of the Hebrew Bible besides English, French and German, each of which has its own special flavour. The Italian, for example, sounds curiously un-scriptural to those (and they probably include most non-Italian readers of the language) who have got used to Dante as the standard Italian example of a serious, formal, yet simple imagery and vocabulary, and it is always a shock to find that the Italian Bible sounds much more like the *Decameron* than like the *Divina Commedia*. There is no limit to the comparing of different trans-lations of the Hebrew Bible or to the different kinds of passages—narrative, prophetic, lyrical, gnomic—whose varying appearance in different languages can be discussed. The Hebrew Bible is the source of many different Bibles, each drawing out some quality in the original which would not at first necessarily strike the reader of the Hebrew text; each is biblical in its own way, yet none can claim to reflect wholly *the* Hebrew Bible. But then what '*the* Hebrew Bible' is can never be fully stated: it, too, has been a different book to different readers and to different generations.

There are other, and perhaps more profound, questions to be asked about the translation of the Bible besides the literary ones. Have different religions, and different denominations, managed to produce renderings which convey a significance peculiar to their own beliefs? This is certainly true of some key passages, for example, in the prophets and in the Book of Job. For I know that my redeemer liveth, and that he shall stand at the latter day upon the earth', is the Authorized Version rendering of Job. 19.25, and the reference is considered to be to the coming of Christ. The American Jewish translation of 1917 renders: 'But as for me, I know that my Redeemer liveth, and that He will witness at the last upon the dust', where the Redeemer is, of course, God. In fact, however, the Hebrew word '*goali*' probably has a legal significance: much of the Book of Job is couched in legal terminology, with Job demanding to know what offence he is charged with and asking for a defending counsel to take up his cause. In this verse he seems to be expressing confidence that eventually a defending attorney will stand up for him (against the satan, who is not the Devil but the angel charged with public prosecutions, as it were, by God). Both Jewish and Christian interpreters have taken a more general, and indeed a more impressive, meaning out of the text, but in doing so have obscured the significance of much of its characteristic imagery. This is in interesting case of the development of religious ideas changing the meaning of the text.

A more obvious case is Isaiah 7.14, where the traditional Christian rendering was for centuries: 'Behold, a virgin shall conceive . . . ' and the passage was taken as a prophecy of the virgin birth of Christ. Modern Christian scholarship recognizes that 'virgin' is a deliberate mistranslation of the Hebrew, and the American Revised Standard Version reads 'Behold, a young woman shall conceive', in agreement with Jewish render-

ings. Then there is Isaiah 14.12, translated in the Authorized
Version as: 'How art thou fallen from heaven, O Lucifer, son of
the morning', in accordance with the traditional Christian view
that this is a reference to the fall of Satan. But the Hebrew word
'*helel*' means 'morning star' (rendered in Latin as 'Lucifer',
'light-bearer') and the prophet is using the term figuratively for
Babylon, which had fallen from its position of power and radiance;
the Babylonians worshipped Istar, the morning star. The American Jewish translation renders: 'How art thou fallen from heaven,
O day-star son of the morning!' while the American Revised
Standard Version renders similarly: 'How you are fallen from
heaven, O Day Star, son of Dawn!' Modern scholars, whatever
their religious beliefs, tend to put accuracy before doctrinal considerations, with the result that there is much less difference
between Jewish and Christian renderings of the Hebrew Bible
today than there was three centuries ago.

More interesting, perhaps, than differences in the rendering of
individual words and phrases are the doctrinal implications of a
translation as a whole. As long as the Catholic Church did not
believe in vernacular translations, and held even the Vulgate to
be what might almost be called a technical work for the professional churchman, there was no attempt to give grace and
polish to biblical renderings. The mediaeval Catholic layman got
his knowledge of the Bible indirectly through sermons and other
intermediary presentations by priests. And when the climate of
opinion eventually moved the Roman Catholic Church to bring
out its own translation, at the beginning of the seventeenth
century, it produced a flinty literal rendering from the Vulgate.
In direct contrast, left-wing Protestantism believed in the Bible
as the only true source of the Christian religion and strove to
make vernacular versions available to all. But the belief in the
literal verbal inspiration of the Bible which accompanied this
attitude led to the Bible being regarded as a sort of divine reference book, to be quoted, regardless of the general context of any
given passage, as a series of separable texts, each with its precise
and literal significance. This produced no more feeling of literary

style than the Catholic belief in the professional and technical nature of the Bible. It was left for the Anglican Church, which believed in vernacular translation without going so far as the bibliolatry of the Puritans, and considered the Bible as a monument of divine eloquence rather than as a divine reference book, to sponsor Bible translation as a work of literature as well as a work of theology. The Authorized Version, more than any other biblical translation in any European language, was a literary rendering; it was not a 'crib' but a work of literature in its own right, written in a style which generations of translators had gradually developed as the appropriate English style for that kind of work. It is interesting that now that the Catholic Church has long regarded vernacular translations as perfectly proper, the modern Catholic translator tries hard to be literary rather than technical in his rendering. Monsignor Knox's translation of the Old Testament is the most 'literary' ever produced; it is written in a deliberately artificial style, with carefully modulated rhythms, paragraphs rising and falling in studied cadence, and sentences flowing in a manner reminiscent of the later George Moore:

Thus Noemi left her dwelling place; and when she set foot on the road that led to the domain of Juda, she turned to her companions, and bade either go back to her own mother's house; May the Lord shew kindness to you, she said, as you have shewn kindness to the memory of the dead, and to me; may you live at ease with new husbands. And with that she gave them a parting kiss. But no, they wept aloud, and declared they would go on in her company, to the home of her own people. Come with me, my daughters? she answered. Nay, you must go back. I have no more sons in my womb to wed you; go back, daughters, and leave me; I am an old woman, past the age for marrying.

This is a remarkable accomplishment, and not merely a stylistic one, for there is much scholarship distilled in each turn of phrase; yet one cannot help feeling that this is almost too literary, that the churchman converted to the view that the Bible which is a basic technical document of his faith is also a supreme work of literature is demonstrating rather too flamboyantly his new state of mind.

To most English-speaking readers, the literary style, or styles, rather, for the Bible has many, made popular by the Authorized

Version seem to be most appropriate, because they are the most familiar, and the problem is to make the Bible more accurate without losing that cherished traditional flavour. The Revised Standard Version, which is a revision of a revision of the Authorized Version, retains some of its magic but it has inevitably also lost much, in its striving after greater accuracy. The American Jewish translation, though it called itself 'a new translation', kept the basic idiom of the Authorized Version more than might have been expected. (For example, it preserved the misleading 'ye' in 'Comfort ye, comfort ye, my people', where the Revised Standard Version has, 'Comfort, comfort my people says your God'.) What do we now demand of an English translation of the Bible? Surely a translation which is both accurate and graceful, based on the soundest available scholarship and expressed in fluent, idiomatic and dignified English. Such a translation is bound to abandon even more of the Authorized Version tradition than either the Revised Version or the Revised Standard Version has done; yet to go to the other extreme and deliberately cut off the poetic overtones of the original (as Dr Gordon sometimes does in his version of Ecclesiastes, rendering, for example, 'Cast thy bread upon the waters' as 'send your goods overseas', which is a dull paraphrase, not a translation) is useless self-denial. A scholarly literary translation, deriving without prejudice or preconception from the best scholarship wherever it is found, and creating its own style as it moves according to the literary forms of the original, about which so much new knowledge is now available, is a desideratum for Jew and Gentile alike. But the problem is not as easy as this. The Bible is not only what modern scholarship holds the text to mean; it is also what the text has meant to generations of devout readers. Modern scholarship, after all, is concerned to reconstruct the meaning originally intended by the first writers or compilers of the text, but that meaning cannot have been constant even for those early writers. The simplest lyric poem, as every modern critic knows, takes on new meanings with each sensitive reading, and how much more so must a work like the Bible! Can modern scholarship in the

English-speaking world conceive of a translation which, while accurate and literary, manages at the same time to convey in its idiom something of what the Hebrew Bible has meant to generations of readers, both Jewish and Christian? The ideal may sound Utopian, but it is surely a task worth attempting.

RELIGION, POETRY AND THE 'DILEMMA' OF THE MODERN WRITER[1]

NEARLY THREE HUNDRED YEARS AGO JOHN MILTON, pondering in his age and blindness over the mysteries of human fate and thinking doubtless of the bitter frustrations and disappointments of his own life, put into the mouth of his hero Samson an almost desperate questioning of God's ways with man:

> God of our Fathers, what is man!
> That thou towards him with hand so various,
> Or might I say contrarious,
> Temper'st thy providence through his short course,
> Not evenly, as thou rul'st
> The Angelic orders and inferior creatures mute,
> Irrational and brute.
> Nor do I name of men the common rout,
> That wand'ring loose about
> Grow up and perish, as the summer fly,
> Heads without name no more remember'd,
> But such as thou hast solemnly elected,
> With gifts and graces eminently adorn'd
> To some great work, thy glory,
> And people's safety, which in part they effect:
> Yet toward these, thus dignifi'd, thou oft,
> Amidst thir highth of noon,
> Changest thy countenance and thy hand, with no regard
> Of highest favours past
> From thee on them, or them to thee of service.

The cry is a familiar one in the history of literature. Why do the wicked prosper and the virtuous suffer? It was a very real question for Milton as he sat in darkness and heard the bells ring out the end of all his political hopes, the end of his dream of being the

[1] Delivered at the Institute for Religious and Social Studies, New York, on 31st January, 1950.

poet and prophet of a new and regenerate England; as he heard
the celebrators of the restoration of Charles II,

The Sons

Of Belial, flown with insolence and wine,

roistering in the streets outside. 'Why standest Thou afar off, O
Lord? Why hidest Thou thyself in times of trouble? . . . For the
wicked boasteth of his heart's desire, and the covetous vaunteth
himself, though he contemn the Lord.' So the Hebrew psalmist
had long before asked the same question. It was Job's question,
too. 'Behold, I cry out of wrong, but I am not heard: I cry aloud,
but there is no justice.' 'Wherefore do the wicked live, become
old, yea, are mighty in power?'

This old question of theodicy, of the justice of God, or, if we
prefer, of the way in which the universe is organized so far as it
affects man, has long been a central theme in literature. The
answer is generally given in terms of attitude rather than of logic.
Job's problem disappears in a note of wonder—wonder at the
grandeur and immensity of creation. The psalmist finds refuge in
faith: 'Better is a little that the righteous hath than the abundance
of many wicked. . . . For the wicked shall perish, and the enemies
of the Lord shall be as the fat of lambs—they shall pass away in
smoke, they shall pass away.' The Prometheus of Aeschylus, on
the other hand, strikes a note of heroic self-confidence—ἐσορᾷς
μ'ὡς ἔκδικα πάσχω 'behold me, how unjust are my sufferings'.
These are very different answers to a single question, but they are
all *literary* answers rather than philosophical solutions. By this
I mean that the answers have force and meaning in virtue of
their poetic expression, of the place they take in the myth or
fable or situation presented, and of the effectiveness with which
they project a mood. Job's solution is no answer if detached from
its eloquent expression and paraphrased as a philosophical position.
Such a procedure would make Job sound merely pusillanimous,
just as it would make the psalmist a naïve self-deceiver and
Prometheus a futile exhibitionist. In other words, we see in
earlier literature a religious (or mythological) tradition and a
literary tradition mutually supporting each other, each depend-

ing on the other for full richness of expression and significance.

Let me try to explain this point more fully by turning again to Milton. We know that the justification of the ways of God to men, the professed theme of *Paradise Lost*, was a major pre-occupation of Milton's throughout his life. We see the problem first stated in 'Lycidas', a poem ostensibly lamenting the death of a young friend who died before he was able to fulfil his promise as poet and teacher but actually concerned with the larger problem of the ambitious idealist in an uncertain and arbitrary world. What is the use of dedicating oneself to a future of service to humanity (in Milton's case, through the writing of poetry 'doctrinal and exemplary to a nation') if one might be cut off at any moment, before even one's period of self-preparation was completed?

> Alas! What boots it with uncessant care
> To tend the homely slighted Shepherd's trade,
> And strictly meditate the thankless Muse?
> Were it not better done as others use,
> To sport with Amaryllis in the shade,
> Or with the tangles of Neaera's hair?

The question is turned this way and that throughout the poem, and every kind of traditional answer suggested before the real answer emerges in the mood and tone of the conclusion:

> Thus sang the uncouth Swain to th' Oaks and rills,
> While the still morn went out with Sandals gray.
> He touch't the tender stops of various Quills,
> With eager thought warbling his Doric lay:
> And now the Sun had stretch'd out all the hills,
> And now was dropt into the Western bay;
> At last he rose, and twich't his Mantle blue:
> Tomorrow to fresh Woods, and Pastures new.

Like God's answer to Job in the whirlwind, this is not a logical disposal of the problem, but the distillation of a mood in the light of which the poet is able to carry on. The quiet sunrise which proclaims a new day brings a note of humility and acceptance to the poet, who now describes himself as an 'uncouth swain'—that is, an unknown or unlearned rustic—and with that comes the determination to do what one can while one can, to enjoy such beauty as life grants and to turn one's hand to what lies to be done without too much speculation on possible accidents: 'Tomorrow to fresh Woods, and Pastures new' has the sound both of peace and of purpose.

When his blindness came, some fifteen years later, Milton again raised the question of God's justice in so dealing with him:

> When I consider how my light is spent,
>   Ere half my days, in this dark world and wide,
>   And that one Talent which is death to hide,
>   Lodg'd with me useless, though my Soul more bent
> To serve therewith my Maker, and present
>   My true account, lest he returning chide;
>   Doth God exact day-labour, light denied,
>   I fondly ask?

But Patience replies, and stills the poet's questioning with a picture of various services rendered by different men actively or passively, God being best served by those 'who best bear his mild yoke'; and the poem ebbs quietly away on the concluding line: 'They also serve who only stand and wait.' Has this answer vindicated God's justice? No; but it has projected a mood in the light of which life seems more interesting, more significant, and more tolerable.

In *Paradise Lost* the justification of the ways of God to men is developed on a more deliberate and even grandiose scale. On the surface Milton, by telling the story of man's fall in Eden, is showing that man fell by a deliberate abuse of his free-will, so that he has himself and not God to blame, and also pointing out that God provided a scheme of redemption which would enable those who made the effort to attain to a state far above that from which Adam fell. Thus man deserved what he got by deliberately doing evil, but God in His mercy brought good out of evil by the Christian scheme of redemption. This is the cold, paraphrasable message of *Paradise Lost*, but it is neither the true meaning of the poem nor the real way in which Milton justified the ways of God to men. The real justification of God's dealings with men lies in the implicit contrast between the ideal idleness of the Garden of Eden and the changing and challenging world of moral effort and natural beauty which resulted from the Fall. This argument is presented obliquely and continuously through mood and imagery: when the beauty of Eve in her unfallen state is described in terms of classical myths which give an atmosphere of ineffable loveliness to the whole picture we get a sense of values which can only emerge in the fallen human imagination. The postlapsarian world (to use the theological term) may lack the bliss of Eden, with its perpetual spring and its freedom from the curse of earning one's daily bread by the sweat of one's brow, but the procession of the seasons which was part of the punishment of the Fall provides some of Milton's most moving imagery, while symbols of rustic labour with its beauty and dignity contradict or at least modify the explicit statement that work was imposed on man as a curse. Even prelapsarian nature, ideal nature before the Fall, can only be made desirable in our eyes in terms drawn from a postlapsarian consciousness, just as good can only be made significant in terms of moral effort against known evil—evil known only in man's fallen state.

The real theme of *Paradise Lost* is man's essential and tragic ambiguity, illustrated in the fact that love is bound up with selfishness (as when Adam follows Eve's example in eating the forbidden apple because he cannot live without her); that good is bound up with evil; that the beauty which adorns the earth as it passes from seed-time to harvest, from the white of winter to the gay colours of spring, is bound up with change, and change, which means growth, also means decay; that the rich pattern of different human civilizations as Milton passes them under review with all the magic of exotic and musical place names and the excitement of geographical discovery was made possible by the curse of Babel; that the dignity and beauty of rustic labour, the basis of some of Milton's finest similes, is the other side of the law which decrees starvation and suffering for those who can find no land or no work. In the personal outburst at the beginning of the third book, what the blind Milton most laments are those

sights of seasonal change which resulted from the loss of Eden's
perpetual spring:

> Thus with the Year
> Seasons return, but not to me returns
> Day, or the sweet approach of Ev'n or Morn,
> Or sight of vernal bloom, or Summer's Rose,
> Or flocks, or herds, or human face divine;
> But cloud instead, and ever-during dark
> Surrounds me, from the cheerful ways of men
> Cut off. . . .

They are 'the cheerful ways of men' still, in spite of 'the sons of
Belial flown with insolence and wine'. And the curse that 'in the
sweat of thy face shalt thou eat bread' can make possible the
imagery of such lines as these:

> As one who long in populous City pent,
> Where Houses thick and Sewers annoy the Air,
> Forth issuing on a Summer's Morn to breathe
> Among the pleasant Villages and Farms
> Adjoin'd, from each thing met conceives delight,
> The smell of Grain, or tedded Grass, or Kine,
> Or Dairy, each rural sight, each rural sound. . . .

This is how Milton justifies the ways of God to men—by
showing through the emotional pattern of his great poem how
everything worth while that we can conceive of is made possible
by the results of the Fall. Again, this is not a logical but a poetic
solution to his problem, like the solution of *Job* and of the
psalmist. A religious tradition and a poetic sensibility co-operated
to produce an effect which needed both but which was wholly
produced by neither.

In *Samson Agonistes* Milton handled this problem for the last
time. Samson the hero was brought pitifully low, apparently
deserted by God, and he recovered only to destroy himself with
his enemies. Samson's moral recovery is a main theme of the
play, but we know from the beginning that there is no going back
to the young heroic Samson doing great deeds for his country.
He recovers only to die. Is that fair or just on God's part? Is that
the only answer to his great cry: 'God of our Fathers, what is

man!'? No: the real answer is an aesthetic one; it lies in the
'katharsis' which the tragedy produces. The chorus sums up the
significance of the action in the well-known conclusion:

> His servants he with new acquist
> Of true experience from this great event
> With peace and consolation hath dismist,
> And calm of mind, all passion spent.

This is Milton's interpretation of the Aristotelian 'katharsis', the
purgation of the emotions through pity and fear, which is
Aristotle's view of the function of tragedy. The calm of mind
produced by the tragic 'katharsis' is at the same time the mood
which accepts God's dealings with men as just. At the end of his
life Milton completely and finally reconciled religion and aesthetics, the Christian and the humanist, by justifying the ways of
God to men in terms of a mood distilled aesthetically by tragedy.
What Professor Douglas Bush has called 'the dilemma of a sacred
poet and a Puritan bred in the congenial air of Renaissance
classicism' was resolved by applying a classical notion of the
function of tragedy to the solution of Job's question.

What I am trying to show is that the interplay between religious
and aesthetic impulses has always been fruitful in literature and
that an appreciation of it is independent of the reader's creed or
philosophical system. One could demonstrate a similar interplay
in Dante and Shakespeare as well as in the Greek dramatists. But
I must hasten on, to ask the questions that we are most concerned
with here. Has the contemporary literary artist anything to learn
from this? Has the disintegration of community of belief which
most observers agree to be a characteristic of our present age
altered the situation so radically that the kind of thing done by
Aeschylus and Dante and Milton—posing questions suggested by
religion and answering them in literary or aesthetic terms—
becomes impossible? Is there an unbridgeable gap between the
past of literature and the contemporary literary artist?

These are not easy questions to answer, and they certainly
cannot be adequately answered here. I am all too conscious of
the dangers of facile generalization and of the ease with which a

showy thesis can be developed by the manipulation of an arbitrary selection of examples. As I try to cast my mind's eye over the vast array of works of literary art from the Book of Job to a poem by Mr Eliot and think of the numerous changes in taste and attitude, the immense diversity of works and of writers, and the vastly different conscious objectives which different artists have set themselves, I can see how tentative and inadequate any answer to the questions I have raised must be even if I were much more of a polymath than I can allow myself to claim. But in the realm of critical ideas nothing significant can be achieved without boldness; so, having listed the dangers, let me now proceed to ignore them.

What does the loss of a common background of religious attitudes and symbols mean to literature? The problem has agitated poets for over a century. Nearly a hundred years ago Matthew Arnold, in his poem 'Dover Beach', expressed a view which is central to our present discontents. Looking out over the Straits of Dover on a calm, moonlit night he listened to the splash of the waves on the shore and thought how Sophocles had heard in that sound 'the turbid ebb and flow of human misery'. He continued:

> The Sea of Faith
> Was once, too, at the full, and round earth's shore
> Lay like the folds of a bright girdle furl'd.
> But now I only hear
> Its melancholy, long, withdrawing roar,
> Retreating, to the breath
> Of the night-wind down the vast edges drear
> And naked shingles of the world.
> Ah, love, let us be true
> To one another! for the world, which seems
> To lie before us like a land of dreams,
> So various, so beautiful, so new,
> Hath really neither joy, nor love, nor light,
> Nor certitude, nor peace, nor help for pain;
> And we are here as on a darkling plain
> Swept with confused alarms of struggle and flight,
> Where ignorant armies clash by night.

P

This mood of what Professor Trilling has called 'controlled self-pity', this elegiac note which enables the poet to face a world without faith, represents a rather different use of poetic devices from that which we find at the conclusion of Job or even in Milton. The earlier writers, it is true, projected a mood, which is what Arnold is doing, but it was a mood which enabled man to achieve new equanimity and go about his business untroubled. In Job, in the older Greek dramatists, in Dante, in many of Shakespeare's tragedies, and in Milton, a 'katharsis' is achieved which frees writer and reader alike from inhibitive brooding. One might even venture a rash generalization and say that these older works freed man for action, while much romantic literature consigns man to perpetual introspection. In fact, this might be if not an adequate at least a workable definition of the two terms, 'classical' and 'romantic'. When Milton grows impatient with God and his destiny he writes a poem which resolves his doubts through projecting a mood of acceptance and preparation for action. Keats, concerned with the same fear that haunted Milton in 'Lycidas', afraid, that is, lest he might die 'before my pen has gleaned my teeming brain', found an answer in pure introspection:

> When I behold upon the night's starred face
> Huge cloudy symbols of a high romance,
> And think that I may never live to trace
> Their shadows with the magic hand of chance;
> And when I feel, fair creature of an hour,
> That I shall never look upon thee more,
> Never have relish in the fairy power
> Of unreflecting love—then on the shore
> Of the wide world I stand alone, and think
> Till love and fame to nothingness do sink.

How different this is from 'Tomorrow to fresh Woods, and Pastures new' or even 'They also serve who only stand and wait'.

Can we go so far as to say that an art with a religious background can achieve 'katharsis' more effectively than one without one? The Romantic poets, who substituted introspective plangency for religious assurance, often saw the function of art quite differently from the way in which Dante or Shakespeare saw it.

Differences between Dante the mediaeval Catholic and Shakespeare the tolerant humanist are numerous and profound enough,
but they are both religious in the sense in which I am using the
term, a sense in which Keats and Tennyson and Matthew Arnold
are not religious. The ending of *Hamlet* or *Macbeth*, with the
reasserting of the norm and the preparation for daily activity is,
in the largest symbolic sense, comparable to the ending of Dante's
Inferno: 'e quindi uscimmo a riveder le stelle' (And thence we came
forth to see again the stars).

The release from troubled introspection into action is, however,
very far from being the objective or the achievement of, say,
Tennyson's 'Break, break, break', Arnold's 'Dover Beach'—we
can all add indefinitely to the list—which cultivate that very state
from which the classical 'katharsis' (I am using the term now
widely and symbolically) seeks to relieve writer and reader. The
cultivation of this state is not, it should be added, peculiar to the
English Romantic poets: there is, in fact, no more perfect example
of it than in that remarkable sonnet 'L'Infinito' by the Italian poet
Leopardi in which a mood of complete surrender to trance-like
contemplation is deliberately cultivated:

> Così tra questa
> *Immensità s'annega il pensier mio:*
> *E il naufragar m'e dolce in questo mare.*

> Thus amid this vastness my thought is drowned,
> And shipwreck is sweet to me in such a sea.

The mood of 'Dover Beach' or 'Break, break, break' is not, of
course, uniquely Romantic: it is not the mood so much as the use
to which it is put in the poem that differentiates Arnold's description of the waves breaking on the lonely shore from similar
descriptions in the classics—from say, the picture of Achilles in
the twenty-third book of the *Iliad* mourning for his dead comrade
Patroclus as he lay ἐν καθαρῷ ὅθι κύματ' ἐπ' ἠϊόνος κλύζεσκον
(in a lonely place where the waves plashed upon the shore).
That is one of the most evocative—if you like, romantic—lines
in Greek literature, but its purpose is not to exploit the temporary

mood of plangent meditation but to prepare the way for the final 'katharsis' of Achilles' anger and grief.

Nevertheless, as Matthew Arnold saw as clearly as anybody, a mood of self-pity, however controlled and beautifully expressed, cannot for long remain a literary norm. In England, the mid and late nineteenth century poets played all possible variations on it and its potentialities were soon exhausted. A classical reaction set in in the second decade of the present century, with T. E. Hulme calling on the poets, in a misquoted line from the seventeenth century dramatist John Webster, to 'end your moan and come away'. Hulme advocated, and prophesied, a period of 'dry, hard, classical verse'. The cry was taken up by Eliot and others, and a revolution in poetic taste was achieved within a generation. 'The poet', wrote Eliot in 1917, 'has not a "personality" to express, but a particular medium, which is only a medium and not a personality, in which impressions and experiences combine in peculiar and unexpected ways.' But in fact neither Eliot nor any other significant poet of our time was content to make of poetry the mere arranging of impressions and experiences in peculiar and unexpected ways. If the classical poets—again using the terms widely and symbolically—had created literature by exploiting the impact of personality on a religious tradition, and the Romantic poets had exploited personality by itself, what was the modern poet to do, who shared the Romantic poets' confusion about religion and at the same time repudiated their exploitation of personality? They could, of course, take Voltaire's position, and say that if God did not exist it would be necessary to create him, and some of the arguments brought forward by Mr Eliot in his prose writing almost suggest that at times this is the line that he took. In his later poetry, however, from 'Ash Wednesday' on, Mr Eliot has been concerned with the impact of personality on a religious tradition, and in the Four Quartets he has been remarkably successful in distilling a mood in the light of which the religious position becomes meaningful if not logically demonstrable. And that, as we have seen, is the way classical art works.

But Mr Eliot's solution is not wholly satisfactory, and certainly not one that can be successfully employed by others, because, however sincerely his religious emotion is felt (and it is not for the literary critic to presume to judge that), the materials it works on are academic and its documents not central to any religious tradition. (Saint John of the Cross, for example, is a more fundamental source of imagery and structure in many of his poems than the Bible or the prayer book, and there is a curious air of coy connoisseurship about his handling of religious documents.) There is, in fact, however much Mr Eliot may repudiate personality in poetry, a highly idiosyncratic personality at work here whose solutions of common problems are *not* really helpful to others, for all the influence of his merely technical procedures on younger poets.

The conflict between faith and reason, between religion and experience, is not the modern problem our contemporary writers have to solve. The more vital the religious tradition, the more real and fruitful has that conflict been: it is, as I have tried to show, in Job, the Greek dramatists, *Paradise Lost*, as well as in Dante and Shakespeare. The modern problem is to find a valid tradition with reference to which literary artists can pit their personality with poetic profit. There is always a gap between a traditional formulation of values and individual experience, and across that gap sparks the poetic insight. You can sometimes get away with making your own tradition, as in a sense Eliot has, for his Christian tradition is not, I venture to think, identical with any of the main forms of the Christian tradition in Western civilization, but there is something both artificial and dangerous about this: for how can there be tension between your personal experience and the impersonal tradition, when the impersonal tradition is something you have discovered or created for yourself? Yet there are ways out of this dilemma—dangerous ways, and not always imitable ways, but nevertheless ways which have on occasion been successfully taken. Let me glance briefly at two of these, that taken by W. B. Yeats and that taken by Dylan Thomas.

There is a well-known statement of his early position made by Yeats in his autobiographical work, *The Trembling of the Veil*:

I am very religious, and deprived by Huxley and Tyndall, whom I detested, of the simple-minded religion of my childhood, I had made a new religion, almost an infallible church of poetic tradition, of a fardel of stories, and of personages, and of emotions, inseparable from their first expression, passed on from generation to generation by poets and painters with some help from philosophers and theologians. . . .

If this was all that Yeats had done, he would not have become the great poet we know him to have been. For to repudiate the religious tradition and to put in its place a tradition derived from the reflection of that repudiated tradition in art and philosophy is neither logical nor helpful. What is religion but the primary expression of those basic myths and values which in turn are used by artists in the way I have tried to suggest? The genuine agnostic can understand and appreciate a religious tradition in life and art, and understand how the tensions between that tradition and individual personality have helped to produce great art, but he certainly cannot go to that art and pick out from it a religious tradition unacceptable to him in its explicit form, though Yeats was not alone in thinking that this could be done. What makes Yeats's statement of his problem so interesting is not the solution he suggests but the awareness of the problem that it shows. He needed a religious tradition to work with, but he could not accept any tradition specifically denominated as religious.

We know, of course, what he eventually did. He built for himself out of the oddest and most miscellaneous material a symbolic system with reference to which he could organize his poetic expression. But if it was his own system, created by himself, how could he set himself over against it to develop those tensions between individual insight and impersonal system which I have suggested are the most significant way in which a poet can use a tradition? The answer is that the conflict in Yeats's poems is not between himself and the system, but between two aspects of the system, which, being a dialectical one, a balancing of opposites, afforded him all the tensions he could handle. The system itself, with its lunar phases and towers and spinning tops and spiral staircases, was based on the perpetual merging of opposites. As you climb the spiral staircase you move through all the points on the circumference of a circle, but when you reach the top of the spiral, which is a circle with an infinitely small circumference, you are at all points in the circumference simultaneously. Yeats's poetic imagery had been from the beginning dominated by a conflict of opposites; in his early poetry we find perpetually the human world contrasted with the supernatural world of faery, the familiar and domestic with the wild and strange, the tame with the heroic, the Christian with the pagan. Later on, his images seem to coalesce into a *tertium quid*, so that simple contrasts disappear and we find symbolic probings into the underlying affinity of apparent opposites. We have this implicitly in the 'Byzantium' poems, and quite explicitly in some of the 'Crazy Jane' poems:

> A woman can be proud and stiff
> When on love intent;
> But Love has pitched his mansion in
> The place of excrement;
> For nothing can be sole or whole
> That has not been rent.

Or consider:

> Bodily decrepitude is wisdom: young
> We loved each other and were ignorant.

Or this, from 'A Woman Young and Old':

> How could passion run so deep
> Had I never thought
> That the crime of being born
> Blackens all our lot?
> But where the crime's committed
> The crime can be forgot.

'Out of our quarrel with others we make rhetoric,' Yeats once remarked; 'out of our quarrel with ourselves, poetry.' Instead of the two poles being personality and tradition, they become opposing aspects of personality. A self-made tradition can only be of value to the literary artist when it contains self-contradictions.

My thesis has been, as will, I hope, be clear by now, that a religious tradition is of value to the literary artist as providing a challenge to individual experience out of which art may result. When that tradition disintegrates, the poet can take refuge in elegiac introspection or he can create or discover a tradition of his own. The former practice may produce much that is valuable, but in the nature of things it cannot be maintained for long, its potentialities being limited and its possibilities soon exhausted. The latter can only work when the created or discovered tradition is complex enough to contain within itself the tensions which the great artist needs; if it does not contain those tensions, then the artist is merely shadow boxing when he employs the tradition, since, being the product of his own imagination, it cannot at the same time be a challenge to his imagination.

Thus Yeats's dialectical symbolic system—if I may use such an ugly term for lack of a better—enabled him to organize the images and ideas in his poetry so as to achieve profound poetic statement. Instead of his own personality wrestling with the tradition, we find opposing elements of his own personality fighting it out and becoming reconciled within the tradition that he pieced together himself. This does not mean that we must understand—still less that we must agree with—the fantastic system which Yeats elaborated in *A Vision* before we can understand or appreciate his poems. Of his best poems it can be safely said that his system is a device to help him achieve the rich and significant patterning of image and idea out of which effective poetic expression is distilled. That significant patterning can be recognized, with all its rich overtones of meaning, in such a poem as 'Byzantium' without any reference to *A Vision*. Indeed, an attempt to interpret the poem too specifically in terms of Yeats's system narrows the meaning unduly and shuts off the reverberating meanings which give the poem its greatness. There are some poems of Yeats which do require the application of the system for their appreciation, but these are his less successful ones.

Dylan Thomas has achieved a very different kind of richly echoing poetic statement, but his success, too, is the result of his creation or discovery of a synthetic tradition in the light of which the proper tensions can be created and resolved. Christianity, Freudian psychology, Welsh folklore, are only some of the elements which he employs together in profound counterpoint to produce some of the most exciting poetry of our time. For a clearer understanding of what modern problem Thomas is solving by this counterpointing of apparently contradictory elements in our culture, let me quote from an author who, in an earlier phase of his career, was painfully aware of the problem, and who has since tried to solve it in a very different way from that chosen by Thomas. Aldous Huxley, in the opening chapter of his novel *Antic Hay* (1923) makes Theodore Gumbril, the disillusioned school master, meditate in the school chapel as follows:

No, but seriously, Gumbril reminded himself, the problem was very troublesome indeed. God as a sense of warmth about the heart, God as exultation, God as tears in the eyes, God as a rush of power or thought—that was all right. But God as truth, God as $2 + 2 = 4$—that wasn't so clearly all right. Was there any chance of their being the same? Were there bridges to join the two worlds?

Gumbril decided that there were not, and therein lay his dilemma. Or again, take the description of the string orchestra in the third chapter of *Point Counter Point* (1928):

Pongileoni's blowing and the scraping of the anonymous fiddlers had shaken the air in the great hall, had set the glass of the windows looking on to it vibrating; and this in turn had shaken the air in Lord Edward's apartment on the further side. The shaking air rattled Lord Edward's *membrana tympani*; the interlocked *malleus*, *incus*, and stirrup bones were set in motion so as to agitate the membrane of the oval window and raise an infinitesimal storm in the fluid of the labyrinth. The hairy endings of the auditory nerve shuddered like weeds in a rough sea; a vast number of obscure miracles were performed in the brain, and Lord Edward ecstatically whispered 'Bach!'

God as a sense of warmth about the heart as opposed to God as $2 + 2 = 4$; music as a series of sound waves impinging on a physiological organism and music as something significant and moving—these are expressed as irreconcilable alternatives. Both explanations seem to be true, yet each seems to deny the other. If the dilemma is posed this way, the only solution would seem to be either complete scepticism or complete irrationality, and neither scepticism nor irrationality can provide a proper environment for great art. What the modern artist needs is some device which will enable him to hold these conflicting attitudes in suspension, as it were, or perhaps it could be better described as a state of tension, or of counterpoint, so that instead of being inhibitive of value they can increase and enrich value.

Huxley's observation about music is neither new nor original. Shakespeare's Benedick, in *Much Ado About Nothing*, remarks in an ironic moment: 'Is it not strange that sheeps' guts should hale souls out of men's bodies?' Unlike Huxley, Shakespeare was not tortured by this perception: he includes it dramatically as one element in the complex and paradoxical nature of things, so that it enriches rather than frustrates his picture of human values in action.

Returning now to Dylan Thomas, we note that his poetic technique enables him to handle in brilliant counterpoint all the different explanations of human situations given by religion, science, and folklore:

> I, in my intricate image, stride on two levels,
> Forged in man's minerals, the brassy orator
> Laying my ghost in metal,
> The scales of this twin world tread on the double,
> My half ghost in armour hold hard in death's corridor,
> To my man-iron sidle.
>
> Beginning with doom in the bulb, the spring unravels
> Bright as her spinning-wheels, the colic season
> Worked on a world of petals;
> She threads off the sap and needles, blood and bubble
> Casts to the pine roots, raising man like a mountain
> Out of the naked entrail.
>
> Beginning with doom in the ghost, and the springing marvels,
> Image of images, my metal phantom
> Forcing forth through the harebell,
> My man of leaves and the bronze root, mortal, unmortal,
> I, in my fusion of rose and male motion,
> Create this twin miracle.

What the modern artist needs is not so much a faith as a poetic principle to enable him to counterpoint against each other the different aspects of knowledge of which the modern world has made him aware. Consider this fact. We know, or we think we know, so much about psychological conditioning, about the psycho-somatic aspects of illness, about the effect of childhood frustrations on adult vices, that we are in danger of being unable to pass any moral judgment on individuals. This man committed rape or murder, but we know that he saw something terrible in the woodshed when he was three, was brought up in a slum, was bullied by a drunken stepfather, had his emotions and instincts warped and frustrated in this way or that, so that we cannot really blame him for what he eventually was driven to do. *Tout comprendre, c'est tout pardonner*, to know all is to forgive all, says the French proverb; but to forgive all is to make it impossible to write the *Divine Comedy* or *Hamlet* or *Paradise Lost*. If we knew all about the inhibitions of King Claudius's childhood, we could not make him the villain in a tragedy. If we knew all Iago's psychological history we might be tempted to spend all our sympathy on him rather than on Othello. And it did not take even that much psychology to make the Romantics turn Milton's Satan into a hero. If our judgments of men are to be dissolved in psychological understanding, we can no longer pattern a tragedy or create any significant work of art with a human situation as its subject matter. Certainly a behaviourist psychology—and I use this term in its widest sense—leaves little room for an appraisal of personality as such, and without an appraisal of personality as such why should Hamlet's death be any more significant than that of Polonius?

Yet Hamlet's death, and all that leads up to it is significant because it is implicitly set against a tradition of what is valuable in human personality, and out of the implicit conflict with this tradition—which held, among other things, that a good man was doing right to punish an evil one—the tragedy emerges. Cannot we too acquire a double vision and set the fact of value in human personality beside the psychological knowledge that would seem to break down the basis of such value, and contemplate the subsequent tensions in art? Cannot the poet, at least, answer Huxley's question by accepting simultaneously both of his alternatives as each true in its own way and finding a richness of observation and expression in which the conflict can be resolved? Even in life, cannot we both forgive a man and pass judgment on him? All the more so, surely, should we be able to achieve this twofold attitude in art, which has so many devices for focussing multiple vision.

The problem of the modern literary artist, therefore, is not to find usable myths so much as to find ways of handling knowledge in a context of value. Knowledge should explain without ever explaining away; proof that Keats's genius flowered early because he had tuberculosis neither explains away the genius nor makes tuberculosis a desirable disease; a study of the nervous system can tell us all sorts of fascinating things about what makes us tick, but cannot alter the basic fact that we *do* tick and the conviction that in the last analysis that fact is mysterious and ineffable; neither physiology nor psychology nor sociology nor economic history, for all the valuable insights they give us into man's behaviour, can alter the fundamental mystery of the god in the machine—man being, as Molly Bloom describes a character in Joyce's *Ulysses*, 'poached eyes on ghost'.

So I dissociate myself from the myth-hunters, who see the modern literary artist's basic need as new myths, as well as from those who deplore the lack of a common religious background in our civilization. I think cultural pluralism is a good thing. I think it is both wise and civilized to realize that no single religious creed represents either the final historical truth about what happened or the final theological truth about the nature of man and his relations with ultimate reality, but that any creed may have valuable insights to contribute. Any piece of faith which is destroyed by new knowledge is destroyed only in its formal expression, not in its fundamental reality—or if it is destroyed in its fundamental reality, then it clearly corresponds to no real need or perception and ought to be abandoned cheerfully. We need neither new knowledge nor new faith, but rather the ability to handle what we have. And that ability, since it involves the counterpointing of apparently contradictory insights, can best be given us by the artist, whose profession it is to distil rich significance out of such counterpointing.

There is then no inseparable gulf between the modern literary artist and his predecessors. If his predecessors enjoyed a more stable background of belief, they still needed to set their individual insights against that background before they could achieve the highest kind of art. We have more balls to juggle in the air, more conflicting claims to focus into a rich pattern of significance, more items of knowledge to organize into a profound and total vision of man's fate. That what should be regarded as an opportunity is often regarded as an inhibition is the result of social and other factors too complicated to be discussed here. Part of the trouble with the modern artist is that he has too many tools and a very indistinct notion of what he should do with them, with the result that he spends a great deal of time simply displaying them. If the artist would spend less time alternately bewailing his 'alienation' from society and flourishing his unemployed skills he might realize the exciting opportunity that awaits him. Everybody is so busy explaining everybody else's lack of success. To the chorus of breast-beaters, prophesiers of doom, *laudatores temporis acti*, beraters of popular taste, deplorers of poets' obscurity, interpreters of the modern dilemma, and all the poetasters, criticasters, and undertakers of the Muse who dance upon the grave of literature in the expectation of being hired to conduct the funeral, I can only say, as the Lord said to Job as he sat wailing among the ashes, 'Who is this that darkeneth counsel with words without knowledge? Gird up now thy loins like a man.'

DATE DUE

JUL - 6 1958

JUL

AUG 18 1960

NOV 22 1961

MAR 5 - 1964